RAILROADS AND LAND GRANT POLICY

RAILROADS AND LAND GRANT POLICY

A STUDY IN GOVERNMENT INTERVENTION

LLOYD J. MERCER

BeardBooks
Washington, D.C.

Library of Congress Cataloging-in-Publication Data

Mercer, Lloyd J.
    Railroads and land grant policy : a study in government intervention / Lloyd J. Mercer.
      p. cm.
    Originally published: New York: Academic Press, c1982.
    Includes bibliographical references and index.
    ISBN 1-58798-154-8 (pbk. : alk. paper)
    1. Railroad land grants--United States--Historty. I. Title

HE1063 .M47 2002
333.1'1--dc21

                                                                               2002034152

Copyright © 1982 by Academic Press, Inc.
Reprinted 2002 by Beard Books, Washington, D.C.

All rights reserved. No part of this publication may be reproduced, stored in a retrieval system, or transmitted in any form, by any means, without the prior written consent of the publisher.

Printed in the United States of America

To Perie, Carolyn, and Janet
Their forbearance helped make it possible

Contents

List of Figures   x
List of Tables   xi
Preface   xv

1. Introduction

Land Grants: Government Intervention in the Market   1
Subsidy, Profitability, and Railroad Investment   3
The Railroad Land Grants   6
Historiography of the Land Grants   8
Objectives of the Study   15

2. Economic Issues in Railroad Land Grant Policy

Building Ahead of Demand   19
External Economies from Railroad Operation   20
Railroads as Natural Monopolies   22
Capital Market Imperfections   24
Hypotheses of the Land Grant Advocates   26
Railroad Land Grants and the Distribution of Income   29
Summary   31

3. Building the Land Grant Railroads

The Central Pacific System   32
The Union Pacific System   38
The Texas and Pacific System   43
The Atchison, Topeka and Santa Fe System   47
The Northern Pacific System   52
The Great Northern Railway System   56
The Canadian Pacific System   60
Summary   67

4. Private Rates of Return

Subsidy Unnecessary   75
Subsidy Necessary but Inadequate   84
Subsidy Necessary and Adequate   87
Summary   97

5. Social Rates of Return

Intraregional Benefits   99
Interregional Benefits   100
Passenger Benefits   105
The Social Returns Stream   107
Tests of Hypotheses B1 and B2   108

6. Building Ahead of Demand

Test of the Fishlow Hypothesis for the Land Grant Systems   119
Estimation of Investment Demand   123
Capacity Utilization   133
The Overbuilding Hypothesis   136
Building Ahead of Demand   138

7. Summary

Economic Rationality of Land Grant Policy   142
Building Ahead of Demand   146
Evaluation of the Railroad Land Grants   147

Appendix A: Investment Expenditure   150
Appendix B: Capital Earnings   178
Appendix C: Net Land Grant Revenue   190
Appendix D: Zero Rent Perimeters   206
Appendix E: Intraregional Benefits   227
Appendix F: Interregional Benefits   233
Appendix G: Passenger Benefits   240
Appendix H: Loan Subsidy Cost   254
Appendix I: Capital Stocks   259

Index   263

List of Figures

Figure 1. Calculation of interregional external benefits.
Figure 2. Increasing net excess demand.
Figure 3. Calculation of interregional external benefits with an increase in demand.
Figure 4. Calculation of direct external benefits to passengers.
Figure D-1. Zero rent perimeters.
Figure D-2. The zero rent perimeter.

List of Tables

Chapters 1–7

Table I. Estimated Private Rates of Return: Central Pacific System

Table II. Investment Expenditures and Land Grant Subsidy by System and Component Aided Railroads

Table III. Investment Expenditures and Loan Subsidy for the Central Pacific and Union Pacific Systems and Component Aided Railroads

Table IV. Estimated Private Rates of Return: Union Pacific System

Table V. Estimated Private Rates of Return: Great Northern System

Table VI. Estimated Private Rates of Return: Texas and Pacific System

Table VII. Estimated Private Rates of Return: Atchison, Topeka and Santa Fe System

Table VIII. Estimated Private Rates of Return: Northern Pacific System

Table IX. Estimated Private Rates of Return: Canadian Pacific System

Table X. Investment Expenditure, Cash and Railroad Subsidies for the Canadian Pacific System

Table XI. Recalculation of Excess Subsidy (Millions of Current Dollars and 1885 Dollars) Using George's Technique with Adjustments

Table XII. New Excess Subsidy Estimate

Table XIII. Alternative Estimates of the Social Rate of Return for the Central Pacific System

Table XIV. Alternative Estimates of the Social Rate of Return for the Union Pacific System

Table XV. Alternative Estimates of the Social Rate of Return for the Texas and Pacific System

Table XVI. Alternative Estimates of the Social Rate of Return for the Santa Fe System

Table XVII. Alternative Estimates of the Social Rate of Return for the Northern Pacific System

Table XVIII. Alternative Estimates of the Social Rate of Return for the Great Northern System

Table XIX. Alternative Estimates of the Social Rate of Return for the Canadian Pacific System

Table XX. Real Accounting Rates of Return and Opportunity Cost of Capital by System (%)

Table XXI. Regression Results by System

Table XXII. Regression Results for the Seven Systems with Normalized Variables

Table XXIII. Free Form Regression Results

Table XXIV. Years for Which Data Are Available and the Regressions Are Fitted for the Seven Systems

Table XXV. Long-Term Elasticities of Capital Stock with Respect to Output, Price, and Relative Profitability

Table XXVI. Normal Rates of Capacity Utilization (Percent of Capacity)

Table XXVII. Normal Capacity Utilization with Capital-Output Elasticity of 1

Table XXVIII. Regression Results by System

Table XXIX. Unaided Rate of Return and Opportunity Cost of Capital by System

Table XXX. Estimates for the Test of Hypotheses A1 and A2

Table XXXI. Estimates for the Test of Hypotheses B1 and B2

Appendixes A–I

Table A-1. Total Current Dollar Value of Construction and Equipment Cost of Individual Railroads in the Central Pacific System, 1863–1889, and Information on Their Entrance into the System

Table A-2. Annual Investment Expenditures by the Central Pacific System

Table A-3. Total Current Dollar Value of Construction and Equipment Cost of Individual Railroads in the Union Pacific System (1864–1889) and Information on Their Entrance into the System

Table A-4. Annual Investment Expenditures by the Union Pacific System

Table A-5. Railroads in the Texas and Pacific System and Information on Their Entrance into the System

Table A-6. Annual Investment Expenditures by the Texas and Pacific System

Table A-7. Railroads in the Atchison, Topeka and Santa Fe System and Information on Their Entrance into the System

Table A-8. Annual Investment Expenditures by the Atchison, Topeka and Santa Fe System

Table A-9. Railroads in the Northern Pacific System and Information on Their Entrance into the System

Table A-10. Annual Investment Expenditures by the Northern Pacific System

Table A-11. Railroads in the Great Northern System and Information on Their Entrance into the System

Table A-12. Annual Investment Expenditures by the Great Northern System

Tables

Table A-13. Railroads in the Canadian Pacific System and Information on Their Entrance into the System

Table A-14. Annual Investment Expenditures in the Canadian Pacific System

Table A-15. Estimated and Book Value Cost per Mile by System and Mileage

Table B-1. Annual Capital Earnings of the Central Pacific System

Table B-2. Annual Capital Earnings of the Union Pacific System

Table B-3. Annual Capital Earnings of the Texas and Pacific System

Table B-4. Annual Capital Earnings of the Atchison, Topeka and Santa Fe System

Table B-5. Annual Capital Earnings of the Northern Pacific System

Table B-6. Annual Capital Earnings of the Great Northern System

Table B-7. Annual Capital Earnings of the Canadian Pacific System

Table C-1. Annual Net Land Grant Revenue of the Central Pacific System (Thousand Current $)

Table C-2. Annual Net Land Grant Revenue of the Union Pacific System (Thousand Current $)

Table C-3. Annual Net Land Grant Revenue of the Texas and Pacific System (Thousand Current $)

Table C-4. Annual Net Land Grant Revenue of the Atchison, Topeka and Santa Fe System (Thousand Current $)

Table C-5. Annual Net Land Grant Revenue of the Northern Pacific System (Thousand Current $)

Table C-6. Annual Net Land Grant Revenue of the Great Northern System (Thousand Current $)

Table C-7. Annual Net Land Grant Revenue of the Canadian Pacific System (Thousand Current $)

Table D-1. Zero Rent Perimeter and Related Estimates by State for the Central Pacific System

Table D-2. Zero Rent Perimeter and Related Estimates by State for the Union Pacific System

Table D-3. Zero Rent Perimeter and Related Estimates by State for the Texas and Pacific System

Table D-4. Zero Rent Perimeter and Related Estimates by State for the Atchison, Topeka and Santa Fe System

Table D-5. Zero Rent Perimeter and Related Estimates by State for the Northern Pacific System

Table D-6. Zero Rent Perimeter and Related Estimates by State for the Great Northern System

Table E-1. Intraregional External Benefits by System with Uniform Distribution

Table F-1. Estimate of External Benefits Accruing to Interregional Shipments on the Central Pacific System by Year

Table F-2. Estimated Annual Average Through Freight Rates per Ton-Mile by Railroad System

Table G-1. Estimate of Alternative Rates per Passenger Mile by Stagecoach and Steamship in 1855

Table G-2. Passenger External Benefits for the Central Pacific System by Year

Table G-3. Passenger External Benefits for the Union Pacific System by Year

Table G-4. Passenger External Benefits for the Texas and Pacific System by Year

Table G-5. Passenger External Benefits for the Atchison, Topeka and Santa Fe System by Year

Table G-6. Passenger External Benefits for the Northern Pacific System by Year

Table G-7. Passenger External Benefits for the Great Northern System by Year

Table G-8. Passenger External Benefits for the Canadian Pacific System by Year

Table H-1. Estimate of Loan Subsidy Cost for the Central Pacific System by Year

Table H-2. Estimate of Loan Subsidy Cost for the Union Pacific System by Year

Table I-1. End-of-Period and Midperiod Capital Stocks (Thousands of 1869 $)

Preface

This book attempts to replace a major part of the railroad land grant legend (according to which the granting of federal and state land to private railroad firms benefitted these firms more than it contributed to society as a whole) with some real numbers and analysis. The present work does not attempt an overall evaluation of railroad land grant policy: noneconomic issues are left to those better qualified to grapple with them, and even several issues that can be considered economic in nature are ignored here because they have frequently been the objects of study elsewhere, at least at a micro level, i.e., for individual railroads. An attempt is made to put the income and wealth distribution impact of the railroad land grants in perspective, but thorough analysis of this issue is not undertaken. The primary question this study does try to illuminate is that of the effect of the railroad land grants on economic efficiency. This emphasis was chosen because it seems clear that improvement of economic efficiency was the major goal that Congress and various state legislatures sought to attain, and thus the examination of economic efficiency questions is fundamental to evaluation of railroad land grant policy. This study will not completely replace the railroad land grant legend (because much is not covered here), but it does represent a considerable diminution of that legend.

My interest in the railroad land grant issue was stimulated by Douglass North's U.S. economic history seminar at the University of Washington.

Yoram Barzel's astute questions about the economic significance of the land grants and his encouragement led me to undertake a study of the Central Pacific System for my Ph.D. dissertation. In later years several of my colleagues contributed through discussion of the economic issues involved in this study. W. Douglas Morgan, M. Bruce Johnson, and Perry Shapiro have been especially helpful. Special thanks are due Stanley Engerman, Roger Riefler, and Jeffrey Williamson, who read earlier versions of the entire manuscript. Their excellent suggestions contributed greatly to its improvement. Perhaps if I had accepted all their ideas it would be better yet.

A large project like this cannot be done without real resources. My major debt here is to the National Science Foundation (grant GS 2259). Without the National Science Foundation's assistance this project could not have been done. Significant financial aid was also provided by the Haynes Foundation and the University of California.

Dennis Heffley, Michael Viren, and especially Anthony Marino provided the research assistance without which I would never have completed this study. Nancy Cabral and Cathy Barrett typed earlier drafts of the manuscript. I am especially indebted to Janice Condit for editorial assistance and the typing of the final draft.

Acknowledgments must be made to the *Journal of Economic History,* the *Business History Review,* and the *Canadian Journal of Economics,* where earlier versions of portions of the book appeared.

This book is dedicated to my wife and daughters, who also have borne part of the burden.

Chapter 1

Introduction

In the nineteenth century, the United States government (like some state governments, particularly that of Texas) found itself the owner of vast amounts of land, the disposition of which occupied a great deal of the attention of both the government and the people. While the federal government never had an explicit land policy, the matter of the transfer of ownership of publicly held property to private firms has been a subject of continuing discussion and debate.[1]

Land Grants: Government Intervention in the Market

A major economic issue that faces us now is the extent (and kinds) of intervention by the government in the market-directed operation of the economy. Many view government intervention in the United States as something that started with the New Deal. This perception is incorrect. Significant intervention in the market by the government has been with us

[1] One of the major reasons that land policy has been the topic of so much discussion is that in general it was inefficient in accomplishing its goals. This inefficiency was primarily the result of the simultaneous pursuit of conflicting goals. There appear to have been four major goals that were the objectives of land policy and that at one time or another were foremost with regard to disposition of the public domain. These were (1) raising revenue for the public treasury, (2) furthering the Jeffersonian ideal of a nation of yeoman farmers, (3) providing aid to various public purposes such as schools, canals, roads, railroads, and veterans' bonuses,

from the earliest days. The New Deal was an intensification of an old phenomenon rather than the creation of a new one.

The nineteenth-century railroad land grants are frequently viewed and evaluated as a simple matter of governmental gifts to business. In fact, the railroad land grant policy is a good example of active government intervention in the operation of the market. What happened in the economy and to particular railroads was determined to a significant extent by this intervention, rather than simply by the working of the market. The rate of growth achieved by the national economy and by particular regions, and the very existence of some railroads, was to some extent a product of the railroad land grants.

In what follows, it must be recognized that the economist's general point of view is that of society. For public policy analysis, the economist is interested in the impact of the policy on the general well-being of society, not on that of specific individuals.

The economist's concern with general welfare manifests itself in an interest in efficiency: the production of any given output with minimal resource use, that is, minimal cost. Thus, the crucial issue in evaluating government intervention is the impact of that intervention on efficiency and therefore on society's overall well-being. From an economic viewpoint, the purpose of government in a democratic society is presumably to undertake those actions that maximize the well-being of society. Rational policy actions must lead to improvement in (or at least maintenance of) the level of economic efficiency and society's well-being.

The railroad land grants were a significant intervention by the government in the operation of the economy. The principal motive of the government (the Congress) in undertaking this intervention was not the transfer or redistribution of income. Private individuals engaged in getting land grants for their railroads were primarily interested in improving their own well-being. Despite this, society's well-being could have been improved by the same action, and the rationality of governmental intervention must be judged by the improvement of society's well-being rather than that of specific individuals. This book presents some tests of the rationality of government intervention in the form of railroad land grants and is intended to increase our knowledge about that strand of land policy that involved gifts from the public domain in aid of (mainly Western) pioneer railroads.

---

and (4) acceleration of the settlement of the West. These four goals conflicted in several ways, and because of these conflicts it was impossible to maximize with respect to all four goals at once. A far better land policy would have been one maximizing with respect to one goal. Unfortunately, the vast amount of land available made it politically easy to pursue many goals in a profligate fashion.

Subsidy, Profitability, and Railroad Investment

Because the provision of federal funds for internal improvements was generally held to be unconstitutional, aid by the federal government for internal improvements in the United States during the first half of the nineteenth century largely took the form of grants of land from the public domain to states.[2] After 1833 the right of way through public lands was frequently granted to railroads, but such grants carried no extra donation of lands. From 1833 on, bills were before Congress to aid various railroads with grants of land from the public domain.[3] The first successful land grant bill was passed in 1850; it provided lands to Illinois, Mississippi, and Alabama in aid of the Illinois Central and Mobile and Ohio Railroads. The 1850 grant consisted of the alternate sections of public land (the odd-numbered sections) within 6 miles of each side of the road so that the granted sections formed a checkerboard pattern.[4] This became the standard pattern for railroad land grants in the United States, with varying amounts of land per mile (mostly larger) provided to later grantees.

By the time the Illinois Central land grant was passed, the general arguments in Congress for and against railroad land grants had been well defined.[5] The main argument for provision of land grants was that the government, as a great landed proprietor, should use its land so as to enhance the value of the total. Many believed that with the improved transportation resulting from the grants, the government's remaining land would have a greater value than the original total. A second argument was the claim by the various states on a share in the public land to be used to aid their development, on the theory both of a proportional distribution of the public domain and of compensation due the new states because the public domain was exempt from taxation. Opposed to these arguments were the objections that the grants were unconstitutional because they were only governmental subsidies in veiled form for internal improvements, and (the objection of the settlers) that the policy resulted in the most desirable lands being obtained by the railroads and their price to the eventual purchaser being increased.

In the decade preceding the Civil War, Congressional discussion concerning land grant policy centered on the question of aid to the "Pacific"

---

[2] John Bell Sanford, *Congressional Grants of Land in Aid of Railroads* (Bulletin of the University of Wisconsin; Economics, Political Science and History Series, II, 3; Madison: Univ. of Wisconsin Press, 1899), p. 11.

[3] *Ibid.*, pp.19–24.

[4] Federal Coordinator of Transportation, *Public Aids to Transportation* (Washington: U.S. Government Printing Office, 1938), II, 105. Hereafter cited as *Public Aids*, II.

[5] Sanford, *op. cit.*, p. 37.

railroads. These were the railroads proposed to provide a transcontinental link between the Midwest and the Pacific Coast. Asa Whitney was the prominent early advocate of a privately owned Pacific railroad to be built with the aid of a federal subsidy. He first presented a plan to Congress in 1845 for government aid for a proposed railroad from Lake Michigan to the Pacific. Whitney's 1845 plan and those that followed were opposed by advocates of governmental construction of the first transcontinental railroad. Neither Whitney's plans for mixed enterprise nor the idea of government construction of a transcontinental railroad made much headway in Congress, because California's entrance into the Union in 1848 greatly increased the number of potential alternative routes across the continent, and the question of route became the crucial stumbling block to Congressional agreement on aid to a Pacific railroad. Agreement on the route for the first transcontinental railroad came only after the Southern states left Congress with the outbreak of the Civil War. The second major issue concerning aid to the Pacific railroads was the type and amount of public assistance to be provided. Governmental construction and operation of the railroads was never actively considered. The question was how much and what type of aid to give private enterprise for the project.

Some Congressmen argued that a large subsidy should be provided for the earliest possible construction of the Pacific railroads because of the immeasurable economic gains that they saw accruing to the nation from the operation of the railroads. This was not a unanimous view. Other members of Congress were less eager to invoke the prospect of economic development to justify aid to the ambitious plans of the railroad promoters. This position was succinctly stated by Representative Garrit Smith of New York, who said in reference to a Pacific railroad:

> If sharp sighted individual enterprise cannot be tempted to undertake it, then it would certainly be a most unprofitable and unwise undertaking for government.[6]

This clash of opinion was resolved in favor of those who visualized enormous economic gains from the operation of the Pacific railroads. A majority in Congress believed that railroad construction would never occur or would be far slower in the absence of government assistance. Land grants were provided for the Pacific railroads, starting with the Pacific Railway Acts of 1862 and 1864, which were primarily for the benefit of railroads forming the first transcontinental (the Central Pacific, Union Pacific, and others), and ending with a grant to the Texas and

[6] Quoted in Robert W. Fogel, *The Union Pacific Railroad: A Case in Premature Enterprise* (Baltimore: The Johns Hopkins Press, 1960), p. 91.

1. Introduction

Pacific Railroad Company in 1871.[7] In the beginning these grants were supported by a wave of popular enthusiasm; however, the revulsion of public sentiment that was fueled by the Crédit Mobilier and other scandals by 1871 forced Congress to refuse additional grants. This change in popular opinion was followed throughout the 1880s by a groundswell of public opinion demanding the recovery of grants to companies failing to observe the requirements of the law.[8]

As the preceding discussion suggests, the economic rationality of the gift of land from the public domain to private railroad firms rested on hypotheses concerning the relationship of the social and private rates of return on investment in those railroads to the opportunity cost of capital. There are four hypotheses that can be specified and that will provide the primary focus for this study. Two of these hypotheses refer to the relationship between the private rate of return on investment in the railroads and the average opportunity cost of capital. The other two hypotheses deal with the relationship between the social rate of return on investment in the railroads and the average and marginal opportunity cost of capital. The average opportunity cost of capital is taken to be the market rate of return, whereas the marginal opportunity cost of capital refers to the highest social rate of return on the project(s) not undertaken as a consequence of the subsidy to the land grant railroads.

For convenience of reference, the specific hypotheses are labeled A1, A2, B1, and B2. Hypotheses A1 is that in the absence of subsidy, the private rate of return on investment in the pioneer (land grant) railroads would be less than the market rate of return. Because subsidy was to be provided by the land grants with the intention of getting the pioneer railroads built, the corollary of A1 is hypothesis A2, namely, that with the land grant subsidy the private rate of return on investment in these railroads would be equal to the market rate of return.

Since it is always possible to find any number of unprofitable projects, the satisfaction of hypotheses A1 and A2 is not sufficient for the land grants to have been economically rational. Some special circumstances are required, and these are reflected in hypotheses B1 and B2. Hypothesis B1 is that the social rate of return on the investment in the land grant railroads would exceed the average opportunity cost of capital, i.e., the market rate of return. Finally, the use of capital for the land grant railroads must be better for society than the best project(s) that are not undertaken, because capital is diverted to the land grant railroads by the provision of subsidy to them. Thus we have hypothesis B2, that the social

---

[7] *Public Aids*, II, 105–107.
[8] David Maldwyn Ellis, "The Forfeiture of Railroad Land Grants, 1867–1894," *Mississippi Valley Historical Review*, XXVIII, 1 (June 1946), 27.

rate of return on the subsidized railroads would exceed the marginal opportunity cost of capital in the United States during the relevant period.

The Railroad Land Grants

This study focuses on the land grants in support of the transcontinental railroad systems. Federal land grants can be divided into three categories: (1) those to transcontinentals, comprising about 77% of the total acreage granted; (2) grants to Midwestern regional railroads, amounting to 15% of the acreage; and (3) grants to Southern Reconstruction railroads, involving 8% of the federal land grant acreage.[9] This acreage distribution justifies focus on the transcontinentals, since it is the acreage granted and the issues deriving from the control of that acreage that have provided the source for discussion and debate during the past century.

Including 2,966,384 acres of forfeited lands for which the Oregon and California Railroad received payment from the federal government, the land grant railroads by the late 1930s had received a net total of 179,187,040 acres: 130,303,668 acres from federal grants and 48,883,372 from state grants.[10] In 1941 the railroads released about 8 million acres of unpatented land still in the process of adjustment in order to take advantage of a clause in the Transportation Act of 1941.[11] The 179 million acre estimated total for the land grants represents about 280,000 square miles, with the final total of federal grants (see footnote 10) representing just over 205,000 square miles.

How does one evaluate the significance of these very large numbers in terms of acres and square miles? The numbers, of course, are huge. But how best to put them in perspective? This is a problem that historians have struggled with for some time.[12] Referring to a slightly larger total

---

[9] *Public Aids*, II, pp. 107–111. Actually the importance in value terms of the Midwest regional grants is considerably greater than suggested by the acreage shares. The nominal (undiscounted) value per acre of the Midwestern grants is almost two and a half times that of the transcontinentals. On the same basis, the Midwestern railroads garnered 31% of the total net proceeds from land grants compared to the transcontinentals' 66%. Given the shorter delay in selling their lands, the value share of the regional railroads would be even larger in present value terms.

[10] *Ibid.*, p. 32. The final total of federal acreage received is about 131 million acres (see U.S. General Land Office, *Annual Report of the Commissioner*, June 30, 1943).

[11] Ellis, *loc. cit.*

[12] See Robert S. Henry, "The Railroad Land Grant Legend in American History Texts," *Mississippi Valley Historical Review*, XXXII, 2 (September 1945), 171–194; the discussion of Henry's article in XXXII, 4 (March 1946); Henry's rejoinder in XXXIII, 1 (June 1946), as well as the note by Charles S. Morgan, "Problems in the Appraisal of the Railroad Land Grants," *Mississippi Valley Historical Review*, XXXIII, 3 (December 1943), 443–454. Morgan was earlier Director, Section of Research, for the Federal Coordinator of Transportation.

1. Introduction

acreage than that cited here, because in the late 1930s the railroads were expected to lay claim to another 4 million acres, the Federal Coordinator of Transportation noted that the total railroad land grants were approximately 7.65% more than the area of Texas and 9.46% of the area of the continental United States.[13] Federal grants alone, in the same comparison, were put at 6.93% of the area of the continental United States, or a little more than the combined area of Indiana, Illinois, Michigan, and Wisconsin.[14] Two prominent historians refer to the grants as "an area equal to Maine, Rhode Island, Connecticut, and New York, with a large slice of Pennsylvania thrown in."[15] Obviously one's geographical frame of reference may have an impact on description of the size of the land grants. With my own frame of reference the federal grants, rather than being larger than New England, were 29% larger than the state of California and 76.6% of the area of Texas, while total land grants are 4.4% more than the combined area of California and Nevada.[16] Listing one or two states in this comparison imparts a slightly different flavor than does a long list of states. The area of the grants is exactly the same either way: immense. However, while discussion of acreage and square miles is nicely descriptive, it does not really illuminate the central issues in land grant policy.[17]

Historians have devoted considerable space and time to attempts at illumination of the land grant policy. The policy of subsidizing pioneer railroads with grants of land from the public domain is a topic discussed in every United States history text that covers the latter part of the nineteenth century. At the same time, an evaluation of the central issue in railroad land grant policy—the economic rationality of the policy—has not been the subject of any considerable volume of significant scholarly research by historians. However, specific topics, including histories of particular land grant railroads, the colonization efforts of land grant railroads, forfeiture of land grants, and the whole land patenting process by the land grant railroads, have been topics of considerable research by historians.

---

[13] *Public Aids*, II, 32.

[14] *Ibid*.

[15] Charles A. and Mary R. Beard, *The Rise of American Civilization*, II (New York: Macmillan, 1927), p. 199.

[16] The final federal land grant total is about 204,688 square miles (see footnote 10), whereas state grants totaled 76,380 square miles, for a total of 281,068 square miles. The area of California is 158,693 square miles, that of Texas is 267,339 square miles, and that of Nevada is 110,540 square miles.

[17] The Federal Coordinator imparted a sense of fairness to his comparisons by noting in *Public Aids*, II, p. 33:

> It should be borne in mind, however, that to a considerable extent the land grant lands were semiarid or broken mountain land, of little value at the time of the grants or today. The Government still holds millions of acres of such lands, from which it derives a moderate return or none at all.

In order to provide an overview of historians' views concerning land grant policy, the following discussion focuses on those views as reflected in the textbook literature.[18] Such a limitation is less severe than it may appear, because the textbook literature undoubtedly gives a broader reflection of historians' views than would the scholarly writings of specialists.

In general, historians have had a negative view of the railroad land grants, but this judgment is not universal, and some historians have presented favorable appraisals of the land grant policy. Thus, it would be a mistake to characterize historians' views on the railroad land grants as monolithic either with respect to overall evaluation of the policy or with regard to the theme used to develop the discussion of the policy and its results. An important point to consider is the (usually) implicit basis of the historians' evaluation. This often appears to be a judgment about (1) the effect of the land grants on income and wealth distribution and (2) some notion of the "correct" income and wealth distribution. Those historians who react negatively to the land grants appear to have concluded that the land grants had an adverse effect on income and wealth distribution, i.e., they made the rich richer without a comparable positive effect on the income of the poor.[19] The question of the income and wealth distribution impact of land policy is considered further in Chapter 2.

Historiography of the Railroad Land Grants

The debate in the historical literature over railroad land grants has generally revolved around a few specific issues. In its crudest form, the central issue has been the question of whether the government drove a sharp bargain with the land grants. At the most naive level, it has been argued that the federal government did not lose anything in the land grant

[18] A notable exception regarding historians' attempts to grapple with the central issues is the discussion in Volumes XXXII and XXXIII (1946) of the *Mississippi Valley Historical Review* replying to Robert S. Henry, "The Railroad Land Grant Legend in American History Texts." Henry's rejoinder in Volume XXXIII, 1 (June 1946), 115–120, is also of interest, as is the separate note by Charles S. Morgan, "Problems in the Appraisal of the Railroad Land Grants." Two other especially noteworthy articles are David Maldwyn Ellis, "The Forfeiture of Railroad Land Grants, 1867–1894," and Leslie E. Decker, "The Railroads and the Land Office: Administrative Policy and the Land Patent Controversy, 1864–1896," *Mississippi Valley Historical Review* XLVI, 4 (March 1960), 679–699. There are also numerous histories of individual railroads as railroad systems, and railroad colonization efforts. The major book on railroad land grants *per se* by a historian is Leslie E. Decker, *Railroads, Lands and Politics* (Providence, Rhode Island: Brown Univ. Press, 1964). This is a useful work, but it deals only with Kansas and Nebraska.

[19] In a technical sense, the implication is that the effect of the land grants was to shift the Lorenz curve for the United States so that the degree of inequality in income (and wealth) distribution with the land grants exceeded that which would have existed without the grants,

1. Introduction

process, because it gave up only one-half the land within the grant area and doubled the price on the acreage it retained. This crude idea was long ago laid to rest.[20] On a more sophisticated level, those making a positive assessment of the land grant transaction probably would agree with Robert S. Henry, who wrote that Uncle Sam was, "a canny landowner using part of his holdings to increase immeasurably the value of the rest, not as a gift but on terms which constituted a bargain shrewder than he realized."[21] Still, in the historian's view, the question of greatest interest has been the fate of the millions of acres of state and federal lands granted to railroads, rather than the issue of whether the government made a shrewd bargain.[22]

Several specific primary questions dominate the historian's consideration of the railroad land grants. The effect of the grants upon the construction of the railroads, the settlement of the West, the pattern and structure of land tenure and ownership, and the establishment of large timber holdings are all issues that loom large in the historian's discussions. The phrases "land monopoly" and "land monopolist" recur frequently in discussions of the railroad land grants. Subsidiary questions concern the swing of Western opinion toward demanding an end to land grants and the forfeiture of unearned grants as well as the role played by the forfeiture movement in the growth of anti-railroad sentiment during the last quarter of the nineteenth century. These questions (and frequently the writer's answer) are at least implicit in the historian's treatment and discussion of the land grant issue.

One of the most common themes in the historical literature is the impact of the railroad land grants on the economic expansion and development of the West. Here it appears that most writers agree to some extent with Henry's argument that the land grants did "what had never been done before—provided transportation ahead of settlement."[23] The developmental theme apparently had its genesis in the Beards' monumental work, *The Rise of American Civilization*.[24] The Beards saw the railroad land grant

---

i.e., the Gini coefficient for the United States income (and wealth) distribution was raised by land grant policy. The further implicit notion here is that there were better policies to accomplish the same aims that would have made income (and wealth) distribution more equal (reduced the Gini coefficient) or which would have been neutral in their effect on income (and wealth) distribution (left the Gini coefficient unchanged).

[20] Cf. Paul Wallace Gates, "The Railroad Land Grant Legend," *Journal of Economic History*, XIV, 2 (Spring 1954), 143–146.
[21] Robert S. Henry, *op. cit.*, p. 189.
[22] David Maldwyn Ellis, *op. cit.*, p. 28.
[23] Robert S. Henry, *op. cit.*, pp. 191–192.
[24] Charles A. and Mary R. Beard, *The Rise of American Civilization* (New York: Macmillan, 1927).

policy as part of the deliberate and well rounded program of the federal government for development of the West.[25] In their view this program was made possible by Northern and Republican control of Congress and the administration following the attempted secession of the South. The resultant program is seen as uniting and benefiting the various elements in the Republican Party, especially the commercial interests of the West, Northern manufacturers, Western farmers, Western miners, the capitalists involved in the railroads, and the politicians who benefited by virtue of their financial interest in Western railroads.[26] A negative note enters this assessment with regard to the Central Pacific and Union Pacific Railroads when it is suggested that

> to the capitalists who furnished the directive impulse the outlook was especially pleasing because they were called upon to contribute so little money relatively and yet were assured handsome profits from the construction of the roadbed and tracks and from the land endowments accompanying the long mileage.[27]

In the Beards' estimation, the other land grant railroads had a more difficult task because they were

> endowed by Congress with magnificent gifts of land but given no such assistance in credits as the Union Pacific and the Central Pacific had received, these later companies found the task of financing their schemes exceedingly difficult.[28]

The Beards appear to conclude that the impact of the land grants was minimal because "railways and promoters, however, merely accelerated a westward movement that was inevitable and indeed was in progress."[29] The Beards' negative evaluation of land grant policy shows through clearly in the end.

> Any one who was squeamish about bald prehension could obtain generous gifts with a show of legality. Within a quarter of a century ending in 1872, the government granted to railway concerns more than one hundred and fifty million acres of public land—an area equal to Maine, Rhode Island, Connecticut, and New York, with a large slice of Pennsylvania thrown in. . . . A chart of the railway land grants in the West looms up like a map of the Roman Empire in the age of Augustus.[30]

[25] *Ibid.*, Vol. 2, especially pp. 127–137.
[26] *Ibid.*, p. 129.
[27] *Ibid.* This and the following quotations are copyright 1927 by Macmillan Publishing Co., Inc., renewed 1955 by Mary R. Beard.
[28] *Ibid.*, p. 137.
[29] *Ibid.*, p. 140.
[30] *Ibid.*, p. 199.

1. Introduction

The theme of the land grants' contribution to economic expansion is retained in the Beards' later textbooks.[31]

Other writers take a more limited approach to the land grant policy issue and merely mention the railroad land grants as being included in the vast amount of land given away by the government. Here the topic is phrased in terms of land-oriented growth with minimal emphasis on railroad expansion. Thus, the theme is still one of development, but with a different emphasis from that of the Beards:

> Within three years after the end of the war the Federal Government was distributing 6,000,000 acres a year of public lands, and although much of this went in grants to the railroads, millions of acres had been turned into farms by new settlers.[32]

Some writers place more emphasis on the railroads and the land grants, devoting a special subsection of a chapter on railroads to the land grants and their effects. This approach is usually characterized by a statistical description of the number of acres given out by the government, and the viewpoint of the writers frequently appears to be on the negative side.

> A complaisant government not only closed these belts to settlement until the railroads had selected their shares, but widened the closed belts to 60 to 120 miles until the railroads had sold such of their land as they chose. . . . Naturally the railroads took every possible advantage of the situation; and insiders who got hold of these lands made fortunes in lumber and minerals.[33]

In a similar vein:

> The "checkerboard" grant to the Union Pacific–Central Pacific Route contained more than 20,000,000 acres of land, spread across the country in alternate sections to a distance of 10 miles on each side of the right of way. Such grants were duplicated elsewhere. . . .
> To them [municipalities in the land grant areas] the railroad meant

---

[31] Cf. Charles A. and Mary R. Beard, *The Beards' New Basic History of the United States* (Garden City, New York: Doubleday, 1960), p. 271. For other writers stressing this theme see: John W. Caughey, *Land of the Free* (Pasadena, Calif.: Franklin Publishing Co., 1965), pp. 438, 442; and John W. Caughey and Ernest R. Moy, *A History of the United States* (Chicago: Rand McNally, 1964), pp. 284–285.

[32] James Truslow Adams, *History of the United States,* III (New York: Charles Scribner and Sons, 1965), 209; for similar approaches see: Oliver Chitwood, *The United States: From Colony to World Power* (New York: Van Nostrand, 1954), p. 836; Ralph Volney Harlow, *The United States from Wilderness to World Power* (New York: Holt, 1949), p. 415; and Ralph V. Harlow, *The Growth of the United States* (New York: Holt, 1951), p. 73.

[33] Leland D. Baldwin, *Survey of American History* (New York: American Book Co., 1957), p. 382. Reprinted by permission of D. C. Heath and Company.

the difference between growth and economic starvation. The fantastic profits that seemed assured drew in private wealth as well. Stocks were peddled from town to town and financiers in the upper ranks laid claim on the fortunes of Europe for billions of dollars.[34]

Many historians prefer to deal with the issue of the railroad land grants as one rife with unscrupulous practices by financiers and lobbyists. They see the land grants as a means by which funds could be obtained for the building of railroads more for private than social benefit:

> Skillful, if none too scrupulous, salesmen persuaded private investors, foreigners as well as Americans, to buy large blocks of railroad securities. Finally, the politicians who sympathized with the aims of the railroads won from Congress grants of federal land to be used in aid of railroad building.[35]

A few historians have seen the land grants as being a better alternative to providing a basis for Western settlement than any other available, and have given positive overall assessments of the railroad land grant policy. Basically, these writers have tried to demonstrate the social benefit derived from the railroad land grants:

> Most of the transcontinental roads . . . were aided by Federal land grants. The value and importance of such aid have long been argued. Much of the land was worthless both then and later, while some of it, such as the timbered areas along the Northern Pacific, became extremely valuable. . . . The final railroad profit is uncertain, while the services of the roads in increasing the wealth of the country are hardly subject to accurate estimates. . . . The only inescapable conclusion is that the construction of the railroads through uninhabited country necessitated tremendous amounts of energy and optimism at a time when more conservative people foresaw only bankruptcy.[36]

---

[34] R. Kent Fielding, *The United States: An Interpretive History* (New York: Harper & Row, 1964), p. 318.

[35] John D. Hicks, *A Short History of American Democracy* (Boston: Houghton Mifflin Co., 1956), p. 301. Concerning this area, there are many writers who expound this viewpoint; cf. Dexter Perkins and Glyndon G. Van Deusen, *The United States of America: A History*, 2 (New York: MacMillan, 1962), 73; T. Harry Williams and Richard N. Current, *A History of the United States*, 2 (New York: Knopf, 1959), 52–53; Morton Borden, *The American Profile* (Lexington, Mass.: D. C. Heath & Co., 1970), pp. 178–179; Merle Curti, *A History of American Civilization* (Freeport, New York: Books for Libraries Press, 1969), p. 368; Avery Craven and Walter Johnson, *The United States Experience in Democracy* (New York: Ginn, 1947), p. 443.

[36] From *The American Story*, by Robert E. Riegel and David F. Long. Copyright © 1978 by the McGraw-Hill Book Co. Used with the permission of the McGraw-Hill Book Company. *Vol. 2, Maturity* (New York: McGraw-Hill, 1955), p. 15. Another reference with this perspective is: Henry Bamford Parkes, *The United States of America: A History* (New York: Knopf, 1953), p. 403.

1. Introduction

Another writer provides a similar positive evaluation:

> Nor should it be casually supposed that land grants and other aids from government were necessarily fraudulently acquired or even socially undesirable. For one thing there was a quid pro quo: the railroads furnished the government with transportation at reduced rates. ... From a social standpoint there was a sound basis for the assistance.[37]

Many historians prefer to deal with the land grants only as a pecuniary factor in the stimulation of railroad development and do not enter into the thicket of questions posed by the policy. Here is an example with an implicit positive evaluation of the policy:

> The supreme achievement was the transcontinental railroads, which were only made possible by large-scale aid from the Federal government in the form of vast land grants and at first—direct loans.[38]

A number of historians have argued that the land grants were sufficient to finance the costs of building the railroad:

> The lands granted to both the Union Pacific and the Central Pacific yielded enough to have covered all legitimate costs of building these roads.[39]

Fred Shannon was an ardent supporter of this view. His strongest statement of this position was contained in his Comment on Henry's "The Railroad Land Grant Legend in American History Texts":

> the half billion dollars in land alone to the land grant railroads was worth more than the railroads were when they were built. Credit from the possession of this land made possible their building and expansion. All additions to the value of the railroads since their building have come from profits obtained from government munificence. If any lobbying is justifiable today it should be from a people's lobby. It should demand that after three-quarters of a century (in some cases almost a century) of private profit from public gifts, it is now time for the

---

[37] Carl N. Degler, *Out of Our Past* (New York: Harper, 1959), pp. 241–242.

[38] H. C. Allen, *The United States of America: A Concise History* (New York: Praeger, 1965), pp. 164–165. Many writers have followed a similar approach: Louis M. Hacker, *The Shaping of the American Tradition*, II (New York: Columbia Univ. Press, 1947), 690–691; Oscar Handlin, *America, A History* (New York: Holt, Rhinehart and Winston, 1968), p. 526; Richard Hofstadter, *The United States, History of a Republic* (Englewood Cliffs, N.J.: Prentice Hall, 1967), p. 518; Nelson Manfred Blake, *A Short History of American Life* (New York: McGraw Hill, 1952), p. 382; and John F. Stover, *The Life and Decline of the American Railroad* (New York: Oxford Univ. Press, 1960), p. 60.

[39] Samuel Eliot Morison and Henry Steele Commager, *Growth of the American Republic* (London: Oxford Univ. Press, 1969), p. 39.

people to take back the property without further recompense, so that in the future the benefits shall be reaped by those who paid.[40]

Historians and other writers who devote themselves exclusively to the topic of railroads and land grants naturally enough allocate a more extensive portion of their work to railroad land grants than the writers of the basic United States history texts. Generally, their comments have presented a balanced view of the railroad land grant policy and its effects.

> Gradually, as knowledge of how railroads were being financed permeated to the general public, the whole affair of railroad promotion, both the honest and the otherwise, was lumped together to make a gigantic and national scandal which has ever since been a milepost in many American history books, many of which have showed maps displaying thick, sinister lines of black indicating the proportion of the public domain that had been granted to railroads. Historians revolted at the exposes of the sharp railroad promoters, wrote angry texts that for the past sixty years have been accepted as gospel in our schools and colleges. Because the historians were angry and because also they really did have reason for anger, many a textbook has been unfair to the railroads and to the administrations that made the land grants.[41]

Other railroad specialists have adopted a definite pro-railroad stance although surprisingly even some of these have argued that the land grants were not necessary:

> These lands have not been the source of wealth to the roads that is commonly supposed. Even in the case of the largest grants the balance for the whole period is quite small and in many cases the land departments are now a source of expense rather than of revenue.... Comparing the building of the roads which received land grants with those that did not, it seems that there was no particular need for most of the grants.[42]

This survey of historians' views reveals several common themes and conclusions. The developmental or economic-expansion aspect of land grant policy, in the sense that construction and operation of the land grant railroads accelerated Western development, seems to be generally accepted.[43] At the same time, most writers do refer to the sharp practices, or

---

[40] Fred A. Shannon, "Comment on 'The Railroad Land Grant Legend in American History Texts,'" *Mississippi Valley Historical Review*, XXXII, 4 (March 1946), 574.

[41] Stuart Hollbrook, *The Story of American Railroads* (New York: Crown Publishing Co., 1947), p. 156.

[42] Slason Thompson, *A Short History of American Railways* (Freeport, New York: Books for Libraries Press, 1971), p. 127.

[43] Besides the economic payoff from land grant policy, the benefits accruing to political unification and national defense do come in for some mention in the literature. Perhaps the strongest statement concerning these latter matters comes from Robert S. Henry. After developing the idea of enormous economic gains produced by the land grant policy he writes: "More important even than these was the contribution of the land grant railroads to

1. Introduction 15

even corruption, associated with the building of at least some of the land grant railroads. Perhaps too frequently, all the land grant railroads are painted with the brush that really should be applied only to some. The historians' consensus seems to be that the land grants, or something like them, were necessary for the acceleration of Western development, but that the policy actually followed was bad because of its deleterious side effects. These include the fostering of crookery and corruption, making the rich richer, and the creation of a monopoly in land with an associated unfavorable structure of land tenure, to the detriment of the average citizen. While there are some who argue that the land grants were unnecessary, this does not appear to be the consensus. Of course, as we will see later, those holding the latter view may in fact be correct at least with respect to some of the land grant railroads on an *ex post* basis. One shortcoming of those who espouse this view is that they make no clear distinction between *ex ante* and *ex post* considerations.[44] For a number of reasons, what is the case *ex post* may be irrelevant to the *ex ante* consideration. Land grant policy was initiated and carried out on the basis of *ex ante* considerations. Evaluation of land grant policy and its effects requires a clear distinction between *ex ante* and *ex post*.

This survey of historians' views suggests that an evaluation of land grants and land grant policy must be built on careful consideration of the parts rather than on an emotional response to the whole. One eminent authority stated the case well when he wrote:

> The dangers of making sweeping generalizations about the wisdom, effectiveness, and consequences of our land grant policy should be obvious.[45]

Objectives of the Study

The primary aim of this study is to provide an empirical evaluation of the central issue in railroad land grant policy: its economic rationality.

---

military security and national unity" (Robert S. Henry, "The Railroad Land Grant Legend in American History Texts," p. 193). On this point, it appears that Colonel Henry significantly overstates the case, at least with regard to land grant railroads in the United States. A more convincing case in this respect can be made for the Canadian Pacific (see Chapter 4).

[44] The reply to this could be that at least some of the promoters knew or believed that the land grants and other subsidies were not really necessary *ex ante*, but merely used the common belief that aid was necessary as a means further to enrich themselves. From the historical record, it would seem that there is a grain of truth in this in that promoters did work to get every bit of aid possible without any fine calculation regarding how much was really necessary. At the same time, it seems abundantly clear that, *ex ante*, some aid was necessary, but the amount provided may have indeed differed from what was actually required *ex ante*, i.e., the aid provided was necessary but nonoptimal.

[45] David Maldwyn Ellis, *op. cit.*, p. 57.

This will be done by testing hypotheses A1, A2, B1, and B2 for seven major railroad systems that received the bulk of land grant subsidy in the United States and Canada. These systems are the Central Pacific, Union Pacific, Texas and Pacific, Santa Fe, Northern Pacific, Great Northern, and Canadian Pacific. Earlier estimates of some of their rates of return have been published elsewhere.[46] The estimates presented here are far more complete than the fragmentary earlier presentations and include important revisions.

An overall, or macro, evaluation of land grant policy is not the goal of this study, which focuses on the central issue of economic rationality. A number of subsidiary (though not unimportant) issues are largely ignored. These include (1) the various effects of withdrawal of land in the primary and indemnity areas while the railroads were selecting and patenting their lands; (2) the scandals (and the sociopolitical effects of these scandals) associated with some of the land grants and land grant railroads; (3) the effect of railroad land ownership and the land grant railroads' performance as land sellers on the pace of settlement and the consequent structure of farm tenure; and (4) the effect of land grant policy on income and wealth distribution.[47]

In Chapter 2 we undertake a more detailed analysis of the economic

---

[46] Earlier estimates of the private rates of return (with and without subsidy) for the Central and Union Pacific Systems, along with an estimate of the social rate of return for the Central Pacific, appeared in Lloyd J. Mercer, "Land Grants to American Railroads: Social Cost or Social Benefit?," *Business History Review*, XLIII, 2 (Summer, 1969), 134–151. Revised and more detailed estimates of the rates of return for the Central Pacific System were given in Lloyd J. Mercer, "Rates of Return for Land-Grant Railroads: The Central Pacific System," *Journal of Economic History*, XXX (September 1970), 3, 602–626. Estimated private rates of return for the Canadian Pacific have been presented in Lloyd J. Mercer, "Rates of Return and Government Subsidization of the Canadian Pacific Railway: An Alternate View," *Canadian Journal of Economics*, VI, 3 (August 1973), 428–437. Estimates of the unaided private rates of return for all the systems were given in Lloyd J. Mercer, "Building Ahead of Demand: Some Evidence for the Land Grant Railroads," *Journal of Economic History*, XXXIV, 2 (June 1974), 492–500.

[47] A number of issues have received careful and detailed study by historians. For some of these, most notably the colonization efforts of the railroads, the forfeiture of land grants, and the performance of the general land office in the land grant process, there are excellent studies in existence (cf. Paul Wallace Gates, *The Illinois Central Railroad and Its Colonization Work* (Cambridge: Harvard Univ. Press, 1941); James Blaine Hedges, "The Colonization Work of the Northern Pacific Railroad," *Mississippi Valley Historical Review*, XII (December 1926), 311–342; James Blaine Hedges, *Building the Canadian West: The Land and Colonization Work of the Canadian Pacific Railroad* (New York: Macmillan, 1939); Richard C. Overton, *Burlington West* (Cambridge: Harvard Univ. Press, 1941); David Maldwyn Ellis, *op. cit.*; Leslie E. Decker, "The Railroads and the Land Office: Administrative Policy and the Land Patent Controversy, 1864–1896"; and Leslie E. Decker, *Railroads, Lands and Politics*.

1. Introduction

issues involved in the land grant policy. Chapter 3 provides a brief history of the seven systems to be studied. The major empirical work in this study involves estimation of the private profitability of the major land grant railroads (Chapter 4) and their social profitability (Chapter 5).[48] The question of "building ahead of demand" is clearly related to notions of private and social profitability and also underlies the discussion of provision of land grant subsidy. Chapter 6 presents a detailed evaluation of the hypothesis of building ahead of demand for the seven systems. This evaluation includes estimation of the investment demand functions, with a neoclassical stock adjustment specification of these functions, for the systems studied. Based on the estimated parameters from these functions, estimates are developed of each system's capacity and capacity utilization, and these are used to examine the question of building ahead of demand.[49] Finally, in Chapter 7 we draw conclusions from the analysis and the estimates of this study.

---

[48] The question of private profitability involves the related question of who paid for the land grant railroads: taxpayers (the people) or investors? For systems included in the present study, some earlier estimates regarding this question were presented in Lloyd J. Mercer, "Taxpayers or Investors: Who Paid for the Land Grant Railroads?," *Business History Review,* XLVI, 2 (Autumn 1972), 279–294.

[49] Some simpler tests which appeared earlier in Lloyd J. Mercer, "Building Ahead of Demand: Some Evidence for the Land Grant Railroads," are also included.

Chapter 2

Economic Issues in Railroad Land Grant Policy

Railroad land grants and land grant policy can be viewed from a number of perspectives; however, it is clear that both the intent and the impact of the policy were basically economic in nature. Historians, as we have seen, have concentrated their discussion of the railroad land grants on economic issues. Naturally enough, economists (myself among them) have also concentrated on the economics of the land grants and land grant policy. The following discussion provides a survey and evaluation of the principal economic issues involved in the land grant policy. This focus does not mean that there are no other issues of substance with regard to land grant policy, but merely reflects the belief that economic issues are paramount for evaluation of that policy.[1]

The primary economic issue with regard to land grant policy involves the question of whether the subsidization of the land grant railroads was required from the standpoint of economic efficiency. Careful consideration of the case for subsidization is required for evaluation of this issue. Notice that the issue of the basis for subsidization is distinct from the question of the optimal means of providing a subsidy if one is required for

---

[1] For the most thorough discussion of these issues in the literature, see Stanley L. Engerman, "Some Economic Issues Relating to Railroad Subsidies and the Evaluation of Land Grants," *Journal of Economic History*, XXXII, 2 (June 1972), 443–463. The discussion in this chapter benefits considerably from Engerman's earlier work.

improved economic efficiency. The land grants were only one of many possible means of providing a subsidy to pioneer railroads. Other major alternatives included cash grants, government loans or guarantees of private loans, government construction of the railroads, etc. The framework for the analysis that follows is economic efficiency. The basic question is whether subsidization of the land grant railroads was necessary to increase (maximize) output, given the existing resource endowments, state of technology, and tastes and preferences of society.[2]

Building ahead of Demand

As we observed earlier, the rationale in the historical literature for public subsidization of the private builders of the land grant railroads rests primarily on the concept that Joseph Schumpeter called "building ahead of demand." The same phenomenon has been termed "developmental construction" by Carter Goodrich in his extensive studies of governmental aid for transportation facilities.[3] The notion of building ahead of demand suggests that an area that is presently unsettled only requires the provision of transportation for settlement and development to proceed. However, transportation is not supplied before settlement for such an area because the railroad (or other transportation system) cannot cover costs in the absence of settlement. Thus, it is argued that government aid is required to support the initial transportation development, which in turn will generate still more settlement, and so on.[4] With regard to the American West, this story suggests that the availability of transportation services was the crucial determinant of the extent of settlement, or at least the pace of settlement.

The hypothesis of building ahead of demand is examined in more detail for the major land grant railroads in Chapter 6. For our present purposes, the important question is whether building ahead of demand provides a

[2] Technically, the question is whether subsidization was required to achieve the *optimum optimorum* (best of the best) with regard to output, i.e., that point on the production frontier at which the marginal rate of transformation among goods in production is equal to the marginal rate of substitution among goods in consumption.

[3] See Carter Goodrich, *Government Promotion of American Canals and Railroads, 1800 to 1890* (New York: Columbia Univ. Press, 1960); Carter Goodrich, ed., *Canals and American Economic Development* (New York: Columbia Univ. Press, 1961); and Carter Goodrich, ed., *The Government and the Economy* (Indianapolis: Bobbs-Merrill, 1967).

[4] In technical terms, the argument is that an increase in supply of transportation services in the unsettled area would result in settlement, with a consequent rise in demand for transportation services so that the transportation facility (railroad, canal, etc.) would earn at least the opportunity cost of its capital. In the absence of settlement, the process described can get under way only with a subsidy to make up some initial shortfall in recovering the opportunity cost of the capital to be committed to transportation in the unsettled region.

justification for subsidization of an investment project. On economic grounds it is easy to see that the condition of building ahead of demand does not by itself justify public subsidy to private entrepreneurs. Most large-scale investment projects, especially those involving new goods and services, are built ahead of demand. Despite this fact, the concept is rarely cited as the basis for subsidy except with regard to transportation facilities. The basic reason for this is that the substantive economic question for any investment project is whether the capital necessary for the project will earn at least its opportunity cost over its lifetime. Capital in transport facilities typically has a long life. If the sequence of provision of transport facilities followed by settlement generating demand (and revenues) for transportation is expected, there is no intrinsic reason why those facilities built ahead of demand should fail to recover their opportunity cost over their lifetime in the absence of governmental subsidy. These considerations indicate that something other than building ahead of demand must provide the justification for subsidization of pioneer railroads.

External Economies from Railroad Operation

The existence of benefits of greater value to society than the price paid by purchasers of railroad services is implicit in the argument by land grant supporters that the land grant railroads would provide some special benefit to society. Such a differential between the value of the benefits to society from an investment project and the value that accrues to private investors involves the concept of externalities. In fact, justification for public subsidy rests at a minimum (or should logically rest) on the existence of some form of externality or divergence between private and social benefits. This differential (externality) is frequently labeled an unpaid benefit. The effect of unpaid benefits is to increase the income and wealth of those who receive them. The existence of unpaid benefits is necessary for subsidization but not sufficient.

In surveying the possible case with regard to externalities, we can assume the existence of perfect capital markets, even though this does not appear to describe the actual situation for pioneer railroads during the land grant era. It makes no difference to the present analysis whether we assume that the land grant railroads were subject to constant, increasing, or decreasing cost.[5]

Private operation of investment projects with significant unpaid benefits

---

[5] For the present purposes, an assumption of decreasing costs, which are frequently supposed to characterize the railroad industry, is not necessary (see Stanley L. Engerman, "Some Economic Issues Relating to Railroad Subsidies and the Evaluation of Land Grants," p. 446). The arguments set forth here apply to the decreasing cost case as well as that involving increasing or constant costs.

2. Economic Issues in Railroad Land Grant Policy

may be possible without subsidy if some of these benefits are internalized, i.e., captured by the firm. A railroad could theoretically capture unpaid benefits by practicing price discrimination. Two general possibilities exist for such multiple pricing policies. First, the submarkets making up the firm's total market could be separated on the basis of price elasticity of demand where the conditions necessary for such separation exist. Then the firm would maximize profits by appropriate prices in the resulting multiple markets. Marginal revenue of the total output must equal marginal revenue in each submarket and marginal cost of the total output for profit maximization. Prices in relatively inelastic markets would be higher than in relatively elastic markets. One can view the practice of differential rates for short and long hauls as an attempt to practice price discrimination in this manner.

A second multiple pricing policy would be for the railroad firm to price as a perfectly discriminating monopolist. Each purchaser would be required to pay the maximum amount he is willing to pay for the quantity of transportation services offered to him. The firm would face a new demand curve—the all-or-nothing demand curve. It would produce that output for which marginal revenue was equal to marginal cost. But, because the marginal revenue curve of the all-or-nothing demand curve is the market average revenue curve, the quantity produced is the same as if the industry were one of perfect competition under conditions satisfying the Pareto optimum conditions. Multiple pricing policies could increase average revenue for the output produced compared with single price profit maximization. Additional cost incurred in utilizing a policy of multiple pricing would be a crucial factor in determining whether profits could be increased by such a policy.

Land grant policy, which permitted the railroads to sell the land to which some of the unpaid benefits accrued, was a means of allowing for internalization of part of the externalities created by the operation of the land grant railroads. If the railroad were a monopoly, internalizing at least part of the externality would have a positive effect on its output decision and would lead to a more socially desirable output than that which would occur without discriminatory pricing or other internalization of unpaid benefits. The substantive point to be drawn from this discussion is that the mere existence of unpaid benefits is not by itself sufficient justification for public subsidy.

In addition to externalities to users of a railroad's services, it is possible that some unpaid benefits could accrue to nonusers. The best known example of this variety of externality arises in the infant-industry argument.[6] In this case the externality to outsiders is the benefit from the

---

[6] *Ibid.*, pp. 446–447.

infant's learning. This spillover of learning from one project to another can result in lower costs of production and a net benefit to society. Here the necessary, but as we have seen not sufficient, condition (justification) for aid exists if there are externalities captured by nonusers of the industry's product in the economy. This potential justification for railroad subsidies has not generally been mentioned in the literature with regard to the land grant railroads, and in fact appears not to have much validity with respect to the pioneer railroads. However, if it existed in that case, such an externality would only be a necessary condition for subsidization. For sufficiency, one would also need to find that hypotheses B1 and B2 are accepted.

Another potential unpaid benefit to nonusers involves the gains associated with political unification and national defense. Even national pride could fit here.[7] Because actual measurement of such benefits is very difficult, if not impossible, we have here the kind of benefit that could be used to support almost anything, since its magnitude depends on the beholder's eye or imagination. While the existence of these benefits has been proposed in the land grant literature, and they are mentioned in at least the legislation regarding the Union Pacific, they appear to be a very weak reed to support subsidization of the United States land grant railroads. By the time the Pacific railroads were built (from the 1860s on), the value of the railroads for national defense and political unification was surely very small. National defense and political unification benefits were probably much larger 20 years earlier, but the railroads were not built then. Thus, what might have been a benefit of substance earlier was much reduced by the passage of time and events and for the analysis here can be safely ignored.[8]

Railroads as Natural Monopolies

Another suggested rationale for subsidization of the land grant railroads rests on the fact that railroads tend to be natural monopolies.[9] This means

[7] It could be argued that this is the major benefit for all those countries providing rather massive subsidies in our own day to national (flag) airlines. Again, for economic efficiency, acceptance of hypotheses B1 and B2 is required.

[8] A related rationale for subsidies would be the existence of option demand by potential users. Option demand refers to the desire to have the service available for potential future use even if there is no demand for the service at present. In the case of the railroads, such an option demand could have been for future military use or national defense even though the railroads were not required for this purpose at the time of the grants.

[9] Stanley Engerman, "Some Economic Issues Relating to Railroad Subsidies and the Evaluation of Land Grants," p. 448, makes the same point, but on the basis of the railroad industry being a decreasing cost industry. It would appear that Engerman meant to refer to

2. Economic Issues in Railroad Land Grant Policy

that demand for the services of individual railroad firms is generally limited relative to the optimum size of the firm (plant). In this case, it is clearly more efficient to have one firm rather than multiple firms in the market.

The condition for a natural monopoly is that marginal cost for the railroad firm must decline over a long range of output relative to its market. For this to occur, marginal productivity of the factors employed by the railroad must rise over a long range of output. This results primarily because of the high degree of indivisibility of the capital used by the railroad. A major reason for this technical characteristic of the railroad is that a railroad between any two points, e.g., A and B, must be built all the way between A and B, whether the number of trains of a given description which are to run between A and B per time unit is the smallest or the largest number physically possible.

The railroad firm as a monopolist follows the same criterion as other firms to select the output that maximizes the profits and wealth of the firm's owners. Since the monopolist's marginal revenue is less than average, single price profit maximization results at less than the social optimum level of output.[10] Under the appropriate circumstances, the railroad could use the multiple pricing policies discussed above to increase profits and move toward the social optimum.

It is sometimes said or implied that the existence of unpaid benefits and a social rate of return on railroad investment that exceeds the private rate of return is the result of the railroad's being a natural monopoly. Thus, intervention by society in the investment decision is thought necessary because the railroad is a natural monopoly. It is true that if the desired result is achievement of the social optimum output or a rate of output more closely approximating the social optimum, some form of subsidy

---

the substantial economies of scale for railroads, resulting from the factors discussed here, rather than to decreasing costs. As is well known, natural monopolies come into existence when the minimum average cost of production occurs at a rate of output so large relative to the market that it is most efficient for a single firm to operate in the particular market [cf. C. E. Ferguson and J. P. Gould, *Microeconomic Theory*, 4th ed. (Homewood, Illinois: Richard D. Irwin, 1975), p. 262]. As one textbook writer points out,

> Decreasing costs, or "external economies" of increasing production, as discussed above must not be confused with "Internal economies of scale" possible for a single firm with a smaller than optimum size of plant.

(Richard H. Leftwich, *The Price System and Resource Allocation*, rev. ed. (New York: Holt, Rinehart and Winston, 1961), pp. 192–193).

[10] By the usual analysis, marginal social benefit (average revenue) exceeds marginal social cost (marginal cost) for the single price profit-maximizing output of the monopolist. Larger outputs increase social welfare until the maximum social welfare is attained for the output at which average revenue equals marginal cost.

may be necessary.[11] A natural monopolist who cannot discriminate may receive negative profit (incur losses) by producing the social optimum output, and would not voluntarily choose that level of output. However, when the policy goal is to have the railroad constructed and operated because of the belief that the social rate of return on the railroad investment exceeds the private (and market) rate, it is clear that the railroad's being a natural monopoly in the usual sense is no proof of the need for provision of public subsidy to the private entrepreneurs. The railroad in this case will be able to find a rate of output yielding at least a normal or market rate of return. The fact that a railroad is a natural monopoly is not by itself a sufficient argument for subsidization of its construction or operation, even if the social rate of return on the railroad investment exceeds the private (and market) rate.

Capital Market Imperfections

A traditional economic justification for subsidies, seldom found in the historical literature, rests on a divergence between the rate of discount, or time preference, in the private sector and the social rate of time preference. This situation may result from imperfection in the capital market. Suppose the rate of discount for future income in the private sector exceeds the (true) rate of social time preference. In this instance the railroads (presumably a particularly profitable investment) would require some subsidy in order for a socially optimal amount of railroad investment to occur. However, because of the divergence between the market rate and the social discount rate, a subsidy to encourage all investments would be socially desirable.[12] This does not, by itself, provide adequate justification for a differential subsidy to railroad construction. Moreover, for the period under consideration, it does not appear likely that the rate of private time preference exceeded the "true" social rate of time preference.

Government intervention (subsidization) in the construction of transportation facilities is sometimes rationalized with the argument that there are imperfections in the capital market that make it impossible for private enterprise to raise the capital required at a cost low enough to make useful

[11] If the railroad owned land whose value would be affected by unpaid benefits created by its operation, and sold the land in addition to charging the purchasers for freight shipped, profit maximization could lead to (or more nearly to) optimum social output. However, there would be only a tendency to this solution when the land grant was for only half the adjacent land (and not necessarily even half the land reaping unpaid benefits from the railroad's operation) and discriminatory pricing is precluded. Despite this, output should be closer to the social optimum than it would be without the land grant.

[12] Such a divergence could exist because of market imperfection or inappropriate intergenerational foresight.

2. Economic Issues in Railroad Land Grant Policy

projects profitable. It is claimed that the government is not subject to these imperfections and can therefore make the investments profitably, because it can obtain the capital at a lower cost. This argument is subject to two important qualifications, which apply not only to investment in transportation facilities but to all investment. First, government financing does not alter the risk of failure of an investment, but merely reduces the risk to the lender. Second, if the rate of return on capital is used as an allocator of capital in the economy, the lower cost to the government does not justify the investment by government in projects whose return is lower than that of alternatives. A difference in interest costs may be a valid argument for government providing capital for economically feasible projects. However, the difference in interest costs is not a valid argument for choosing one project over another. The government loans to the Union Pacific and the Central Pacific are not specifically an issue in this study. However, these loans significantly lowered the cost of capital to the firms involved and reduced an important risk involved in railroad promotion, namely, the risk that the promoters would run out of funds before completing the railroad and lose the entire investment.[13]

Land grants to the Pacific railroads performed a function similar to that which government loans could have performed or did perform with respect to reducing imperfections in the capital market. The grants provided the railroads with an additional asset of value. Obtaining this asset essentially added nothing to the cost of construction of the railroad.[14] Sale of this asset presumably raised the return on the railroad investment above that obtainable by purely private enterprise for the same project. The land grant asset also promised some security against loss to investors in the railroad. Thus, the land grants were a means to reduce somewhat imper-

---

[13] Robert W. Fogel, *The Union Pacific Railroad*, p. 109. Fogel argues that if the government had built the road or supplied the funds for the Union Pacific, this risk would not have existed. The government reduced this risk by providing a relatively low cost loan which covered a major portion of the construction costs.

[14] It might be argued that the land grants did in fact cost at least the Union Pacific and the Central Pacific railroad firms something, given the "excessive" speed at which they were built in order to obtain as much land grant acreage and as large a loan as possible. Some promoters of the Union Pacific stated that the speed at which the Union Pacific was built increased the cost of the road by 25%. This argument, however, ignores the fact that slower construction would have also involved an additional cost. That additional cost would be the present value (at the market rate of interest) in the year that construction begins, of the income that would have been lost if it had taken $T + T'$ years to construct the railroad rather than T years. The race for land grants thus does not necessarily result in additional cost in a real sense. Fogel, in his study of the Union Pacific, finds that if construction costs were raised by 25% by faster construction, the additional cost of slow construction as defined here (assuming that construction proceeds at half the actual rate) would have exceeded the additional cost of fast construction. (Fogel, *The Union Pacific Railroad*, p. 104).

fections in the capital market for the railroad firms and to make it possible for them to obtain capital with a lower risk premium. Despite this consideration, it is still the case that the inability of private entrepreneurs to raise the necessary capital at a cost low enough to ensure profitability of their projects is not by itself a sufficient justification for public subsidy of those projects. The two qualifications cited above support this conclusion.

A seemingly similar justification for subsidization of the land grant railroads rests on the supposed need to provide a subsidy in order to offset private evaluations of the riskiness or uncertainty of individual projects. Stanley Engerman has suggested that this is apparently the best justification for subsidy in the case of the land grant railroads.[15] This situation can be viewed as one of imperfection in the capital market. In this case the *ex ante* view is that individual railroads would be unprofitable because of the high degree of risk or uncertainty associated with the projects. On average it may have been expected that capital devoted to the pioneer railroads would earn its opportunity cost from operations. Yet given the uncertainty of the individual projects, investors demanded a risk premium as a condition of undertaking them, because even if the railroads on average would be profitable, financial failure in operation of any single one was always possible.

The crucial issue here with regard to public policy is the social rate of return on the investment in the land grant railroads. If the expected social returns from the land grant railroads were sufficiently high, some kind of government intervention to overcome the impact on the capital market of the perceived high risk or uncertainty for private investors could be desirable. This argument suggests an expectation that the unaided private rate of return on individual investments in the land grant railroads would be less than the opportunity cost of capital (market rate of return).

Hypotheses of the Land Grant Advocates

Those who supported land grants to pioneer railroads did argue that the grants would be beneficial to society.[16] Land grant advocates also believed

[15] Stanley L. Engerman, "Sound Economic Issues Relating to Railroad Subsidies and the Evaluation of Land Grants," p. 450.

[16] Their position is summed up in the following statement by Senator William M. Gwin of California, as quoted in Fogel, *The Union Pacific Railroad*, p. 91, with regard to the operation of the pioneer railroads: "Our population would be increased, our resources doubled, and the continent covered with people and states from the Atlantic to the Pacific. Our wealth would be more than doubled; so would our products. A new impulse would be given to our agriculture, manufacturing, mining, commercial and navigating interest." At the same time few doubted that these railroads would fail, in fact would not be built for some period of time, without the aid of the government.

2. Economic Issues in Railroad Land Grant Policy

that the rate of return on private investment in the railroads would be less than the market rate. Thus, while the railroads were expected to be socially beneficial, rational private investors would not undertake construction of the roads. At the same time, it was expected that the land grant subsidy would raise the private rate of return on the railroads to at least the market rate. This set of expectations demonstrates the two hypotheses regarding private rates of return: hypothesis A1, that the unaided private rate of return on investment in the land grant railroads would be less than the market rate of return; and hypothesis A2, that the land grant subsidy would make that private rate at least equal to the market rate.[17] It is important to note that these were *ex ante* expectations—expectations before the fact. The empirical test of these hypotheses for the railroad systems included in this study (see Chapter 4) is on an *ex post* basis—on the basis of what actually happened. In effect, the hypothesis tests of this study evaluate the question of whether what happened with regard to private (and social) rates of return (*ex post*) corresponds with what was expected (*ex ante*).

For rationality in respect of economic efficiency, two additional hypotheses must have been included in the arguments of land grant supporters. Hypotheses A1 and A2 alone are insufficient to support the economic rationality of the land grant subsidy. Supporters of the land grant policy clearly believed that the land grant railroads would be beneficial to society. However, the mere fact that a project will be beneficial to society is not by itself sufficient justification for public subsidy to private investors. Product X or Product Y may be very beneficial to society, but that alone does not justify public subsidy to the private investors in products X and

---

[17] Land grants were not the only means available to accomplish this result if it were considered socially desirable. Two major alternatives were possible. First, various actions would reduce the private risk of loss without changing the expected value of the projects. Government guarantee of private securities or use of government rather than private securities to finance investment would accomplish this goal. The latter was in fact used for several land grant railroads, suggesting that capital market conditions were crucial in determining the extent of government intervention. A second major possibility involves provision of a nonrelated subsidy to in effect diversify the investors' portfolio. The expected value of the package (railroad plus the nonrelated subsidy) would be higher, but that of the railroad unchanged, while the risk of investor loss on the railroad would be reduced. Provision of an asset of value, e.g., land grants in an already settled area, cash grants, etc., in conjunction with the railroad securities would accomplish this goal. The land grants did not accomplish this because they promised a higher expected return, highly correlated with the return from operations of the railroad, without a large reduction in risk. From these considerations we can see that the land grants were not the most efficient form of subsidy in economic terms, although in terms of political feasibility they may have been best. For a detailed discussion of these points, see Stanley L. Engerman, "Some Economic Issues Relating to Railroad Subsidies and the Evaluation of Land Grants," pp. 450–452.

Y. The proponents of land grant aid seem to have believed that while the land grant railroads would be privately unprofitable, they would at the same time be sufficiently socially profitable to make their subsidization economically rational. This implies the two additional hypotheses discussed earlier: hypothesis B1, that the social rate of return on investment in the land grant railroads would exceed the average opportunity cost of capital (the market rate of return); and hypothesis B2, that the social rate of return would exceed the marginal opportunity cost of capital. The latter refers to the social rate of return on projects curtailed or abandoned as a consequence of the diversion of capital to the land grant railroads with the provision of the land grant subsidy. The empirical tests (*ex post*) of hypotheses B1 and B2 for the land grant systems included in this study are reported in Chapter 5. The earlier comments with respect to hypotheses A1 and A2 and *ex ante* and *ex post* considerations apply also to the evaluation of hypotheses B1 and B2.

For a specific investment project (railroad system), one can clearly argue that the land grant policy was beneficial to society if a test of the four hypotheses leads to acceptance of (failure to reject) all four.[18] If either hypothesis B1 or hypothesis B2 is rejected, it is equally clear that, in terms of economic efficiency, the land grant policy was not beneficial to society. Rejection of hypotheses A1 and A2, but acceptance of (failure to reject) hypotheses B1 and B2, makes it much less clear whether the land grant policy was or was not beneficial to society.[19] The way out of this tangle seems to be to draw a clear distinction between *ex ante* and *ex post* considerations. The test here of hypotheses A1 and A2 is on an *ex post* basis. Land grant policy was formulated on *ex ante* expectations. From the historical record it seems clear that hypotheses A1 and A2 are correct on an *ex ante* basis. If we reject hypotheses A1 and A2 on an *ex post* basis, the meaning of this rejection is simply that what happened with regard to private rates of return did not correspond with what was expected. However, land grant policy may have been beneficial for society even if hypotheses A1 and A2 are rejected (*ex post*) for all land grant railroads. All that is required to conclude that land grant policy with regard to a specific

---

[18] Acceptance of hypotheses A1 and A2 when the private rate of return with the subsidy is greater than the market rate indicates that subsidy was required, but that the amount provided was nonoptimal (in this case too large).

[19] One could argue that subsidization accelerated the construction and operation of the land grant railroads and thus led to more rapid or earlier economic growth than would have otherwise occurred if hypotheses B1 and B2 are accepted. On this basis, the land grants could be viewed as beneficial to society. It has been suggested that the acceleration of construction was 10 to 15 years at most [cf. Robert Edgar Riegel, *The Story of Western Railroads* (New York: Macmillan, 1926), p. 43]. This, of course, is simply an educated guess and there are others who argue that no acceleration of construction occurred.

2. Economic Issues in Railroad Land Grant Policy

railroad was beneficial for society, that is, economically rational, is acceptance of (failure to reject) hypotheses B1 and B2 on an *ex post* basis.[20]

We see from this survey that the best justification for subsidization of the land grant railroads remains the necessity for an offset for private evaluation of the riskiness or uncertainty involved in the projects. The evaluation of this justification here will be done by tests of the hypotheses A1, A2, B1, and B2 discussed above for the seven land grant railroads included in this study.

Acceptance of the hypotheses proposed here would not show that land grant policy was the most efficient means of accomplishing the social goals involved in land grant policy. In fact, for the subsidization rationale involved in hypotheses A1, A2, B1, and B2 land is not the preferred method of subsidizing construction because the land grants provided a higher rate of return without reducing risk and the value of the subsidy was highly correlated with the return from railroad operations. Thus, land grant policy, as it was actually implemented, was not efficient; that is, it was not the best subsidy for promotion of the appropriate investment and output decisions.

Railroad Land Grants and the Distribution of Income

One further economic issue that is worth a brief note is the question of the impact of the land grants on income and wealth distribution. The railroad land grants represented a transfer of wealth from common holding (the public domain) to a relatively few favored individuals. There surely is little doubt that this action operated to increase the inequality of the distribution of wealth holding and the distribution of income. The question of substance is, how important was this alteration in wealth and income distribution?

First, how much did the land grant railroads receive from the land subsidy? The Federal Coordinator of Transportation reported net proceeds from sale of land grants of $409,564,256 through 1927.[21] This total was made up of $363,248,503 from federal grants and $46,315,753 from

---

[20] Note that the policy may have been beneficial without being the best policy possible. Society may have gained from the policy, despite its being not the most economically efficient. Here factors beyond economics enter into the evaluation. In particular, the political feasibility of alternative subsidies must be considered. Given constitutional scruples about cash assistance, the land grants were probably the cheapest form of subsidy in political terms.

[21] *Public Aids,* II, 115. This does not include income received from the granted lands other than by their sale. It also does not include the value of unsold lands.

state grants. A later report shows total net proceeds from both federal and state land grants through 1941 of $434,806,671 plus an estimated value of unsold lands of $60,684,036.[22] The $495,490,703 total was composed of $440,400,051 from federal land grants and $55,090,652 from state land grants. For purposes of comparison, let us take the $495 million figure as the total net proceeds from the land grants. This, of course, refers to the sum of a flow over a period of more than 70 years and includes the almost $61 million estimated value of unsold lands. The comparisons presented here are with valuations of stocks at points in time. Because of this stock-flow problem, these comparisons are only indications of the impact of the land grants on wealth and income distribution.

Lee Soltow reports that if Andrew Carnegie acquired $500 million before giving it away, he would have accounted for only 0.5% of total wealth.[23] The $495 million total for net land grant sales proceeds would on this basis be equal to 0.5% of total wealth. The $495 million total is 3.8% of the estimated 1900 value of farm land in the United States.[24] Compared to the estimated value of all land in the United States in 1900, net land grant proceeds represent 1.65%.[25] If we use total estimated 1900 asset (wealth) value for the comparison, the $495 million in net land grant receipts is equal to 0.5%.[26]

The comparisons presented here suggest that while the land grants contributed to greater inequality of wealth and income distribution in the

[22] U.S. Board of Investigation and Research, *Report and Comments on H. R. 4184 . . . to the Committee on Interstate and Foreign Commerce of the House of Representatives*, March 9, 1944, p. 28.

[23] Lee Soltow, *Men and Wealth in the United States, 1850–1870* (New Haven: Yale Univ. Press, 1975), p. 113.

[24] The value of farm land in 1900 is estimated by Alvin S. Tostlebe to be $13.058 billion [see Alvin S. Tostlebe, *Capital in Agriculture: Its Formation and Financing since 1870* (Princeton: Princeton Univ. Press, 1957), p. 54]. These comparisons could be made for various years. In general, the values with which the land grant proceeds are being compared rose over time. Thus, if one selected a 1930 or 1940 basis for comparison, the value of the grant proceeds relative to the comparison value would be smaller: 1.4% in 1930; 2.1% in 1940, when the basis of comparison is the estimated value of U.S. farm land. On the other hand, an earlier basis of comparison, e.g., 1880, would produce a higher value, in the case of the value of farm land: 6.6%. The year 1900 is used here because it is approximately the midpoint of the period included in land grant sales.

[25] The estimated 1900 value of all land (in 1929 dollars) is $60.1 billion. In current dollars this is about $30 billion [see Raymond W. Goldsmith, "The Growth of Reproducible Wealth of the United States of America from 1805 to 1950," p. 310, in *Income and Wealth of the United States: Trends and Structures* (Cambridge: Bowes & Bowes, 1952), Simon Kuznets, ed., for the estimate of the value of land (in 1929 dollars) and p. 324 for national wealth deflators to convert to current dollars].

[26] *Ibid.*, p. 310, for the components of total asset (wealth) value and p. 324 for national wealth deflators.

United States, the impact was negligible:[27] too small to make income distribution a dominant issue in evaluation of land grant policy. The major issue remains whether the land grants were economically rational, i.e., whether they made a positive contribution to economic efficiency.

Summary

This study is not intended to provide a complete (macro) evaluation of railroad land grant policy and the land grant railroads. Its goal is to provide some answers with regard to those important issues involved in the testing of the four hypotheses and some further examination of the question of building ahead of demand. The following analysis and estimation is conducted at a micro, rather than a macro, level on the principle that for the land grant railroads

> each enterprise must be studied individually before it can be determined whether a land grant was necessary, helpful, ineffectual, or harmful.[28]

---

[27] Another way of viewing the comparison of net land grant sales to total assets (wealth) in 1900 is on per capita terms. Population of the United States in 1900 was 76 million. Per capita wealth (in current dollars) was $1,262, while the per capita value (in terms of the 1900 population) of net land grant sales was $6.50.

[28] David Maldwyn Ellis, *op. cit.*, p. 58.

Chapter 3

Building the Land Grant Railroads

Good economic history requires a solid foundation in the corresponding history as well as the requisite economic theory and quantitative methods. The starting point for evaluation of land grant policy must be the history of the policy and the railroads affected by it. In order to meet these objectives, this chapter presents a brief history of each of the seven land grant systems included in the study. These histories provide both a general description of the formation of the systems and an outline of the timing of their construction and expansion during the time periods used for the rate of return calculations. The details of land grant policy with regard to each system and its component railroads are also included. These histories of the railroads and land grant policy give us the necessary background for the quantitative analysis and hypothesis testing that follow.

The Central Pacific System

The railroad system that is labeled here as the Central Pacific System eventually became the Southern Pacific System. The name of the nucleus of the original system (the Central Pacific Railroad) is used as the system title in this study. The Central Pacific System defined here included 20 separate railroads (see Table A-1, Appendix A).

3. Building the Land Grant Railroads

The Central Pacific of California was organized on June 28, 1861. The initial promoter of the company was the engineer, Theodore Judah, who in 1860 discovered a practical route for a railroad over the Sierra Nevada. Armed with this information, Judah attempted to interest capitalists in San Francisco and Sacramento in financing his project. Although he was unsuccessful in San Francisco, he did interest enough people in Sacramento, including the "Big Four"—Leland Stanford, Charles Crocker, C. P. Huntington, and Mark Hopkins—to form the company and raise the money for a full instrumental survey from Sacramento to the Truckee River in the summer of 1861. After that survey, Judah thought a railroad from Sacramento to the state line would cost $12,380,000 or $88,428 per mile.[1] The line surveyed in the summer of 1861 is essentially the line of the Central Pacific today.

After the 1861 survey, the Sacramento capitalists involved in the Central Pacific, now led by Huntington and his friends, were inclined to see the project through, provided reasonable government assistance could be secured.[2] Judah journeyed to Washington to lobby for the necessary legislation, which emerged in the form of the Pacific Railroad Acts of 1862 and 1864. The primary subsidies provided in the act of 1862, aside from the right of way on government land, were 10 alternate sections of public land on each side of the railroad per (straight line) mile of railroad and the loan of United States 6% 30-year bonds. The bond loan was in the amount of $16,000 per mile for the line west of the western base of the Sierra Nevada, $48,000 per mile for the 150 miles east of the western base of the Sierra Nevada, and $32,000 per mile east of the mountainous section. The bonds were not redeemable by the government until maturity and the government was to pay the interst until that time.

The Pacific Railroad Act of 1864 was much more generous to the affected railroads than the 1862 act. The 1864 act doubled the land grant provided by the first act. A provision of even greater importance changed the lien of the United States bond loan from a first mortgage to a second mortgage. This alteration made it possible for the railroads involved to sell their own first mortgage bonds, which provided the necessary attraction for the financial resources needed not only to begin construction, but also to carry it to completion. These resources had not come forward before the act of 1864. This act was the crucial key to the successful financing of the building of the Central Pacific Railroad (and the Central Pacific System).

Construction of the Central Pacific Railroad began at Sacramento on

---

[1] Stuart Dagget, *Chapters on the History of the Southern Pacific* (New York: Ronald Press, 1922), p. 19.

[2] *Ibid.*, p. 20.

January 8, 1863. During 1863 the federal government aid was augmented by various city and county government bond subsidies. The total realized from these sources was $1,050,000.[3] The state of California also contributed by assuming the interest for 20 years on $1,500,000 of 7% bonds. With the financing provided by these sources, construction proceeded slowly from Sacramento, with various small contractors building sections of the road. Charles Crocker and Company built the first 18 miles and others built miles 19 to 29.[4] After completion of section 29 and the passage of the Pacific Railroad Act of 1864, Charles Crocker and Company was given the contract to build the railroad to the California state line. Crocker's contract for construction from section 43 eastward called for payment to be five-eighths in gold and three-eighths in capital stock at 50% of face value. The latter provision was later changed to 30% of face value.

In late 1867, as construction on the Central Pacific approached the California state line, the Big Four and others formed a new company, the Contract and Finance Company, to carry on the further construction of the railroad. The Central Pacific agreed to pay $86,000 per mile, half in cash and half in Central Pacific stock, for the Contract and Finance Company's construction of the remainder of the Central Pacific line. In addition to completing the Central Pacific main line, the Contract and Finance Company built a portion of the California and Oregon Railroad (part of the Western Pacific), the entire San Joaquin Valley branch of the Central Pacific from Lathrop to Goshen, and portions of the Southern Pacific of California before being dissolved in 1874.

The Central Pacific was opened in January 1868 to the California state line, 278 miles from Sacramento. Construction went forward rapidly in 1868 with 362 miles of road built. The Central Pacific reached the summit of Promontory Point on April 30, 1869, and the famous gold spike ceremony, signalling the linkup of the Central and Union Pacific Railroads, was held on May 10.[5] The Central Pacific then added 47.5 miles from Promontory Point to a point 5 miles west of Ogden by purchasing the line from the Union Pacific. Later, the Central Pacific leased the remaining 5 miles into Ogden for 999 years, thus establishing the proper junction of the Central and Union Pacific.[6]

---

[3] *Ibid.*, p. 21.

[4] Apparently Judah's influence prevented Crocker from building sections 19 to 29. There were a number of differences of opinion between the Big Four and the other original Central Pacific promoters led by Judah. The Big Four were able to dominate the situation completely only after Judah's death in November 1863.

[5] George Kraus, *High Road to Promontory* (Palo Alto: American West Publishing Company, 1969), p. 256.

[6] John Debo Galloway, *The First Transcontinental Railroad* (New York: Simmons-Boardman, 1950), p. 165.

3. Building the Land Grant Railroads

The work of putting together the Central Pacific System did not wait until the completion of the transcontinental line. By the end of 1867 the Big Four owned five railroads: the Central Pacific, the Western Pacific, the California and Oregon, the California Central, and the Yuba.[7] The consolidation of these lines with the Central Pacific occurred after 1867. In addition to the lines mentioned, the Big Four were also considering the acquisition of the Southern Pacific Railroad by 1867. The California and Oregon, Western Pacific, and Southern Pacific were all land grant railroads; however, the Big Four did not get the Western Pacific land grant with their acquisition of that railroad.[8]

In order to dominate the traffic between Sacramento and San Francisco Bay, the Big Four gained control of the California Pacific Railroad in 1871. The California Pacific's route from Sacramento to Oakland was much shorter than the circuitous route of the Central Pacific by way of Stockton, and as a result the California Pacific was a formidable competitor to the Central Pacific for Sacramento–Oakland traffic. As was the case with several other smaller railroads, the owners of the Central Pacific simply exercised financial control of the California Pacific for a number of years rather than legally merging it with their developing system. In 1876, the California Pacific was leased to the Central Pacific on terms very favorable to the latter.[9]

The Southern Pacific Railroad was favored in July 1866 with a grant by Congress of right of way and 10 alternate sections of land on either side of its proposed line in the state of California. This line ran from San Francisco to San Diego and then eastward to the state line. At this time, an existing railroad, the San Francisco and San José, already ran between its namesakes. Some time in 1868, the San Francisco and San José and the Southern Pacific Railroad companies fell under the control of the Huntington group.[10] On October 12, 1870, the San Francisco and San José Railroad, the Southern Pacific, the Santa Clara and Pájaro Valley Railroad, and the California Southern (a new company organized on paper only) consolidated into a new corporation: the Southern Pacific Railroad of California. Central Pacific interests clearly controlled this new company.[11]

The Southern Pacific Railroad of California came to be divided into two parts: the Northern Division, running south from San Francisco, and the Southern Division, including all the lines south of Goshen in the San

---

[7] Kraus, *op. cit.*, p. 168.
[8] Galloway, *op. cit.*, p. 116.
[9] Daggett, *op. cit.*, pp. 117–118.
[10] *Ibid.*, pp. 122–123.
[11] *Ibid.*, p. 123.

Joaquin Valley. The Northern Division, which included the old San Francisco and San José, was extended from San José to Tres Pinos by 1872. The construction effort then shifted to the San Joaquin Valley and through the desert to Mojave by 1876; however, the 240-mile stretch from Mojave to Needles was not completed until 1883. This latter line was leased to the Atlantic and Pacific Railroad (Santa Fe System) in August 1884. In the meantime, the Southern Pacific acquired the Los Angeles and San Pedro Railroad in 1874, providing itself with a southern (Los Angeles) terminal in advance of completion of the main line. The Los Angeles and San Pedro Railroad was largely built in 1868 and 1869 by Phineas Banning, a stagecoach line owner who had no connection with the Central Pacific System.[12] Under an 1872 agreement with the county of Los Angeles (which netted the railroad a grant of over $500,000 from the county), construction began north and south from the city of Los Angeles.[13] San Fernando and San Pedro were reached in 1874 and Anaheim in 1875. The link with the main line coming down from the San Joaquin Valley occurred in September 1876. Construction of the Southern Pacific mainline continued south through the Imperial Valley, reaching Fort Yuma in 1877.

Until 1874, construction on the Southern Pacific of California was undertaken by the Contract and Finance Company. This company was dissolved in 1874 and a new construction company, the Western Development Company, was created to take its place. The Western Development Company completed the major part of the Southern Pacific of California, and built part of the Northern Railway and the San Pablo and Tulare Railroad in addition to various other construction jobs for the Central and Southern Pacific and their owners. In turn, the Western Development Company was dissolved in 1878 following the deaths of Mark Hopkins (one of the Big Four) and David D. Colton, who had been a major associate of the Big Four. Mr. Colton had a one-ninth share in the Western Development Company. The replacement for the Western Development Company was the Pacific Improvement Company, created in late 1878.[14]

The Pacific Improvement Company constructed the Southern Pacific of California between Mojave and Needles and extended the Northern Division from Soledad and San Miguel. It also completed the Los Angeles and San Pedro, California and Oregon, and Oregon and California Railroads

---

[12] Franklyn Hoyt, "The Los Angeles and San Pedro: First Railroad South of the Tehachapis," *California Historical Quarterly*, XXXII (December, 1953), 329–332.
[13] *Ibid.*, pp. 128–129.
[14] The last of the construction companies was the Southern Development Company, which completed construction east of the Arizona state line. The Southern Development Company was of minor importance compared to its predecessors.

3. Building the Land Grant Railroads

and extended the Northern Railroad in the Sacramento Valley from Willows to Tehama. Between 1878 and 1880 the Southern Pacific of Arizona was built and equipped by the Pacific Improvement Company. This was followed by construction of the Southern Pacific of New Mexico, which reached El Paso, Texas, on May 19, 1881.[15] Huntington then used the financial leverage provided by his interest in the Galveston, Harrisburg and San Antonio Railroad to force an agreement between the latter road and Jay Gould of the Texas and Pacific, which resulted in the Texas and Pacific giving up its corporate rights west of El Paso and the operation of the two roads as one continuous line.[16]

Following his absorption of the Galveston, Harrisburg and San Antonio, Huntington purchased Morgan's Louisiana and Texas lines, thus enabling the Southern Pacific to enter New Orleans. By January 1883, through cars were running from New Orleans to San Francisco on what became the Southern Pacific's Sunset Route.[17] The Central Pacific System considered in this study does not include the line east of El Paso, Texas. The accounting information available allows this simplification. Moreover, for evaluation of land grant policy this specification of the Central Pacific System is adequate.

The various parts of the Central Pacific System were held together by a combination of leases and stock control. By 1877 the Huntington group held all or a majority of the stock of all companies included in the system. Initially, the Central Pacific was the lessee. The only exception was the Northern Division of the Southern Pacific of California, which was never included in the lease of the Southern Pacific to the Central Pacific. In 1884 the Southern Pacific Company of Kentucky was organized as the central company in the associates' empire. The Southern Pacific Company leased the Southern Pacific Railroad of California and the subsidiaries comprising the through line to New Orleans for 99 years from February 10, 1885. Prior to this, the Southern Pacific Company issued $100,000,000 in capital stock and acquired in exchange for its certificates the stock of the three Southern Pacific Railroads (California, Arizona, and New Mexico). The Southern Pacific Company also leased the Central Pacific Railroad and its subsidiary lines for 99 years from April 1, 1885.

The apparent reason for this change in organization was that by 1884 the ownership of the Central Pacific had become scattered, with Huntington and his friends holding less than 30% of the stock; the stock of the South-

---

[15] Virginia H. Taylor, *The Franco-Texan Land Company* (Austin & London: Univ. of Texas Press, 1969), p. 177.
[16] *Ibid.*, pp. 177–178.
[17] *Ibid.*, p. 179.

ern Pacific meanwhile continued to be closely held by the original associates.[18] The cause of this development was the creation of an active market for Central Pacific securities before one could be found for Southern Pacific securities. Sale of Central Pacific securities was apparently an important source of cash to finance the later expansion of the system. Thus, the system that existed by 1889, the final year of the period included in the present analysis, was truly a product of the Central Pacific Railroad, and for that reason is labeled the Central Pacific System.

The Union Pacific System

The prospect of constructing and operating a railroad across the great American "desert," the interior lands west of the 100th meridian, had intrigued such visionaries as Horace Greely, but even as late as 1862 had not generated excitement among capitalists. Nor was the interest of capitalists greatly stimulated by the provisions of the Pacific Railroad Act of 1862, offering 10 sections of land per mile and a 30-year loan of government bonds (currency sixes) in the amount of $16,000, $32,000, or $48,000 per mile, depending on the difficulty of the terrain. Under the provisions of the 1862 act, the government was to have a first mortgage on the property in return for its loan, and was to withhold provision of the loan until each succeeding 40 miles of construction had been approved by the government commissioners for the yet-to-be-formed company.

In September 1862 a group of congressionally designated commissioners, including two representing the government, met in Chicago to elect a temporary set of officers and launch a stock subscription drive.[19] The goal was the sale of 2,000 shares to raise $2 million, so that a permanent management could be legally elected. In 6 months only $300,000 was raised. During the next 6 months, Thomas C. Durant (a former New York medical man) rounded up enough subscribers to raise the total stock subscription to $2,177,000. Durant did this in part by supplying three-fourths of the necessary 10% down payment himself.[20] The stockholders met at the end of October 1863 for the formal organization of the company. The new management then had to wrestle with the substantial problem of raising enough money to get construction underway.

After a winter of lobbying by Durant and others, Congress passed the Pacific Railroad Act of 1864, which was signed on July 2, 1864. This act doubled the land grant and reduced the government's claim for its bond

---

[18] Daggett, *Chapters on the History of the Southern Pacific*, pp. 146–149.
[19] The Union Pacific Company, with five commissioners representing the national government, was created by the Pacific Railroad Act of 1862.
[20] Robert G. Athearn, *Union Pacific Country* (New York: Rand McNally, 1971), p. 30.

3. Building the Land Grant Railroads

loan to a second mortgage, while also providing for the release of the government bonds after completion of every 20 miles rather than every 40 miles. Despite this rather considerable liberalization of the terms of the 1862 act, capital still did not come forward in sufficient amounts to enable construction to begin. A major factor in this low level of interest by investors is said to have been their search for quick profit in the highly inflationary Civil War economy.[21] Operation of the Union Pacific Railroad certainly did not promise quick profit.

Durant and his associates finally did come up with a vehicle of sufficient attraction to entice investors interested in quicker profits than those to be obtained from running a railroad across the Great Plains. The new attraction created by Durant and his associates was a construction company to build the railroad. Initially named the Pennsylvania Fiscal Agency, the construction company was soon renamed the Crédit Mobilier of America. The Crédit Mobilier provided limited personal liability for the investors, general limited liability laws not being in existence in 1864, and created the possibility of earlier profits at less risk than those attainable with the railroad alone. With the creation of the Crédit Mobilier, the financing necessary to initiate construction finally materialized.

Tracklaying on the Union Pacific did not begin until July 10, 1865 (over 18 months after the start of construction on the Central Pacific) and then proceeded very slowly due to continuing financial difficulties. In August 1865 the tottering company was momentarily saved by the purchase of $1 million of Crédit Mobilier stock by Oakes and Oliver Ames, and a loan of $600,000 by Oakes Ames, a wealthy New England shovel manufacturer and member of Congress. Contributions of other New Englanders, impressed by the Ames brothers' example, brought the total new investment to $2.5 million. By mid-October 1865 about 15 miles of track had been completed. Two months later the construction crews were laying 1 mile of track per day and the Union Pacific was finally on its way to becoming a reality rather than a vision.

By the spring of 1867, about 400 miles of road had been completed, two trains daily ran each way between Omaha and North Platte, Nebraska, and a new financial crisis erupted. This crisis was accompanied in mid-May by the removal of Durant from control of the Crédit Mobilier and installation of Sidney Dillon in his place. Durant remained as vice-president and general manager of the Union Pacific until the road was completed in 1869.[22] In these positions, he blocked the award of further construction contracts until he became a trustee for the later contracts, which were then administered for the benefit of the stockholders of the

[21] *Ibid.*, p. 32.
[22] Galloway, *op. cit.*, pp. 210–211.

Crédit Mobilier. Various additional schemes were resorted to in the effort to attract new financing during the summer of 1867. These were successful enough that the immediate financial crisis was weathered. On November 13, 1867 the track reached Cheyenne, then in Dakota Territory.[23]

Durant and Dillon thought the Union Pacific would reach Salt Lake City before the end of 1868. Instead, the tracks had barely entered Utah by year's end. Moreover, the northerly route around the Great Salt Lake was chosen so that the railroad did not even pass through Salt Lake City. Ogden was reached on March 8, 1869.

Congress, by joint resolution of April 10, 1869, set the meeting point of the Union Pacific and Central Pacific at Promontory Summit.[24] By this time the grading crews of the competing lines had overlapped for a month or more and a good many miles. The Central Pacific spent $751,954 on rights of way and construction east of Promontory and the Union Pacific spent a larger sum on grading work west of Promontory.[25] Much of this was wasted, because it resulted in two parallel graded roadbeds across almost 200 miles of desert, with only one being used in the end.[26] The official connection, complete with the appropriate ceremonies, occurred on May 10, 1869.

The Union Pacific Railroad from Omaha, Nebraska to Ogden, Utah formed the nucleus of the Union Pacific System as it was built up in the years after 1869. As defined here, the Union Pacific System by 1889 included 47 railroad companies (see Table A-3, Appendix A). Although it is beyond the scope of the present work to discuss the development of the system during 1869–1889 in great detail, a brief outline of the system's development is given here.

Under its charter, contained in the Pacific Railroad Act of 1862, the Union Pacific Railroad was not allowed to build branches. However, it was not denied the right to enter into agreements with other railroads, including purchase. As a result, the Union Pacific System was built by a process of consolidations, purchase of other roads, purchase of controlling interest in other roads, and lease of other roads. The work of building the system began early, the more farsighted promoters of the Union Pacific having realized before reaching Promontory that feeder lines were necessary to funnel business into the main system.[27] Despite this early recognition of what was required for long-term success, the financial difficulties of the Union Pacific were such that creation of the Union Pacific

---

[23] Wyoming Territory was created in August 1868.
[24] Athearn, *op. cit.*, p. 98.
[25] Galloway, *op. cit.*, p. 103.
[26] *Ibid.*, p. 164.
[27] Athearn, *op. cit.*, p. 213.

3. Building the Land Grant Railroads

System did not get underway in earnest until the late 1870s, except for the addition of the Utah Central, in which a controlling interest was obtained in 1872.

An area of early expansion for the Union Pacific was in the Colorado Rockies. The Colorado Central, which had a standard-gauge line from Golden, Colorado to Cheyenne and a narrow-gauge line from Golden to Central City and Georgetown, was effectively under Union Pacific control by 1876, although it was not formally leased to the latter until 1879. The Colorado Central track paralleled the Denver Pacific (a branch of the Kansas Pacific System) track from Denver to Cheyenne, and its completion contributed to the financial difficulties of the Denver Pacific and the Kansas Pacific. The Kansas Pacific had gone into receivership in 1873, and in 1879 was taken over by Jay Gould. Gould proceeded to put together a system that included the Denver Pacific, Kansas Pacific, Kansas Central, the old Central Branch of the Union Pacific, and the Missouri Pacific. Gould's system threatened to become a transcontinental competitor to the Union Pacific. With all this in mind, he arranged a very favorable sale of his railroads (excluding the Missouri Pacific) on January 14, 1880, to the Union Pacific.[28] The new company was renamed the Union Pacific Railway Company. With this acquisition the Union Pacific doubled in size and now had a substantial system in Kansas and Colorado in addition to its main line. The financial health of the system was weakened, however, by the purchase of the Gould roads for far more than they were worth.[29] The Colorado portion of the system was expanded in the next year (1881) with the completion of the Julesburg branch to complete the link between Julesburg, Colorado and Denver. In addition, several roads were added in 1881 to tap the mining country of the Colorado Rockies.

During the late 1870s, considerable agricultural branch line expansion occurred in Nebraska. Some of these lines were also intended to reach into the new mining area of the Black Hills of Dakota Territory. These branches were built by independent organizations, owned by the Union Pacific, or purchased either in receivership or from another railroad. The Nebraska-based branches added in these ways between 1876 and 1879 included the following: the Omaha and Republican Valley Railroad; the Omaha, Niobrara and Black Hills Railway; the Hastings and Grand Island Railroad; the Saint Joseph and Western Railroad; and the Manhattan and Blue Valley Railroad. With these acquisitions the Union Pacific had a considerable system in eastern Nebraska.

By 1883 the Union Pacific owned 20 branch railroads of varying size and

[28] *Ibid.*, p. 227.
[29] *Ibid.*, p. 228.

had controlling interest in five others. The consolidation of 1880 yielded a system of 1,821 miles. In 1883 the Union Pacific System was almost twice as long: about 3,600 miles.[30]

The other major area of expansion of the Union Pacific System prior to 1889 was west and north of Ogden. Various lines in Utah were gathered into the system between 1872 and 1880. The most important of these was the Utah and Northern Railway (formerly the Utah Northern). The Utah Northern had built a line from Ogden to Franklin, Idaho (just over the Idaho–Utah boundary) by mid-1874. Construction then ceased until Union Pacific interests apparently took full control of the road after its sale at foreclosure in 1878. The Utah and Northern was then pushed north to a connection with the Northern Pacific at Garrison, Montana, in November 1882. Running from Ogden to Garrison, the Utah and Northern Railway became an important mainline feeder for the Union Pacific.

The last major expansion of the Union Pacific prior to 1889 was the construction of the Oregon Short Line and the development of its feeder lines and connecting lines in the area from the headwaters of the Snake River to Portland, Oregon. A survey line had been run down the Snake River to the Columbia River and the Pacific in 1867–1869.[31] Construction of the Oregon Short Line began in 1881 at Granger, Wyoming, with approximately 600 miles of railroad completed to the western terminus of Huntington in eastern Oregon by late 1884. This included a 70-mile branch line from Shoshone, Idaho to Ketchum, Idaho, to serve the Wood River mining district. The Oregon Short Line connected with the Oregon Railway and Navigation Company at Huntington, and by this connection established a through road from Omaha to Portland.[32] In 1887 the Oregon Short Line leased the Oregon Railway and Navigation Company for 99 years.[33] From January to June 1888, the Northern Pacific managed to become the joint lessee of the Oregon Railway and Navigation Company. The Union Pacific withdrew from the joint lease in June 1888. In June 1889 it successfully regained sole control of the lines west of Huntington. The Oregon Short Line and Utah Northern Railway Company was created by consolidation on August 1, 1889. The new company included its two namesake branches plus the Utah Central, the Salt Lake and Western, the Utah and Nevada, the Ogden and Syracuse, the Nevada Pacific, and the Idaho Central. In addition to the Oregon Railway, which was still operated

[30] *Ibid.*, p. 234.
[31] *Ibid.*, p. 312.
[32] James Blaine Hedges, *Henry Villard and the Railways of the Northwest* (New York: Russell & Russell, 1967), p. 134.
[33] *Ibid.*, p. 145.

3. Building the Land Grant Railroads

under lease, this new subsystem had over 1,400 miles of track.[34] The construction and development of this western subsystem completed the Union Pacific System as it enters into this study.

The Texas and Pacific System

The Texas and Pacific System is by far the smallest system included in this study, but it received (and lost most of) one of the largest land grants in acreage. The Texas and Pacific Railroad Company was chartered by act of Congress on March 3, 1871.[35] The charter provided for construction from Marshall, Texas to San Diego, California, via El Paso. In addition, branch lines from Marshall to New Orleans and from a point 100 miles east of San Diego to a connection with the Southern Pacific were included in the charter. The 1871 act provided for a federal land grant (estimated to be 18 million acres) of 20 sections per mile in California and 40 sections per mile in the territories of New Mexico and Arizona.[36] The Southern Pacific of California, in the same legislation, was authorized to build from San Francisco to Los Angeles and from a point at or near Tehachapi Pass to a connection with the Texas and Pacific at or near a point on the Colorado River.[37] The Texas and Pacific Railroad was the principal firm in the Texas and Pacific System, which included six railroads by 1900 (See Table A-5 in Appendix A for a listing of the separate railroads).

With the usual difficulties of raising the necessary capital, the progress of the Texas and Pacific was slow. On March 21, 1872 the Texas and Pacific purchased all the assets of the Southern Pacific Railroad Company (a Texas railroad, not the Southern Pacific of California). This was followed on March 30, 1872 by the purchase of the entire assets of the Southern Transcontinental Railway Company.[38] In October 1872 the Texas and Pacific purchased all the property and franchises of the Memphis, El Paso, and Pacific. These acquisitions established the Texas and Pacific as the major railroad power in Texas at the time.

On May 24, 1871 the Texas Legislature had passed, over the Governor's veto, a grant of $10,000 per mile, not to exceed a total of $6,000,000, in 8%, 30-year state bonds to be divided equally between the Southern

---

[34] Athearn, *Union Pacific Country*, p. 329.
[35] S. G. Reed, *A History of the Texas Railroads* (Houston, Texas: St. Clair, 1941), p. 151.
[36] Henry V. Poor, *Manual of the Railroads of the United States for 1878* (New York: H. V. and H. W. Poor, 1878), p. 859. Hereafter cited as *Poor's Manual* for the appropriate annual volume.
[37] Taylor, *op. cit.*, p. 76.
[38] *Ibid.*, pp. 86–87.

Pacific Railroad Company and the Southern Transcontinental Railway Company. The act provided that future legislation might grant these companies or their successors 24 sections of land per mile in place of the bonds if the state constitution were changed to permit land grants. Another provision was that the newly chartered Texas and Pacific should succeed to all the rights and privileges of the two companies if it consolidated with them.[39]

An amendment to the Texas constitution ratified by popular vote on March 19, 1873 allowed the legislature to make land grants of up to 20 sections per mile to aid railroad construction. The Texas and Pacific, which had succeeded to the bond-subsidy rights of the Southern Pacific Railroad Company and the Southern Transcontinental Railway Company, agreed to accept 20 sections per mile in lieu of bonds. The legislature, on May 3, 1873, agreed to this compromise. Despite these actions the Texas and Pacific did not receive any land for a great part of its line and averaged only 5,000 acres (7.8 sections) per mile for its trackage in Texas.[40]

On May 2, 1872 Congress passed a new act, which changed the name of the Texas and Pacific Railroad Company to the Texas and Pacific Railway Company. The 1872 act required 100 consecutive miles from Marshall to be completed and in operation within 2 years, with at least 100 miles of road built per year and the whole line completed within 10 years of the date of the act.[41] The 1872 act was amended by an act of June 2, 1874, which required construction to commence at San Diego within 1 year, with 10 miles to be in operation within 2 years and an additional 25 miles each year thereafter.[42]

When the Texas and Pacific acquired the Southern Pacific Railroad Company, the latter extended eastward from Marshall to Hallville, Texas. The Memphis, El Paso and Pacific had work underway when it was acquired, on 45 miles of road from Moore's Landing to Jefferson and an additional 25 miles west from Jefferson.

In an effort to speed up construction, Thomas A. Scott, the president and chief promoter of the Texas and Pacific in its early years, offered the position of Chief Engineer to General Grenville M. Dodge, who had performed that function for the Union Pacific during its construction to Promontory. Dodge accepted, at four times his Union Pacific salary of $5,000 per year, and organized the California and Texas Construction Company to build the railroad. This company had first been incorporated as the Domain Land Company in Pennsylvania and was reorganized on

[39] Reed, *op. cit.*, pp. 151–152.
[40] *Ibid.*, p. 152.
[41] *Ibid.*, p. 361.
[42] *Poor's Manual*, 1877–1878, p. 345.

3. Building the Land Grant Railroads

June 17, 1872 for the purpose of building the Texas and Pacific.[43] It was organized along the lines of the Crédit Mobilier, with the stockholders of the railroad company exchanging their shares dollar for dollar for the paid-in stock of the construction company, which then became the owner of the Texas and Pacific Railway Company.[44] On August 6, 1872 a contract was entered into for the construction of the Texas and Pacific from the eastern boundary of Texas to San Diego. Work began on October 1, 1872.

During the first year, the California and Texas Construction Company completed a little more than 195 miles of road, so that the Texas and Pacific had 251 miles of road: Longview to Dallas, 130 miles; Brookston to Sherman, 54 miles; and Marshall to Texarkana, 67 miles. Unfortunately, the Panic of 1873 brought construction on the Texas and Pacific to a halt.[45] In March 1874 the contract with the construction company was cancelled. These developments meant that the Texas and Pacific was threatened with the loss of its land grant unless construction could be resumed soon. Scott, as an independent contractor, managed to grade 11 miles west from Sherman, build about 8 miles west from Dallas, and extend the southern line to Eagle Ford by the end of the year. A 1-year extension granted by the legislature on April 30, 1974 temporarily protected the Texas and Pacific. A further 6-month extension was provided by the Texas Legislature's act of March 15, 1875.[46] The Texas and Pacific entered into a new contract with the California and Texas Construction Company on March 27, 1875.

In 1874 Scott had petitioned the federal government for a $60,000,000 subsidy over and above the land grants. This was later changed to a request for a guarantee of 5% interest annually for 50 years on $38,000,000 to cover estimated costs of $25,000 per mile on easier construction and $40,000 for the more difficult portions.[47] In the end, the company proposed a straight $27,368 per mile and offered to mortgage to the government a portion of its future earnings and the line west of Fort Worth.[48] The Texas and Pacific bill was reported favorably out of committee in both the House and Senate in early 1878. However, by joint resolution the House Judiciary Committee was then instructed on March 25, 1878 to investigate the Texas and Pacific's title to the 600 miles of road to be constructed between Fort Worth and El Paso and the company's ability to execute a

---

[43] Taylor, *op. cit.*, p. 93.

[44] *Ibid.*

[45] The Panic of 1873 was a general financial panic following the September 18, 1873 closure of Jay Cooke and Company of New York as a result of that company's connection with the Northern Pacific Railroad.

[46] Taylor, *op. cit.*, p. 164. Numerous additional requirements on timing and location of future construction were written into this act.

[47] *Ibid.*, p. 105.

[48] *Ibid.*, p. 122.

valid mortgage on that road. On June 4, 1878 the Texas and Pacific bill was laid aside until the next session, and in the end it was never picked up.[49]

Not only had the Texas and Pacific's attempt to obtain a further federal subsidy failed, but its lack of construction finally led to the automatic expiration, on July 1, 1877, of its right to receive further land grants from the state. By that time it was becoming clear that the Texas and Pacific would never build west of El Paso, and it appeared unlikely that it would even build as far west as El Paso itself. This also meant that the federal land grant (for construction in New Mexico, Arizona, and California) would not be obtained.

The 28-mile extension of the Texas and Pacific from Fort Worth to Weatherford, Texas was finally begun, with local assistance, in late 1878. Grading was completed on January 21, 1880, but the first train did not arrive until June 4.[50] In the meantime, Jay Gould had taken the helm of the Texas and Pacific when it became clear that Scott, who died in May, 1881, would receive no financial aid from Congress. Gould and Russell Sage formed a new construction company, the Pacific Improvement Company, to build from Fort Worth to El Paso and beyond, with General Dodge in charge of the work. The construction company agreed to build to El Paso by January 1, 1882. This set the stage for the final big construction push on the Texas and Pacific and the race between Gould and Huntington (who was pushing the Southern Pacific eastward toward El Paso). The Texas and Pacific lost this race and its connection with Huntington's Galveston, Harrisburg and San Antonio occurred 90 miles east of El Paso at Blanco Junction (Sierra Blanca, Texas) on December 1, 1881.[51]

With completion of the line to Sierra Blanca, the Texas and Pacific had 994 miles of railroad in Texas. During 1881 the Texas and Pacific also completed by construction and purchase (of the New Orleans and Pacific Railroad) a line from Shreveport to New Orleans. Except for some small branch lines and construction of its own line between Shreveport and Waskom (17.6 miles) in 1898, which allowed it to give up the lease of the Vicksburg, Shreveport and Pacific for that connection, the Texas and Pacific System included in this study was completed in 1881.

On the evidence presently available, the expansion of 1880 and 1881 was financially indigestible for the Texas and Pacific. In addition, severe weather conditions in 1884 made the Louisiana portion of the system unusable for part of the year and probably helped push the company over the financial brink. In any event, financial reorganization was required when the firm failed to pay all its bond coupons in 1884.

[49] *Ibid.*, p. 132–133.
[50] *Ibid.*, p. 175.
[51] *Ibid.*, pp. 177–178.

One result of the financial difficulties of the Texas and Pacific was an apparent cessation of investment in the years 1885 and 1886. This was followed by a considerable sum of investment for general improvements to the line in 1887 and 1888. The heavy expenditure for this purpose was one of the conditions in the program for reorganization.[52]

The Atchison, Topeka and Santa Fe System

Although it had modest beginnings, the Atchison, Topeka and Santa Fe became the largest among the United States systems included in this study. The original promoter of the Santa Fe was a former Pennsylvania lawyer, Cyrus K. Holliday. In 1859 Holliday got a charter from the Kansas Territory Legislature for the Atchison and Topeka Railroad to run between those two cities. An act passed by Congress in 1863 provided a land grant of 10 sections per mile to the state of Kansas to aid in the construction of a railroad from Atchison via Topeka to the western boundary of the state in the direction of Santa Fe, New Mexico.[53] On November 24, 1863 the name of the railroad was changed to Atchison, Topeka and Santa Fe. This railroad became the nucleus of the Santa Fe system, which included 32 railroads by 1900 (see Table A-7 in Appendix A for a listing). The state legislature passed an act to accept the federal land grant (February 8, 1864) and to give it to the Atchison, Topeka and Santa Fe as 20-mile sections of "first-class" railroad were completed. The federal legislation required that the railroad from Atchison to the Colorado–Kansas state line be completed and in operation within 10 years (by March 3, 1873).[54]

In 1868 the Santa Fe, by act of Congress, was able to buy 340,000 acres of fertile Indian lands near Topeka for $1 per acre. These lands, plus promised bond aid of $150,000 to $250,000 each from five counties (which was never paid), finally provided the financing to get the Santa Fe off the drawing board and on its way.[55] A construction company called the Atchison Associates was organized, and in the winter of 1868–1869, 10 miles of grading and a bridge over the Kansas River at Topeka were completed. Excellent coal deposits dictated the choice to build southwest from Topeka rather than from Atchison. During 1869 only the 28 miles of road to Burlingame were completed. Finances remained the main obstacle to more rapid construction. The Atchison Associates withdrew as the con-

---

[52] *Poor's Manual*, 1886, p. 188, and 1889, p. 812.
[53] L. L. Waters, *Steel Rails to Santa Fe* (Lawrence, Kansas: Univ. of Kansas Press, 1950), p. 31.
[54] *Ibid.*
[55] *Ibid.*, pp. 33–36.

struction contractor after completing the road to Burlingame, and construction beyond Burlingame was carried on by the railroad itself.

In mid-1870 the railroad was completed to Emporia and in 1871 through Florence to Newton. The 137 miles completed to Newton were about one-fourth of the total required to earn the original land grant. On March 22, 1872 the Board of Directors voted to complete the road by the deadline (March 3, 1873) despite the tight money market and potentially higher costs due to haste. In less than 9 months about 360 miles of road, including the section between Atchison and Topeka, were completed, and cars were run to the state line by December 28, 1872.[56] The first branch line, under the charter of the Wichita and South Western Railway Company, was also built in 1872 from Newton to Wichita. This line was leased to the Santa Fe on completion and was later consolidated into the system.

The structure of the Santa Fe System is clearer if we note that the system consisted of the Atchison, Topeka and Santa Fe Railroad in Kansas, to which were added a large number of other railroads built in one way or another in the interests of the Santa Fe. Once the Santa Fe itself was established, the smaller lines were financed by the process of security exchanges between them and the Santa Fe. The subsidiary roads gave their securities, for which there was no substantial market, to the Santa Fe and received in return Santa Fe securities for which there was a larger market. The proceeds from the Santa Fe securities then provided the necessary funds for construction of the smaller lines. At the same time, ownership of the securities of the smaller lines gave the Santa Fe control of these lines.

The Santa Fe survived the Panic of 1873, but for about 2 years was unable to raise the funds required for further expansion. During this period the major bright spot for the Santa Fe was the substantial shipments of cattle and buffalo hides and bones from Dodge City.[57] In May 1875 the extension west of Granada, Colorado began. Construction was carried forward under the name of a Santa Fe subsidiary, the Pueblo and Arkansas Valley Railroad (formerly the Colorado and New Mexico Railroad, the Pueblo and Salt Lake Railroad, and the Arkansas Valley Railroad), which had a charter to build in Colorado. Pueblo, Colorado was reached February 29, 1876, following a struggle with the Kansas Pacific, which also wished to build to Pueblo. Lease of the Kansas City, Topeka, and Western in 1875 provided expansion to the east and entrance to Kansas City. During 1877 only 31 miles of track (a branch line down Walnut Creek from

[56] *Ibid.*, p. 95.
[57] James Marshall, *Santa Fe: The Railroad That Built an Empire* (New York: Random House, 1945), pp. 69–72, 91.

3. Building the Land Grant Railroads

Florence) were completed; however, considerable improvements were undertaken on the Pueblo extension.[58]

The big expansion of the Santa Fe system began in 1878. At the end of 1875 the Santa Fe had 786 miles of track. This was expanded to 7,000 miles by September 1889.[59] On February 8, 1878 a charter was granted in the name of the New Mexico and Southern Pacific Railroad to build south from Pueblo, Colorado to New Mexico. The Pueblo and Arkansas Valley Railroad was responsible for this new construction. Train service to Las Vegas, New Mexico via Raton Pass began in July 1879. The main line then swung south to Albuquerque, but Santa Fe was finally reached with a branch line in early 1880. Several branch or feeder lines in Kansas were also undertaken in 1879, and an abortive attempt was made by the Pueblo and Arkansas Valley to build from Pueblo to Leadville.[60] Although the Santa Fe won the "battle" of Raton Pass with the Denver and Rio Grande Railway, it lost the line to Leadville. In retrospect, it is clear that the Santa Fe won the more lasting victory.

Albuquerque was reached in April 1880, and 6 months later an additional 100 miles had been completed into San Marcial, New Mexico. About this time, the Santa Fe reached an agreement with the Southern Pacific to connect with the latter at Deming, New Mexico. This connection was made on March 8, 1881. During construction to Deming the Santa Fe also built from San Marcial to El Paso. From San Marcial to the Texas boundary this construction was accomplished in the name of the Rio Grande, Mexico and Pacific Railroad; the Rio Grande and El Paso Railroad was the vehicle for construction from the Texas line to El Paso.[61] In March 1882 the Santa Fe acquired the Sonora Railway, running from Benson, Arizona to Guaymas, Mexico. The Sonora Railway is not included in the Santa Fe System in this study.

Rather than relying on the connection with the Southern Pacific in southwestern New Mexico, the directors of the Santa Fe wanted their own line to the Pacific coast. To further this goal they acquired a half-interest in the Atlantic and Pacific Railroad from the new St. Louis and San Francisco Railroad (Frisco) in early 1880. Under the agreement between the two roads, the Santa Fe was to construct the 35th-parallel line of the Atlantic and Pacific from Albuquerque to California. The Atlantic and Pacific was one of the oldest railroad enterprises in the west, with a charter (for the Southwest Railroad) from the state of Missouri dating

[58] *Ibid.*, p. 93.
[59] *Ibid.*, p. 115.
[60] Waters, *op. cit.*, pp. 57–59.
[61] *Ibid.*, p. 61.

from 1849. Little work was ever accomplished on the proposed railroad, and with the state threatening foreclosure, John C. Frémont obtained the charter of the company (the Southwest Railroad, which later became the South Pacific Railroad Company) in 1866. Frémont then obtained a charter for a new company, the Atlantic and Pacific Railroad, by act of Congress, on July 27, 1866. The South Pacific joined the Atlantic and Pacific in 1870.[62] After going into receivership in 1875, the Atlantic and Pacific was acquired by the Frisco in 1876. The 1866 act had authorized the Southern Pacific of California to connect with the Atlantic and Pacific at a point on the California boundary selected by the former. Starting in the spring of 1880, the Santa Fe pushed construction by the Atlantic and Pacific Railroad through to a connection with the Southern Pacific at Needles, California in August 1883.

The Santa Fe's hopes for a terminus on the Pacific in the United States were not satisfied by the line to Needles. At the same time, San Diego, which had been promised a railroad by the Southern Pacific of California and the Texas and Pacific, was still waiting for those promises to materialize. Several San Diego groups and the leaders of the Santa Fe established the California Southern Railroad Company in 1880. This company's line was completed from National City (south of San Diego) to San Bernardino, California in September 1883. Realizing that a connection between the California Southern and the Atlantic and Pacific at Needles would greatly reduce the value of its Mojave Division (the 240-mile section from Mojave to Needles), the Southern Pacific leased that section of line to the Atlantic and Pacific in August 1884.[63] In November 1885 the gap between San Bernardino and Mojave was spanned by the California Southern. The Santa Fe then had a Pacific outlet (in the United States), 17 years after the first spade of dirt was turned in Kansas.

While the push to the west was proceeding, the Santa Fe was expanding in its home territory. In late 1880 the Santa Fe acquired control of the Kansas City, Lawrence, and Southern Railroad, whose 365 miles provided an excellent complement to the main line. Five additional small branch lines with a total of 114 miles of road were built in Kansas under various corporate names in 1881 and 1882. Three short branches were also built in New Mexico during 1882. About 200 miles of branch construction were started in 1883 but little was completed. During 1884 four branches in Kansas and two in New Mexico were completed, for a total of 245 miles of track.[64] The branch line additions of 1880–1884 gave the Santa Fe a well

---

[62] *Ibid.*, p. 64.
[63] *Ibid.*, p. 73.
[64] *Ibid.*, p. 76.

3. Building the Land Grant Railroads

developed network in Kansas and an adequate branch system in New Mexico.

An expansion started by the Santa Fe in 1884 extended the system from Kansas to the Gulf of Mexico. Expansion through Indian Territory required authority from Congress, which was forthcoming in 1884 to the Southern Kansas Railway Company (a Santa Fe creation). While the Southern Kansas received permission to build south through Indian Territory, the Gulf, Colorado and Santa Fe (GC & SF) was given authority to build north. Informal cooperation between the Santa Fe and the GC & SF began in 1884, and in 1886 the Santa Fe purchased controlling interest in the GC & SF. Counting its branches, the GC & SF possessed 695 miles of lines in 1886. The main line ran from Galveston to Brownwood and a major branch ran from Temple to Fort Worth in the direction of Indian Territory. This branch was extended from Fort Worth to Purcell in Indian Territory, to connect with the Santa Fe (Kansas Southern) under the terms of the 1886 agreement. In the fall of 1886, construction of a second line of the Southern Kansas Railroad began from Kiowa, Kansas through Indian Territory to the Texas boundary. From there to Panhandle City, Texas, construction was continued in late 1887 by the Southern Kansas Railway Company of Texas.

While the drive to the Gulf was underway, numerous small additions were made to round out the system. A number of these in Southern California were combined in the California Central Railway Company, established in 1887. In Kansas the majority of small additions (over 400 miles of line) were brought into the system by a new subsidiary, the Chicago, Kansas and Western Railroad Company.

During the Santa Fe's great building period, its president was William B. Strong, who ruled from 1881 to 1889. Strong is quoted as having said that "when a railroad ceases to grow, it begins to decay."[65] The final burst of growth of the Santa Fe system, and implementation of Strong's philosophy, was the expansion of the system from Kansas City to Chicago. The Chicago, Santa Fe and California Railway Company was organized and obtained the necessary Illinois and Iowa charters in late 1886. The whole new line was completed in 1 year. Several other small additions were made to the system in 1887, including the Denver and Santa Fe from Pueblo to Denver. The year 1887 saw the end of the great construction period of the Santa Fe system.

In 1890 the Santa Fe acquired the St. Louis and San Francisco (Frisco) system and the Colorado Midland Railway. Both of these roads were in serious financial difficulties. Their purchase proved to be a grave mistake.

[65] *Ibid.*

After the reorganization (and foreclosure sale) of 1895, both the Colorado Midland and Frisco were separated from the Santa Fe.[66] They are not included in the Santa Fe system in this study.

In late 1889 the Santa Fe carried out a voluntary reorganization, including the issuance of new bonds. The general result was to raise the system's funded debt and reduce the annual fixed charges. This financial reorganization appreciably eased the Santa Fe's position. The improvement was short-lived, because the 1890 purchase of the Frisco system and the Colorado Midland and the replacement of a large volume of income bonds with $100 million in new second mortgage bonds, coupled with the onset of a protracted depression, spelled financial disaster for the Santa Fe. The Santa Fe System went into receivership on December 23, 1893. A number of reorganization schemes were proposed in the following 2 years. An acceptable plan was developed and the reorganized Atchison, Topeka and Santa Fe Railway Company was chartered on December 12, 1895.

From 1895 to 1900 the Santa Fe concentrated primarily on extension and acquisition of branch lines. One important move was the trade of the New Mexico and Arizona Railroad and the Sonora Railroad to the Southern Pacific Company (in 1897) for the Mojave Division of the Southern Pacific of California. The major expansion of the period was the purchase of the stock and completion of the construction of the San Francisco and San Joaquin Valley Railway. This provided entrance to San Francisco and lines in the rich San Joaquin Valley. Because freight operations did not begin until May 1, 1900 (and passenger service until July 1, 1900), this railroad is not included in the Santa Fe System of this study.

The Northern Pacific System

The Northern Pacific Railroad was chartered by act of Congress on July 2, 1864. The Northern Pacific System, including 36 separate railroads by 1900 (see Table A-9 in Appendix A), was developed, with the Northern Pacific Railroad as its base. The Northern Pacific was authorized to construct a railroad from Lake Superior to Puget Sound with a branch line to Portland, Oregon. No pecuniary subsidy, like the loans to the railroads comprising the first transcontinental, was provided for this ambitious undertaking, but a land grant of 20 sections per mile in states and 40 sections per mile in territories was provided. The date for completion of the railroad was initially set as July 4, 1876, but this was extended 2 years by the act of May 7, 1866 and an additional year by the act of July 1, 1868.[67]

---

[66] Marshall, *op. cit.*, p. 251.
[67] *Poor's Manual*, 1885, p. 718.

3. Building the Land Grant Railroads

The Northern Pacific Railroad was not formally organized until December 6, 1867. On March 1, 1869 Congress authorized the railroad company to issue mortgage bonds, which the original act of 1864 had forbidden.[68] After Jay Cooke and Company had undertaken the contract for the sale of the mortgage bonds, Congress authorized, by joint resolution of May 21, 1870, the issuance of mortgage bonds on all the railroad's property, including its land grant. The same resolution also provided for relocation and construction of the main line to some point on Puget Sound via the valley of the Columbia River, with the right to locate and construct its main branch from some convenient point on the trunk line across the Cascade mountains to Puget Sound.[69]

Construction on the Northern Pacific began at Duluth, Minnesota in July 1870. Also during 1870, the Northern Pacific purchased the St. Paul and Pacific Railroad and the St. Paul and Pacific Railroad: First Division. Construction extended the Northern Pacific main line 450 miles to Bismarck, Dakota Territory by 1873. Construction on the west coast started in 1870 at Kalama, Washington Territory and in 1873 reached Tacoma, Washington Territory (the new terminal city which the Northern Pacific had laid out). The crash of Jay Cooke and Company and the ensuing Panic of 1873 brought an abrupt end to construction. There was almost no railway construction on the Pacific coast during the next 4 years.[70] In subsequent reorganizations the Northern Pacific lost the St. Paul and Pacific railroads, which later became the seed for the Great Northern System. The Northern Pacific defaulted on its bond interest on January 1, 1874, and the entire property went into receivership in April 1875. The road and franchises were sold under foreclosure to a committee of the bondholders, and the company was reorganized in September 1875.[71]

During 1876 the Puyallup Branch (31 miles) was undertaken from Tacoma to the coal fields (Wilkeson, Washington Territory) in the foothills of the Cascades. This construction helped silence critics in Oregon and Washington Territory and in Congress, who were demanding the forfeiture of the land grant across the Cascades on the ground that it was not being used.[72] The line to the coal fields was completed in late 1877.

The Western Railroad of Minnesota, from Brainerd to Sauk Rapids, was leased for 99 years by the Northern Pacific in 1878. Construction on the eastern end of the main line got underway again in 1879 with an extension 59 miles west from Bismarck. The Casselton Branch Railroad, running 32 miles from Casselton to Elm River, Dakota Territory, was constructed by

---

[68] *Ibid.*
[69] Hedges, *op. cit.*, p. 22.
[70] *Ibid.*, p. 26.
[71] *Poor's Manual*, 1876–1877, p. 394.
[72] Hedges, *op. cit.*, p. 29.

the Northern Pacific in 1880. Construction on the main line proceeded westward (159 miles) in 1880 to Glendive, Montana Territory. Another 221 miles were also completed between Wallula Junction, Washington Territory (at the confluence of the Snake and Columbia Rivers) and the boundary of Idaho Territory near Lake Pend d'Oreille. By early 1882 the section eastward from Wallula Junction to the Idaho line was completed, and the main line was extended another 143 miles to Big Horn River, Montana Territory. Several branch lines and extensions in Dakota Territory were also completed during 1881. Construction proceeded rapidly in 1882 and 1883, with the main line being completed to a connection with the Oregon Railway and Navigation Company at Wallula Junction and the Kalama-Tacoma line extended to Portland by September 1883.[73] The Oregon Railway and Navigation Company provided the link from Wallula Junction to Portland.

Completion of the transcontinental road was cause for celebration, but was accompanied by severe financial difficulties. Construction expenditures had so far outrun the estimates that by October 1883 there was a deficit of almost $9.5 million in terms of the excess of expenditures over receipts from the $40 million general mortgage bonds, and Henry Villard, President of the Northern Pacific, estimated that another $5.5 million would be needed.[74] To resolve this problem, $20 million worth of new second mortgage bonds were sold, increasing the total Northern Pacific bond issue to $61.6 million.[75] This substantial increase in the system's debt was followed by a sharp fall in the value of Northern Pacific stock and the resignation of Villard.[76]

By the middle of 1884, the Northern Pacific operated 2,453 miles of railroad, including 478 miles of branch roads. Construction activities focused on the 253-mile Cascade Branch during the years 1885 to 1887, with the road being built from both the western (Tacoma) and the eastern (Pasco, Washington Territory) ends. Trains started running over the Cas-

[73] *Ibid.*, p. 109.
[74] *Ibid.*, p. 114.
[75] *Ibid.*
[76] *Ibid.*, p. 111. In late 1880 and 1881, Villard and some associates had gained control of the Northern Pacific by purchase of its stock. Villard was concerned that the proposed Cascade route would strip his railroad, the Oregon Railway and Navigation Company, of a substantial part of its income. After gaining control of the Northern Pacific, Villard set up a third company, The Oregon and Transcontinental Company, to own the majority of the stock of the other two companies and to supply the means for building and equipping branch lines of the Northern Pacific. The depreciation of Northern Pacific stocks after the construction deficit had a significant adverse effect on the Oregon and Transcontinental. Villard also resigned from the presidencies of the Oregon Railway and Navigation Company and the Oregon and Transcontinental in early 1884.

3. Building the Land Grant Railroads

cade Branch in July 1887, using a switchback in place of a 1.9-mile tunnel, which was not completed until the summer of 1888. Only about 70 miles were added to branch lines elsewhere from mid-1884 to mid-1886.

With completion of the Cascade Branch in sight, branch line construction and acquisition accelerated after mid-1886. The Spokane and Palouse, Helena and Red Mountain, and Duluth and Manitoba Railroads (about 180 miles in all) were added during the fiscal year (July 1 to June 30) of 1886–1887. During the following fiscal year, four new branch lines were added, and major extensions were completed on three old ones, so that branch lines on June 30, 1888 totaled 1,035 miles, a gain of 300 miles during the year.[77] Operating lines were extended only about 50 miles in the succeeding year, but by the end of 1890 another 500 miles had been added to the system by construction, lease, and purchase. More than half of this (264 miles) was in the Northern Pacific and Manitoba Railroad, which had previously been operated independently (in the interest of the Northern Pacific) but which was formally turned over to the management of the Northern Pacific by contract of July 1, 1890.[78]

The Northern Pacific System made a major addition on April 1, 1890 by leasing the Wisconsin Central lines (887 miles), comprising the Wisconsin Central Company and its leased roads (395 miles) and the Wisconsin Central Railroad Company and its leased lines (492 miles).[79] This lease was cancelled on September 27, 1893 as a result of the default of the Northern Pacific on the August 1 rental.[80]

The combination of its large bond debt with fixed interest payments and the depression starting in 1892 proved too much for the financial health of the Northern Pacific. Receivers were appointed for the Northern Pacific Railroad Company on August 15, 1893, with separate receivers appointed in October 1893 for the leased and branch lines.[81] The branch line receiverships were vacated in November 1894. The charter of the Superior and St. Croix Railroad Company, which was approved by the Legislature of Wisconsin in 1870, was acquired by the reorganization managers of the Northern Pacific Railroad Company in 1895. In July 1896 the company assumed the corporate title of Northern Pacific Railway Company.[82] On September 1, 1896 the new company took over the property, rights, and franchises of the Northern Pacific Railroad Company, which had been sold under foreclosure in July, 1896.

[77] *Poor's Manual*, 1889, p. 847.
[78] *Ibid.*, 1891, p. 394.
[79] *Ibid.*, 1893, p. 494.
[80] *Ibid.*, 1894, p. 601.
[81] *Ibid.*
[82] *Ibid.*, 1897, p. 575. The reorganization plan is outlined in *Poor's Manual*, 1896, p. 690.

The Northern Pacific Railway Company obtained the properties of the old Seattle, Lake Shore, and Eastern Railway Company in April 1898, and put into effect a plan to reorganize the company. Two new companies were created to succeed to the property of the old line. These were the Seattle and International Railway, Seattle to Sumas, Washington (125 miles), and the Spokane and Seattle, Spokane to Davenport, Washington (50 miles). With the exception of 4 miles leased to the Great Northern, the latter road was not operated. The Northern Pacific also purchased a controlling interest in the 180-mile Washington and Columbia River Railway in 1898 and reacquired the lease on the 109-mile Central Washington Railroad Company (renamed Washington Central Railroad in its 1898 reorganization).[83] These 1898 acquisitions essentially completed the Northern Pacific System as included in this study, although there were another 100 to 200 miles of branch lines constructed or acquired in the 4 years following the 1896 reorganization.

The Great Northern Railway System

In 1857 the legislature of Minnesota provided a charter to the Minnesota and Pacific Railway Company. The charter gave the company authority to build a railroad from Stillwater to St. Paul and through St. Anthony to Breckenridge, with a branch by way of St. Cloud to St. Vincent on the Canadian boundary. (Apparently the legislature intended this to be a "saintly" railroad!) Construction of the Minnesota and Pacific Railway was to be financed with first mortgage bonds. Because state bonds were more readily salable than the bonds of a fledgling railroad, $600,000 of the company's bonds were given to the state as security for a loan of an equal amount of state bonds.[84] The company defaulted on the interest payments on both its own first mortgage and the state bond loan after 62.5 miles of roadbed from St. Paul to near St. Cloud had been completed (except for placement of the superstructure). In 1860 the State of Minnesota purchased the railroad's property for $1,000 at a foreclosure sale.

The St. Paul and Pacific Railroad Company was incorporated for the purpose of taking over the rights and property of the Minnesota and Pacific, and in 1862 the legislature conferred those rights on the new company, including the land grant to 10 sections per mile provided by act of Congress on March 3, 1857 and amended July 12, 1862.[85] The St. Paul and Pacific completed the 10 miles from St. Paul to St. Anthony and had

---

[83] *Ibid.*, 1900, p. 584.
[84] Harold M. Sims, "History of the Great Northern Railway Company," *Shipper and Carrier* (February 1925), 3.
[85] *Public Aids*, II, 106.

3. Building the Land Grant Railroads 57

that line in operation on July 2, 1862. The First Division of the St. Paul and Pacific Railroad Company was organized and took over the property and rights of the St. Paul and Pacific in February 1864. The First Division completed the lines from St. Anthony to Sauk Rapids and Breckenridge and in 1871 undertook to construct the lines from St. Cloud to St. Vincent and Brainerd. At the end of 1871 a total of 283 miles of railroad had been completed.[86]

In 1870 the First Division of the St. Paul and Pacific Railroad was purchased by the Northern Pacific Railroad Company, but operated independently.[87] The First Division was to connect with the Northern Pacific at Brainerd. During 1872 an additional 35 miles of road were opened on the First Division from St. Cloud to Melrose.[88] The financial collapse of the company led to a cessation of construction, and on August 1, 1873 that portion of the road from St. Paul to Sauk Rapids and St. Cloud to Melrose (the St. Vincent and Brainerd Extension) was placed in receivership. It was later sold under foreclosure and reorganized as a separate company.[89] During the receivership period, construction was completed on 236.75 miles of the St. Vincent Extension portion of the St. Paul and Pacific. Further extension of the line resulted from the lease of the Red River and Manitoba Railroad (30 miles) and Red River Valley Railroad (10.75 miles).[90] During its own reorganization in 1873 the Northern Pacific surrendered the main line and branches of the First Division to the bondholders. A plan for the reorganization of all the St. Paul and Pacific Companies, including the First Division, was finally agreed upon in early 1879.

James J. Hill and his associates enter the story at this point with the organization of the St. Paul, Minneapolis and Manitoba Railway on May 23, 1879, and the June 1879 purchase of the various St. Paul and Pacific properties, as well as the two leased roads of the St. Vincent Extension.[91] Since the State of Minnesota had enforced forfeiture of the uncompleted line from Sauk Rapids to Brainerd in 1877 (on the grounds of default by the company with regard to conditions imposed on it by the legislature), the St. Paul, Minneapolis and Manitoba came into possession of 560 miles of railroad, all located in Minnesota.[92]

---

[86] *Poor's Manual*, 1872–1873, p. 577.
[87] *Ibid.*, 1875–1876, p. 255.
[88] *Ibid.*, 1874–1875, p. 621.
[89] *Ibid.*, 1877–1878, p. 784.
[90] *Ibid.*, 1880, p. 829.
[91] *Ibid.*, p. 826. An important factor in this purchase was the act of the Minnesota Legislature on March 6, 1876, which allowed railroads chartered by the state to be sold at foreclosure and reorganized with their land grants intact [see Pierre Berton, *The Impossible Railway* (New York: Knopf, 1972), pp. 186–188].
[92] Sims, *op. cit.*, 7.

In 1879 and 1880 the gap in the St. Vincent Extension from Alexandria to Barnsville and the line from Fishers Landing to Grand Forks, Dakota (Territory) were completed by construction and the Brown's Valley Railroad from Morris to Brown's Valley, Minnesota, was purchased. Also under a separate organization (Dakota Extension), the main line was built from Barnsville to Moorhead.[93] With the completion of the latter to Grand Forks, the company had 860 miles of railroad in operation by April 30, 1881. To obtain an outlet to the Great Lakes, an interest was obtained in the St. Paul and Duluth Railroad Company, running from St. Paul to the head of Lake Superior. Another 66.5 miles was built under the charter of the Minneapolis and St. Cloud Railroad Company from St. Cloud to Hinckley on the St. Paul and Duluth, and opened for operation by the end of 1882. A land grant of 10 sections per mile was attached to the charter of the Minneapolis and St. Cloud.[94]

Hill became president of the company in 1882 and began the push to the Pacific in earnest. With the completion of various extensions and branches in Dakota Territory and Minnesota, the company had 1,058 miles of railroad in operation by mid-1882. An additional 292 miles were added in the following year. The westward push stalled, apparently due to financial difficulties, and the following 2 years (to July 1, 1885) were quiet ones on the construction and acquisition front, with only 117 miles added to the system. At the end of 1885 about 1,470 miles of railroad were operated by the company.

The Montana Central Railway Company, incorporated in 1886, quickly came under control of the St. Paul, Minneapolis and Manitoba interests and provided the vehicle for construction of the main line and branches in Montana.[95] Construction was completed from Great Falls to Helena in 1887, and to Butte in 1888. In the meantime the extension from North Dakota was pushed forward rapidly, with approximately 645 miles of track laid westward from Minot, North Dakota to a connection with the Montana Central at Helena during 1887. Several branch lines in Dakota and Minnesota were also completed and put into operation during the year. Further branch line construction and acquisition brought the total mileage of the system to 3,260 miles by the end of 1890.

Under the authority of various acts of the Minnesota Legislature, including one of March 6, 1869, the company had the power to change its name or that of any of its branches or divisions. On September 18, 1885 the company filed notice of a change in name to the Great Northern Railway Company.[96] This was accompanied by the issuance of the pre-

---

[93] *Ibid.*, 8.
[94] *Poor's Manual,* 1882, p. 739.
[95] Sims, *op. cit.,* 12.
[96] *Poor's Manual,* 1891, p. 224.

3. Building the Land Grant Railroads

ferred stock of the new company to stockholders of the St. Paul, Minneapolis and Manitoba at 50% of its face value, the other 50% being paid by transfer of all securities owned by the old company to the new.[97] On February 1, 1890 the St. Paul, Minneapolis and Manitoba Railway was leased for 999 years by the Great Northern Railway Company. The Great Northern System included 15 separate railroads by 1900 (see Table A-11 in Appendix A).

The stockholders also decided, in 1889, that the system should be extended to the Pacific Coast. The route selected covered a distance of 819 miles, from Pacific Junction, Montana to the Pacific terminus at Everett, Washington. The Pacific Extension was placed in operation on July 1, 1893.

Feeder lines to the north in the State of Washington were established in 1898 by developing branch systems on both the east and west sides. The Seattle and Montana Railroad Company was organized to skirt the shore from Seattle north to the Fraser River in British Columbia. This new company acquired the properties of the Seattle and Montana Railway Company, the Fairhaven and Southern Railroad Company, and the Seattle and Northern Railway Company, as well as the capital stock of the New Westminster Southern Railway, to form a through line from Seattle to New Westminster, British Columbia. The Great Northern also acquired the four railroads and the 217 miles of road of the Spokane Falls and Northern System in 1898, with a through road from Spokane Falls, Washington to Nelson, British Columbia, and a branch from Northport, Washington to Rossland, British Columbia.[98]

In the middle and late 1890s numerous other branch railroads were constructed, extended, or acquired to provide traffic for the Great Northern trunk line. Considerable improvements were also undertaken on the main line itself. On December 31, 1900 (the end of the period under consideration) the Great Northern System operated more than 5,000 miles of railroad.

The original reason for including the Great Northern System in this study is that it was essentially privately built at a later date in competition with the most subsidized United States land grant system—the Northern Pacific. The Great Northern did benefit from a land grant subsidy, but that benefit was virtually a happenstance. Federal land grants ended with the act of March 3, 1871 in favor of the Texas and Pacific Railroad Company.[99] The Great Northern System was an outgrowth of the St. Paul, Minneapolis and Manitoba Railroad, which was formed May 23, 1879, considerably after the end of the land grant era. The St. Paul, Minneapolis and

---

[97] *Ibid.*, p. 225.
[98] Sims, *op. cit.*, pp. 17–18.
[99] *Public Aids*, II, 107.

Manitoba was initially formed out of the foreclosed St. Paul and Pacific Railroad, which had come into possession of a federal land grant created by an act of March 3, 1857.[100] The unsold portion of that old grant passed to the new company and became the major part of the land grant of the Great Northern System. In 1880–1881 the St. Paul, Minneapolis and Manitoba acquired the charter of the Minneapolis and St. Cloud Railway Company, to which was attached a land grant from the State of Minnesota in the amount of 10 sections per mile.[101] This grant formed the remainder of the land grant of the Great Northern System, which became the beneficiary of efforts to subsidize predecessor railroads that were, unlike the Great Northern, truly pioneer efforts.

The Canadian Pacific System

In the sense in which the term usually appears to be used in the historical literature, i.e., building where there were relatively few people, great open spaces, and little immediate prospect of sufficient earning power for financial survival, the Canadian Pacific was the most clearly built ahead of demand of the railroad systems included in this study. The Canadian Pacific, of the systems examined, also illustrates most clearly the importance of the factors of political unification and national defense as grounds for governmental subsidization.

The Confederation of the British North American provinces of Nova Scotia, New Brunswick, and Canada occurred on July 1, 1867. A basic factor in the entry of New Brunswick and Nova Scotia into Confederation was the agreement to build the Intercolonial Railway to connect Montreal and Halifax.[102] Manitoba joined the Confederation in July 1870, followed by British Columbia in July 1871 and Prince Edward Island in July 1873. British Columbia joined with the promise to start construction of a railway to connect that province with the rest of the country within 2 years and to complete it within 10 years.[103]

The Canadian House of Commons in 1871 passed a resolution stating that the proposed railway "should be constructed and worked by private enterprise, and not by the Dominion Government; and that the public aid to be given to secure that undertaking, should consist of such subsidy in money or other aid, not unduly pressing on the industry and resources of the Dominion . . ."[104] Two financial groups then proceeded to incorpo-

---

[100] *Ibid.*, 106.
[101] *Poor's Manual*, 1900, p. 748.
[102] J. Lorne McDougall, *Canadian Pacific* (Montreal: McGill Univ. Press, 1968), p. 14.
[103] *Ibid.*, pp. 15, 19.
[104] John Murray Gibbon, *The Romantic History of the Canadian Pacific* (New York: Tudor, 1937), pp. 167–168.

3. Building the Land Grant Railroads

rate and submit proposals to the government for the construction of the railroad. The first of these groups was the Canada Pacific Railway Company; the second was the Interoceanic Railway Company. Since the two groups represented the provinces of Quebec and Ontario, and it was not politically feasible to choose one and exclude the other, strenuous efforts were made to amalgamate the two companies. Because these efforts failed, a new charter was drawn up in February 1873, creating a new company, the Canadian Pacific Railway Company, with men from both of the old groups. The company was to have a capital of $10 million and was to build from Lake Nipissing to the Pacific Coast, with branches to Lake Superior and Pembina.[105] The Canadian Pacific was offered a subsidy of $30 million and 50 million acres for the main line and additional land grants for the branches. The railroad was to be completed to the Pacific Coast by July 20, 1881.

In the spring of 1873 the Canadian Pacific attempted, but failed, to raise the necessary money to begin construction. This was followed by the onset of the most severe Canadian depression between the 1850s and 1930s. Strong recovery did not get underway until 1879.[106] This combination of events appeared to put an end to the hope that a private company would be able to build the Pacific railway. The government offered a subsidy of $10,000 and 20,000 acres of land per mile constructed. With no takers, the cash offer was raised to $30 million and a guarantee of 4% on expenditures beyond that sum.[107] When there were still no takers, the government decided to construct the railway itself under the Department of Public Works.

Construction of the Canadian Pacific Railway started about 4 miles from the mouth of the Kaministiquia River on June 1, 1875. By the end of 1876 work was well under way on two important sections: one from Fort William westward to Selkirk; the second from Selkirk southward through Winnipeg to Pembina on the border with the United States. The connection of the 83-mile Pembina Branch with the St. Paul and Pacific occurred in December 1878. To placate demands for more action from British Columbia, contracts were let for 127 miles of railway along the Fraser River in British Columbia to a young engineer, Andrew Onderdonk.[108] Construction began in 1878 on this section of the road, which became known as the Onderdonk section. Late in 1878, with a new government coming into power, another section of railroad was ordered to run 200 miles west from Winnipeg.

[105] McDougall, *op. cit.*, p. 23.
[106] *Ibid.*, p. 24.
[107] Gibbon, *op. cit.*, p. 180.
[108] *Ibid.*, p. 186.

Dissatisfaction with the progress of public construction and the manner in which it was being carried out led to the creation of a Royal Commission in 1880 to consider charges of disorganization in the governmental construction effort. The Commission's report concluded that government construction was very wasteful and inefficient.[109] This finding set the stage for another attempt to find a private company to build the railroad with public assistance.

Three private groups were involved in the negotiations for a new contract and charter. A Canadian syndicate led by George Stephen, who was to become president of the Canadian Pacific Railway Company, was finally selected. The bill containing the contract and the charter of the Canadian Pacific Railway Company was pushed through Parliament and became law on February 15, 1881. The government was to provide a cash subsidy of $25 million, a land grant of 25 million acres, and was to turn over to the company the lines built with public funds (the Onderdonk section in British Columbia, the Pembina Branch, and the Thunder Bay to Red River line). In addition, there were a number of other smaller subsidies.[110] In return for this assistance, the company agreed to build the road in 10 years and operate it efficiently. The Canadian Pacific Railway Company was the nucleus of the Canadian Pacific System, which included 24 separate railroads by 1900 (see Table A-13 in Appendix A).

During 1881 the Canadian Pacific made only limited progress, with a mere 100 miles of new line opened. In addition to this new construction, a total of 162 miles of railroad (the Pembina Branch and the road from Selkirk east to Cross Lake) were taken over from the government.[111] During the same year, the gap from the eastern end of Lake Nipissing to Ottawa (290 miles) was filled by purchase of the Brockville and Ottawa Railway and the Canadian Central Railway.[112] This purchase provided the company with access to the other railways of Ontario and Quebec.

An important development for the Canadian Pacific's future occurred in late 1881 when Stephen, on the advice of James J. Hill, hired W. C. Van Horne as general manager of the Canadian Pacific to oversee construction and operation.[113] During Van Horne's first year, 646 miles were added to the main line and 113 miles to branches by construction.[114] Another 347 miles of main line were purchased and 435 miles of main line and 65 miles of branches were turned over by the government. By the close of 1882 the

[109] McDougall, op. cit., pp. 29–30.
[110] See Pierre Berton, op. cit., pp. 216–217, for a complete listing.
[111] McDougall, op. cit., p. 51.
[112] Poor's Manual, 1882, p. 907.
[113] McDougall, op. cit., p. 52.
[114] Ibid.

3. Building the Land Grant Railroads

main line was completed and in operation to Swift Current, 512 miles west of Winnipeg, and track was laid 94 miles further west.[115] Construction in 1881 and 1882 was, to a large extent, financed by the sale of $10 million in land grant bonds. Unfortunately, by the end of 1882 the land boom was over and the immediate market for land grant bonds was exhausted.[116] Only $1 million of land grant bonds, out of the $15 million balance, were sold in 1884–1885.

Sale of common stock provided over $20 million during 1883. This financed a further vigorous expansion, with almost 700 miles of railroad built during the year. The Manitoba Southwestern Colonization Railway was leased as the start of a system of branch lines to feed the main line in the west. Also, in 1884, the Canadian Pacific leased the Ontario and Quebec Railway and its leased lines, the Credit Valley Railway, the Toronto, Grey and Bruce Railway, and the Atlantic and Northwest Railway. By the end of 1884 construction on the main line in the west had reached a point near the summit of the Selkirk Mountains, providing a continuous rail connection west from Montreal for nearly 2,500 miles. Rails had also been laid on the government sections of the tidewater terminus from Port Moody, British Columbia, to Savona's Ferry, and work was well advanced on the 203-mile gap between Savona's Ferry and the end of track near the summit of the Selkirks.

The burst of activity in 1884 was made possible by a loan from the government. Stephen had proposed this loan to the Minister of Railways and Canals on January 15, 1884. The government accepted the proposal, and by act of Parliament in March 1884 authorized a loan to the company of $22.5 million, due May 1, 1891, with 5% interest payable semiannually. An additional $7.4 million was to be advanced to cover guaranteed dividends on outstanding stock. The company was to complete the main line by May 1886. As security for these loans the government took a first lien against all the property of the Canadian Pacific. If the company was in default on either interest or principal for 12 months its right to either cash or land subsidy was to end, the land grant bonds held by the government were to become its property, and all employees of the company would become employees of the government.[117] Because it was so inclusive, the act had the result that the company could borrow nowhere else, because all of its assets were tied up.

Construction in 1884 used up the new loan, so that by the end of the year the company was once again skating on the edge of bankruptcy. The personal fortunes of the prime movers in the company were pledged to

[115] *Poor's Manual*, 1883, p. 960.
[116] McDougall, *op. cit.*, p. 53.
[117] *Ibid.*, p. 58.

borrow the funds to pay the February 1885 dividend and to keep the company afloat from day to day.

On March 26, 1885 an event occurred which led to a demonstration of the value of the Canadian Pacific and provided the political means by which the company was finally able to establish the necessary financial base for completion of the main line. The Saskatchewan (or Second Riel) Rebellion started in earnest at Duck Lake, Saskatchewan, with an attack on a detachment of the North West Mounted Police by a group of rebels led by Louis Riel.[118] Despite gaps totaling 100 miles in the road around Lake Superior, the Canadian Pacific offered to move troops from the east to Saskatchewan. Over a 2-week period more than 3,300 troops were moved from various eastern points to Qu'Appelle, Saskatchewan.[119] Units that were loaded in the east on March 30 were in Winnipeg on April 4, and less than a week later the first of these columns moved out of Qu'Appelle for Riel's headquarters at Batoche.[120] The quick movement of the troops led to a swift end to the rebellion. Without the railroad they could not have moved until after the opening of navigation. By that time the outcome of the rebellion would have been much less certain.

Construction of the Canadian Pacific represented the fulfillment of a promise made to get British Columbia to join the Confederation in 1871. Because of this it can be argued that there were significant political unification benefits derived from the Canadian Pacific. At the same time, the Second Riel Rebellion demonstrates that there were also significant national defense benefits associated with the Canadian Pacific. This situation with regard to national defense and political unification benefits is quite different from the case of the United States' railroads. For the latter these benefits did not significantly differ from zero when the railroads were finally built. In the case of the Canadian Pacific, however, these benefits were very substantial.

By act of Parliament on July 20, 1885, the Canadian Pacific finally got off the financial treadmill it had been on throughout its existence. The act authorized (a) cancellation of $35 million of unissued shares; (b) issuance of $35 million of 5% bonds with a maximum term of 50 years; (c) an immediate loan of $5 million secured by $8 million of the bond issue and a further $7 million loan secured by an equal sum in bonds if the company desired it; (d) postponement of payment of the $29.9 million government debt until May 1, 1891; and (e) acceptance by the government of $20 million of the bonds as security for an equal amount of the government

---

[118] Berton, *op. cit.*, pp. 468–475.
[119] *Ibid.*, p. 484.
[120] McDougall, *op. cit.*, p. 60.

3. Building the Land Grant Railroads

debt and a first lien on the company's unsold bonds, subject to the outstanding land grant bonds for the balance.[121]

The Canadian Pacific soon placed $14.6 million of the bonds with Baring Brothers in England for 90% of par. During the first half of 1886 Baring's took the remainder of the issue at 99.4% of par. With this financial transfusion, construction was pushed on and the main line was completed on November 7, 1885. Regular train service on the through line from Montreal to Port Moody began in June 1886. Also in 1886, the company paid off the last of its debt to the government: $19,150,700 with interest in cash, and $9,880,912 with interest in land surrendered from the land grant at $1.50 per acre.[122]

With the main line completed, construction and acquisition of extensions and branches proceeded, with an average of about 300 miles per year added to the system. In late 1885 control of the North Shore Railway from St. Martin's Junction to Quebec (159 miles) was acquired. Also during 1885, the company undertook construction of a major branch from Algoma Mills to Sault Ste. Marie (183 miles). The latter line was opened in January 1888. The extension of the main line from Port Moody to Vancouver (14 miles) was opened in May 1887.[123]

The year 1890 saw several major acquisitions. In June the Canadian Pacific gained a controlling interest in the Duluth, South Shore and Atlantic Railroad Company and the Minneapolis, St. Paul and Sault Ste. Marie Railroad Company. Since the operation of these companies is recorded separately and they were not fully integrated with the Canadian Pacific System before 1900, they are not included in the estimates for the system here. The 446-mile New Brunswick Railway (including its leased lines) was leased in July 1890 and operated as a part of the Canadian Pacific System from September 1, 1890.[124] Two more roads, the Montreal and Ottawa Railway and the Tobique Valley Railway, were acquired in 1891. This was followed in 1892 with the lease of the Montreal and Lake Maskinongé Railway and the Alberta Railway and Coal Company.

The Canadian Pacific leased the Naksup and Slocon Railway (34 miles) in 1893 and Section 5 of the Atlantic and Northwest Railway (18 miles) in 1894. Various minor branch extensions were constructed in 1895. The Toronto, Hamilton and Buffalo Railway completed its extension from Hamilton to Toronto in 1896 and was then leased to the Canadian Pacific.[125]

---

[121] *Ibid.*, pp. 62–63.
[122] *Ibid.*, p. 64.
[123] *Poor's Manual*, 1889, p. 932.
[124] *Ibid.*, 1891, p. 1014.
[125] *Ibid.*, 1896, p. 992.

After completion of the main line in 1885, the last important economic area in Canada that was cut off from the rest of the national economy was southeastern British Columbia. Socially, that area was an extension of the United States.[126] The mineral wealth of the region could not be developed without better transportation, partly because good cheap coking coal was needed to operate the necessary smelters. Such coal was available in the Crow's Nest Pass area on the eastern edge of the region, but without a railroad it was economically useless. The Province of British Columbia chartered the Crow's Nest and Kootenay Lake Railway Company (later renamed the British Columbia Southern Railway Company) in 1888 to build from the provincial boundary to Nelson.[127] In 1890 the Province authorized a land grant of 20,000 acres per mile of railway constructed, and in 1891, 1893, 1894, and 1895 requested federal assistance in the form of a cash subsidy for the proposed line. Nothing came of these requests, although the government had been giving cash subsidies of $3,000 per mile to any railway getting Parliament's attention since 1882, and double this amount for any which could bring forward reasonable claim for special consideration.[128]

Between 1893 and 1896, the Canadian Pacific and the government exchanged proposals and counterproposals regarding a cash subsidy for construction of a railroad from Lethridge, Alberta (the end of the Alberta Railway and Coal Company line) through Crow's Nest Pass to Nelson, British Columbia. An agreement was reached and enacted into law on June 28, 1897, with the formal agreement between the government and company signed on September 6, 1897.[129] The agreement provided for a cash subsidy of $11,000 per mile, with the total not to exceed $3,630,000, and for specified reductions in the Canadian Pacific's existing freight rates.

The Canadian Pacific had started construction westward from Lethridge prior to the agreement with the government. The railroad was within 12 miles of the summit of the Rockies by the end of 1897. In October 1898, under the charter of the British Columbia Southern Railroad Company (which had been acquired in 1897), the road reached Kootenay Landing. The line was continued from Proctor to Nelson, and a train ferry on Kootenay Lake was used to bridge the 34-mile gap from Kootenay Landing to Proctor in order to provide through train service to Nelson. The cash subsidy received, $3,404,720, was about one-third of the cost of construction and equipment of the railroad from Lethridge to

---

[126] McDougall, *op. cit.*, p. 74.
[127] *Ibid.*, p. 75.
[128] *Ibid.*, p. 78.
[129] *Ibid.*, p. 79.

3. Building the Land Grant Railroads

Nelson.[130] Completion of the Crow's Nest branch (340 miles) marks the last major extension of the Canadian Pacific System during the period included in this study.

Summary

This brief review of the corporate history and building of the seven land grant systems for which hypotheses A1, A2, B1, and B2 are to be tested illustrates the generally precarious financial conditions of even the subsidized railroads during their formative periods. Investors were relatively slow to come forward even for the Central and Union Pacific, where the government loan substantially reduced one major risk: the risk that insufficient financing would be forthcoming to complete the project. This lack of investor interest is still more pronounced in the case of the other systems, with the exception of the Great Northern. Since the Great Northern started with several hundred miles of railroad that had been in existence under various corporate titles for some time, it was much more attractive to investors.

In general, this survey shows that on an *ex ante* basis investors believed these railroads would be unprofitable without subsidy, but profitable with the assistance of the land grant (and other) subsidy. Given the historical record, it seems reasonable to accept (*ex ante*) the four hypotheses proposed here. In order to move beyond this qualitative judgment based on the historical record it is necessary to make a quantitative evaluation of what actually happened with regard to the four hypotheses *ex post*, so that the contribution of land grant policy to economic growth can be assessed. This is the task to which we now turn, starting with the private rates of return.

---

[130] *Ibid.*, p. 80.

Chapter 4

Private Rates of Return

Evaluation of hypotheses A1 and A2 for the seven railroad systems rests on the estimates of the private rates of return reported here. The unaided private rate and the private rate with land grant aid are estimated for each United States system. For the Canadian Pacific System, the "unaided" rate includes the effect of some of the numerous subsidies provided that railroad. It is not feasible to separate out all of these relatively minor subsidies. The value of the three major subsidies (land grant, cash, and construction expenditures) provided to the Canadian Pacific is measured and the private rate of return is estimated with various combinations of these subsidies and with the entire subsidy package.

In addition to evaluation of hypotheses A1 and A2, the rate of return estimates also make possible estimation of the divergence of actual subsidy from optimal subsidy for each system. These latter estimates provide a basis for judgment on the optimality of the subsidy policy (on an *ex post* basis) and illustrate the extent to which the policy diverged from an optimal one. Where investment in a railroad was unprofitable an optimal policy would have provided a subsidy just sufficient to allow the capital devoted to the project to recover its opportunity cost. If a system were profitable (*ex post*) the optimal policy would have been one of zero subsidy.

Two general methods of calculating rates of return are commonly found in the literature. The most frequently used technique involves computing

4. Private Rates of Return

one of the two alternate accounting rates of return. One of these is the annual ratio of net earnings to net assets (both earnings and assets adjusted for depreciation). The second is the annual ratio of gross earnings to gross (undepreciated) assets. For convenience these techniques are labeled the ratio or accounting method.[1]

A second algorithm for calculating rates of return rests on economic rather than accounting reasoning and involves computation of the internal rate of return for an investment project. To compute the unaided private rate of return for a finite period, let

OR = the annual value of the total revenue produced by the operation of the investment project,
OC = the annual value of operating (noncapital) costs for the investment project,
GI = annual gross investment in the investment project,
TA = an end (terminal) year adjustment,
r = a rate of discount,
PV = the present value of the net receipts stream,
T = the number of years used in the estimation of the internal rate of return minus one,
t = a time subscript,

where

$$PV = \sum_{t=0}^{T} \frac{OR_t - OC_t - GI_t}{(1 + r)^t} + \frac{TA}{(1 + r)^T}.$$

Rate of return estimates for this study are calculated using the internal rate of return method. These rates of return are the value of r for which the present value of the appropriate net receipts stream is zero.

The equation $PV = f(x)$, where

$$f(x) = \sum_{t=0}^{T} \frac{OR_t - OC_t - GI_t}{(1 + r)^t} + \frac{TA}{(1 + r)^T},$$

---

[1] Robert W. Fogel uses neither of these measures, but uses instead the ratio of net earning to gross assets (accumulated construction expenditures) in his estimation of the average annual unaided private rate and social rate of return for the Union Pacific Railroad during the decade 1870–1879. See Robert W. Fogel, *The Union Pacific Railroad*. Fogel's estimate of the unaided private rate of return is 11.6% (p. 96). He concludes that the Union Pacific was profitable. Peter J. George (pp. 750–751 and fn. 30–32) in "Rates of Return in Railway Investment and Implications for Government Subsidization of the Canadian Pacific Railway: Some Preliminary Results," *Canadian Journal of Economics* (November 1968), 740–762, believes he himself has a biased measure of the net profitability ratio, but his measure is actually the gross profitability ratio. George estimates what he calls the (unaided) private rate for the Canadian Pacific over the decade 1886–1895.

is a polynomial with real coefficients and $T + 1$ roots. One difficulty with the internal rate of return method is that there may be more than one real positive root for which $f(x) = 0$ and thus multiple internal rates of return. Descartes' rule of signs allows us to determine the maximum possible number of real positive roots and to state a necessary condition for the existence of only one real positive root and one internal rate of return. The number of real positive roots is $m - 2k$, where m is the number of variations of sign between successive terms of the polynomial written according to descending powers of the variable, and k is a positive integer or zero. Thus, the maximum number of real positive roots is m, the number of sign variations, and the necessary condition for the possibility of only one real positive root for $f(x)$ and the existence of only one internal rate of return is that there be an odd number of sign variations. Because the net receipts streams for all of the rates of return computed in this study have an odd number of sign variations, the necessary condition is satisfied.

The PV curve for each of the rates of return in this study was computed by intervals of one percentage point (0.01) for values of r from 0 to 2.00. These curves demonstrate that the PV functions estimated here have only one real positive discount rate for which $PV = 0$. In each case, $PV > 0$ with $r = 0$ declines at a decreasing rate $[f'(x) > 0]$ to a negative minimum as r increases and then increases at a decreasing rate $[f'(x) < 0]$ toward a negative asymptote as r increases toward infinity.[2]

On an *ex post* basis, the internal rate of return is always the true rate of return, while the ratio or accounting method using the annual ratio of net earnings to net assets (the net profitability ratio) yields the true rate of return only under very restrictive conditions, and the accounting rate of return using the annual ratio of gross earnings to gross assets (the gross profitability ratio) is always biased.[3] The net profitability ratio can equal the economic rate of return only if the depreciation schedule used in the firm's accounts is defined as the time rate of change of the present value of the gross earnings stream. Thus, the accounting method of computing rates of return would produce the true rate of return only by chance, and only if the ratio of net earnings to net assets is used.

The finite period included for each system studied here is intended as an approximation to the life of the original investment in that system. Estimation of the internal rate of return over a finite period requires an adjust-

---

[2] The negative asymptote results in each case because of the negative value of net receipts (OR-OC-GI) in year zero for each system.

[3] Thomas R. Stauffer, "The Measurement of Corporate Rates of Return: A Generalized Formulation," *The Bell Journal of Economics and Management Science*, 2, 2 (Autumn 1971), 466–467. This article has an excellent discussion of the relationship between economic and accounting rates of return.

4. Private Rates of Return

ment to the usual net receipts stream $(OR_t - OC_t - GI_t)$, as noted in the PV equation above for the unaided private rate of return, where the net receipts stream (NR_t) is $OR_t - OC_t - GI_t + TA$. The value of r for which $PV = 0$, computed on the basis of the usual net receipts stream over a finite period, will be an understatement of the true rate of return. This is because the capital stock whose formation is represented by the investment expenditure stream over the finite period is not completely used up in the terminal year of that period. Thus, without adjustment, the costs associated with forming the capital stock are all included in the net receipts stream, but the entire earnings stream of that capital is not included.

Two general techniques might be used to correct for the understatement described. One is to estimate that portion of the firm's future capital earnings $(OR - OC)$ stream which is attributable to the capital stock in existence at the end of the terminal year. This would be an expensive procedure and would involve construction of "synthetic statistics" whose reliability would be difficult to judge by tests of consistency or sensitivity.[4] A second possibility is to make an adjustment in the terminal year of the calculated net receipts stream to account for the inherent understatement of the stream. This solution is both cheaper and much more straightforward. Moreover, the sensitivity of the result (the rate of return) to various terminal adjustments can be readily tested. Addition of a terminal adjustment to the net receipts stream is adopted here to take account of the understatement of the stream when it is calculated over a finite period that does not include the full life of the capital created during the period.

Addition of a terminal adjustment to the net receipts stream creates a new problem because the magnitude of the terminal adjustment has a significant effect on the rate of return estimate. To illustrate the sensitivity of the rate of return to the size of the terminal adjustments, four adjustments are tested with each system. For convenience these alternative terminal adjustments are labeled A, B, C, and D. Terminal adjustment A is an estimate of the market value of the firm's outstanding securities (bonds and stocks). In the case of the Central Pacific and Union Pacific systems, the value of the firm's outstanding debt to the United States government (for its loan of government bonds and accumulated interest to railroads included in the system) is added to the market value of private securities to compute the value of terminal adjustment A.[5] This value is adjusted in

---

[4] On the general basis for testing such synthetic statistics see Alfred H. Conrad, "Econometrics and Southern History," *Explorations in Entrepreneurial History*, 2nd Series, 6, 1 (Spring–Summer 1968), 34–74.

[5] Common (or other) stock and bonds are valued at the daily low on the New York or London Stock Exchange (as appropriate) for the terminal year. The value of outstanding

each case for the estimated contribution of future land grant revenues to the market value of private securities in the terminal year.[6]

The year-to-year movement of market prices for a firm's securities is often substantial (perhaps for autonomous reasons unconnected with the expected profitability of the firm's operations). One might then arrive at a quite different estimate of the internal rate of return in, for example, the case of the Central Pacific System, if 1888 or 1890, rather than 1889, had been the (arbitrarily) selected terminal year. An alternative terminal adjustment which is some proportion of the terminal-year value of all bonds and stocks illustrates the sensitivity of the result to the arbitrary year selected. Terminal adjustment B used here is 50% of the value of terminal adjustment A.[7]

Still another potential terminal adjustment is the estimated terminal-year value of the system's capital stock. This is terminal adjustment C, which is defined here as the terminal-year value of capital stock estimated by the perpetual inventory method. With this technique, capital stock in any year t is computed from the equation

$$K_t = K_{t-1}(1 - \delta) + GI_t\left(1 - \frac{\delta}{2}\right),$$

where

K = value of capital stock, end of period,
GI = value of investment expenditures during the period,

---

public debt is added based on the following reasoning. The government bonds constituted a second mortgage on the appropriate properties of the Central and Union Pacific System. Some of the bonds of those systems were first mortgages, and of course the common stock represented a residual claim after mortgage claims were satisfied. Thus, if the first mortgage bonds and the common stock had positive market value (above the present value of future land grant revenues) in the terminal year (which they did for both the Central and Union Pacific), it was expected that the existing capital stock would generate sufficient earnings to pay off all mortgages, including the public debt, and still leave something for residual claimants. The value of the outstanding public debt must then be a part of terminal adjustment A. What is in effect added to the net receipts stream in the terminal year is the present value (at the internal rate of return) of the payments to discharge the principal and accumulated interest of the government debt.

[6] See Appendix C for the estimation and presentation of net land grant revenue by system.

[7] The proportion chosen could, of course, be greater than 1. Given the usual "large" size of terminal adjustment A, it appears reasonable to test only on the down side here. Terminal adjustment B is accomplished simply by adding 50% of the terminal-year value of bonds and stocks to the net receipts stream in the terminal year. For the Central Pacific and Union Pacific the same proportion of the 1889 present value (at the internal rate of return) of the payments to discharge the government debt is also added. Terminal adjustment B is adjusted for the effect of unsold land grant acreage in the same manner as terminal adjustment A.

4. Private Rates of Return

δ = a constant rate of depreciation, and
t = a time subscript.

The important unknown here is the value of δ. In the nineteenth century railroad firms did not do depreciation accounting.[8] For the five systems other than the Central Pacific and Union Pacific, the constant value of δ used is 1.97%. This is Larry Neal's estimate of the average annual depreciation rate for the period 1897–1914 and appears reasonable for use with the system built originally with steel rather than iron rails.[9] This is less applicable to the Central Pacific and Union Pacific Systems, whose original lines were built with iron rails in the 1860s.

Available information for the Central Pacific and Union Pacific allows the calculation of two alternative average depreciation rates. For the Central Pacific System the alternative double-declining balance depreciation rate based on construction of the original Central Pacific Railroad is 3.69%. This is arrived at in the following manner. On the basis of the investment expenditure estimates the three major components of capital stock—(1) structures, (2) track, and (3) equipment—accounted, respectively, for 65.9, 23.6, and 10.5% of the total investment expenditures during the 1863–1869 construction period. Given reported average length of life for these components, the respective straight-line depreciation rates are 2, 10, and 5%.[10] Track replacement was reported as a current operating expense and thus is not included in investment expenditures after initial construction. One can assume that the track component is constantly maintained and not included in the depreciation rate to be charged against the capital stock. The weighted straight-line rate of depreciation is then 1.843%, i.e., (0.659)(0.02) + (0)(0.236) + (0.105)(0.05) + 0.01843. The double-declining balance rate is 3.69%.

The report of J. L. Williams, a governmental director, on the cost of construction and equipment of the original Union Pacific Railroad provides a basis for estimating the weights for the three components of the capital stock for that line.[11] Assuming the same straight-line depreciation rates for the components, the weighted straight-line depreciation rate for the stock is 1.578%, i.e., (0.354)(0.02) + (0)(0.472) + (0.174)(0.05) = 0.01578. The double-declining balance rate is 3.156%.

---

[8] In fact, they started depreciation accounting only in the twentieth century under protest and after being forced to do so by the Interstate Commerce Commission regulations of 1907, which were not made enforceable until 1910.

[9] Larry Neal, "Investment Behavior by American Railroads: 1897–1914," *Review of Economics and Statistics*, LI, 2 (May 1969), 132.

[10] Fogel, *op. cit.*, pp. 96 and 97.

[11] U.S. Senate Executive Documents, No. 69, 49th Congress, 1st Session, p. 54.

Because of the construction over the Sierra Nevada Mountains, the original Central Pacific involved a far greater proportion of structures in total investment expenditures and proportionally less in track and equipment than did the Union Pacific. The estimated Union Pacific rate is much more likely to represent the average rate for the Central Pacific System than the estimated Central Pacific Railroad rate. Thus, the estimated Union Pacific rate is used in the calculation of terminal adjustment C for both the Central Pacific and Union Pacific Systems.[12]

Finally, the range of possibilities is well illustrated if a fourth terminal adjustment is employed. Terminal adjustment D is the simplest of all—no terminal adjustment is made. This does nothing to correct for the obvious understatement involved in the calculation of the net receipts stream from annual data over a finite period. It does, however, add to our knowledge about the sensitivity of the calculated rate of return to the magnitude of the terminal adjustment. Moreover, given the other inputs into the internal rate of return computation, terminal adjustment D provides a clear lower-bound estimate of the rate of return in question.

All data used to calculate rates of return in this study are in real or constant dollar terms. For the United States systems a number of price indexes were considered for this purpose. The Snyder–Tucker general price index, based on wholesale prices, cost of living, and rents and wages, appears to be the best index both in terms of the techniques and methodology used to construct it and the breadth of coverage.[13] It is used here for the United States systems, with the base of the index shifted to 1869.

As illustrated by the discussion in Chapter 3 of the histories of the seven land grant systems, the financial success of the land grant railroads varied considerably. The remainder of this chapter is organized to reflect this and will deal in turn with three (*ex post*) outcomes with respect to the subsidy policy, as revealed by the rate of return estimates. These three outcomes are: (1) subsidy unnecessary; (2) subsidy necessary but inadequate; and (3) subsidy necessary and (at least) adequate.

---

[12] The upward bias is suggested by a report of another government director of the Union Pacific, C. N. Snow, as reported in Senate Executive Document No. 69. Snow reports the cost of the heaviest section of line (between Cheyenne, Wyoming and the 1,000-mile post) on the original Union Pacific, from which the capital components can be calculated. The percentages for structures, track, and equipment are 38.3, 43.8, and 17.9, respectively. The weighted straight-line rate is 1.661%, i.e., $(0.383)(0.02) + (0)(0.438) + (0.179)(0.05) = 0.0166$. The double-declining balance rate is then 3.332%, which is higher than 3.156% and not greatly different from the 3.69% rate estimated for the Central Pacific Railroad.

[13] U.S. Bureau of the Census, *Historical Statistics of the United States: Colonial Times to 1945*, (Washington: U.S. Government Printing Office, 1949), pp. 231–232.

Subsidy Unnecessary

It probably will not surprise anyone that some of the land grant railroad systems were privately profitable investments (*ex post*). What is surprising is that two of the three systems that were privately profitable according to the present estimates were among the earliest built in the West and were components of the first transcontinental railroad.

The Central Pacific System

Investment expenditure estimates are discussed in Appendix A. Table A-2 presents annual investment expenditure estimates for the Central Pacific System during the period 1863–1889. Operation of the Central Pacific Railroad began in 1864. Table B-1 in Appendix B (Capital Earnings) provides the estimated capital earnings of the Central Pacific System for the years 1864–1889. Land sales by the Central Pacific Railroad did not begin until 1869. Table C-1 in Appendix C (Net Land Grant Revenue) provides estimates of the net land grant revenue of the Central Pacific System for the years 1869–1927. Net land grant revenue is added to the unaided private net receipts stream to calculate the aided private rate of return. Net land grant revenue during 1890–1927 is also used to adjust the market value of securities (terminal adjustments A and B) for the contribution of future land revenue to that value in the terminal year. This is done by subtracting the terminal-year present value (at the market rate of return) of land sales beyond the terminal year from net receipts in that year. This procedure is followed for all systems.

The unaided and aided private rates of return estimated for the Central Pacific System with the alternative terminal adjustments are presented in Table I. To make a judgment concerning hypotheses A1 and A2, we need to compare these estimated private rates of return with the average alter-

TABLE I

Estimated Private Rates of Return: Central Pacific System

Terminal adjustment[a]	Unaided private rate (%)	Aided private rate (%)
A	13.2	13.9
B	11.3	12.2
C	10.6	11.6
D	8.0	9.5

[a] See text for definition of alternative terminal adjustments.

native private rate available in the economy during the same period. Two possibilities for comparison (in terms of available data) are the average yield on railroad bonds and the average earnings/price ratio of all common stock on the New York Stock Exchange.

The mean annual yield on railroad bonds during the period 1863–1889 is calculated from data on railroad bonds that Frederick R. Macauley used in his index of railroad bond yields.[14] The annual average earnings/price ratio of all common stock on the New York Stock Exchange for 1871–1889 was obtained from a study of common stock indexes.[15] The mean annual rates are 5.9% for the yield of railroad bonds and 7.7% for the earnings/price ratio. These are money rates.

The earnings/price ratio is used here as a proxy for the average opportunity cost of capital (market rate) in the economy during the rate of return estimation period for each system. Because only the value of equity shares and not that of bonds is included in the denominator, the earnings/price ratio overstates the market rate. Since the estimated rates of return in this study are real rates, the mean annual earnings/price ratio must be adjusted from a money rate to a real rate. This is done using the approximation that if R_m = the money rate of interest, R_r = the real rate of interest, P = the general price level, and ΔP_e = the expected change in the general price level, then

$$R_m = R_r + \frac{\Delta P_e}{P} \quad \text{so that} \quad R_r = R_m - \frac{\Delta P_e}{P}.$$

The Snyder–Tucker price index (1869 = 100) is used to represent the general price level in the case of the United States systems. It is assumed that the change in the price level that actually occurred between years t and $t + 1$ was expected in year t. The mean real earnings/price ratio for 1871–1889 is 9.03%, which is used as the market rate for comparative purposes with the Central Pacific System.

Given the estimated market rate of 9.03%, the rate of return estimates of Table I indicate that hypothesis A1 must be rejected for the Central Pacific System unless terminal adjustment D is selected as the correct terminal adjustment. The Central Pacific System was privately profitable *ex post* with any of the other terminal adjustments suggested. The terminal adjustment we prefer and will accept in this study is terminal adjustment C, the estimated value of the end-of-period capital stock in the final year.

---

[14] Frederick R. Macauley, *Some Theoretical Problems Suggested by the Movement of Interest Rates, Bond Yields and Stock Prices in the United States since 1856* (New York: National Bureau of Economic Research, 1938), pp. A37–A60.

[15] Alfred Cowles III and Associates, *Common Stock Indexes, 1871–1937* (Bloomington, Indiana: Principia Press, 1938), p. 404.

4. Private Rates of Return

The rates of return accepted for the Central Pacific System are 10.6 and 11.6%, for the unaided and aided private rates, respectively. We see *ex post* that land grant aid to the Central Pacific System was a mistake. Land grant aid was not required for private profitability and simply raised an already adequate private rate of return by 9.4% or 1 percentage point. On an *ex post* basis, the land grant subsidy policy was not optimal with respect to the Central Pacific System because no land grant subsidy was required.

The test of hypotheses A1 and A2 provides one measure of the contribution of land grant aid to the Central Pacific System. The differential between the estimated unaided and aided private rates of return indicates that although land revenues made a significant contribution to the return of the firm, they were at the same time a relatively small part of the total returns. Many writers in the past have argued that the land grants paid for the construction of the land grant railroads.[16] One basic fault with this contention is that systems, rather than their components, i.e., individual railroads, are the relevant units to consider. Moreover, given the usual time lag between receipt and sale of the land, this question can be correctly analyzed only if we place the streams of investment expenditures and net land grant earnings in the same time dimension. Comparison of the absolute totals of investment expenditures and subsidies is inadequate for this purpose. Analysis of the land grant's direct contribution to paying the investment cost of the land grant railroads requires that the streams of net land earnings and investment expenditures be viewed in present value terms for a common point in time. For the Central Pacific System, this is done by computing the 1863 present value (at a 9.03% rate of discount) of investment expenditures and subsidies. The 1863 present value of the land grant is $5.089 million, compared to $40.324 million of investment expenditures for the specific railroads receiving land grants and $61.381 million for system investment expenditures through 1889.[17] Here it is clear that the land grants did not pay for the Central Pacific System nor even for specific land grant railroads in that system. For the latter, the land grants were equivalent to an 1863 capital grant from the government, which

---

[16] Cf. Fred A. Shannon, *America's Economic Growth* (New York: Macmillan, 1940), p. 363, and Samuel Eliot Morison and Henry Steele Commager, *The Growth of the American Republic* (New York: Oxford Univ. Press, 1942), II, pp. 112–113. At the other extreme, Robert S. Henry argued in a famous article that "the net realizations from sales, particularly during the period of construction, were but a tiny fraction of the cost of building the railroads" (see Robert S. Henry, "The Railroad Land Grant Legend in American History Texts," p. 186). For a more detailed discussion of this, see Lloyd J. Mercer, "Taxpayers or Investors: Who Paid for the Land-Grant Railroads?".

[17] The land grant railroads included are the Central Pacific, California and Oregon, and Southern Pacific of California.

amounted to 12.6% of the 1863 present value of investment expenditures in the land-grant-aided railroads of the Central Pacific System.

Before leaving the question of the Central Pacific System's private profitability and related issues, it will be instructive to consider a second major subsidy to that system. The federal government loaned almost $28 million worth of its 6% currency bonds to the Central and Western Pacific Railroads. This loan involved a cost to society and a subsidy to the firms.[18] In addition to this direct construction loan, the government in effect made a second loan (with an interest charge of zero) to these railroads by not requiring full payment of the annual interest on the bonds until (after) the loan was due, and a third loan by extending the time for payment of the construction loan and accumulated interest when these obligations fell due in the second half of the 1890s. A measure of this cost and subsidy is the difference between the annual payments by the railroad on the government loan and interest and the payments it would have been required to pay private lenders for a loan yielding the same funds.[19] The total real value of this loan subsidy to the Central Pacific System is $50.105 million. The 1863 present value of the real land and loan subsidies (at a discount rate of 9.03%) is $15.631 million, whereas that of the real investment expenditures is $42.537 million for the subsidized roads and $61.381 million for the system.[20] In terms of 1863 present value, the loan subsidy ($10,542 million) was worth twice as much as the land grant, and represented an 1863 capital value equal to 36.7% of the 1863 present value of investment expenditures of the aided railroads. This was indeed a significant subsidy, and was far more important than the land grant, which has been so much more discussed in the literature.

[18] In addition to the one discussed here, a further subsidy was involved in the relegation of the federal loan to a second mortgage, which then allowed the firms to sell a like amount of their own first mortgage bonds. They obtained more funds at lower cost from the latter than would otherwise have been the case, for two reasons: first, because they represented a first rather than a second mortgage, and because the proceeds from the second mortgage greatly reduced the risk of failure due to an inability to obtain the resources for the entire project, and second, because the asset position of the borrower was much enhanced by the proceeds from the sale of the second mortgage, which carried a government guarantee. These same considerations apply to the constituent roads of the Union Pacific System which received the same government loans.

[19] See Appendix H for a discussion and presentation of the annual estimates for the Central Pacific and Union Pacific Systems.

[20] The present value of the specific railroads' investment expenditures refers to the present value of the stream of expenditures actually made, whereas that for the system refers to the stream of investment expenditures attributed to the system. Because of the way in which mergers, leases, etc., are treated in constructing the system investment expenditure stream, these two streams are not the same with respect to the point in time at which investment costs are recorded for railroads that merged with the Central Pacific (or were leased) after some or all of their original construction had taken place.

4. Private Rates of Return

For the bond-aided railroads alone, the Central and Western Pacific, the 1863 present value of real investment expenditures is $31.222 million. In present-value terms the loan subsidy was equivalent to a capital grant in 1863 equal to 33.8% of the 1863 present value of investment expenditures for those railroads through 1870. For the Central Pacific System the land grant and loan subsidies were equivalent to a capital grant of 25.5% of the 1863 present value of the system investment expenditures.[21] Viewed in the proper perspective, neither the land grant nor the loan subsidies, nor even the two together, paid for the investment in either the Central Pacific System or the subsidized railroads considered alone. On the other hand, the land and loan subsidies did make a significant contribution to the success of the system, with the often neglected or underestimated loan subsidy being twice as large as the land grant subsidy.[22]

Table II shows the present values of land grant subsidies and investment expenditures (and the ratio of these present values) for all seven systems and their land grant railroads. In each case the estimated market rate of return relevant for the system is used as the rate of discount and the present values are computed for the first year in the time period considered. Table III presents this same information for the loan subsidy and investment expenditures of the Central Pacific and Union Pacific Systems and their bond-aided railroads. In all cases we see that although the subsidies made significant contributions, they did not literally pay for the investment in either the specifically aided railroads or the systems.

The Union Pacific System

Annual investment expenditure estimates for the Union Pacific System during the period 1864–1869 are shown in Table A-4 of Appendix A. The Union Pacific Railroad did not begin operation until 1866. Table B-2 of Appendix B presents the estimated capital earnings of the system for 1866–1889. Estimated net land grant receipts for the years 1865–1889 are listed in Table C-2 of Appendix C. Alternative estimates of the aided and unaided private rates of return are shown in Table IV. The average esti-

---

[21] These calculations of the value of the subsidy are gross of the reduced rate benefit accruing to the federal government (and therefore taxpayers) for the movement of federal government freight and passengers. While these were large in absolute size, most of this benefit was realized 70 to 80 years later (during World War II). Moreover, the land grant rate reductions were given the government by non-land-grant railroads as well. A consideration of these benefits would not significantly change the conclusions based here on 1863 present values at a discount rate of 9.03%.

[22] One authoritative source, *Public Aids*, II, 60, estimates the total loan subsidy for all railroad construction loans by the federal government at $48 million. About $64.6 million of such loans were made. The total current dollar loan subsidy estimated in this study (see Appendix H) is $72 million, or 50% more than the estimate of the Federal Coordinator of Transportation.

TABLE II

Investment Expenditures and Land Grant Subsidy by System and Component Aided Railroads

System and land grant railroads	Investment expenditures present value [a] (thousand 1869 or 1900 $)	Land grant subsidy present value (thousand 1869 or 1900 $)	$\dfrac{PV_{igr}}{PV_{ie}}$ [b]
Central Pacific	61,381	5,089	0.083
land grant RR [c]	40,381	5,089	0.126
Union Pacific	64,840	9,950	0.153
land grant RR [d]	66,580	12,348	0.185
Texas and Pacific	38,702	7,530	0.195
land grant RR [e]	26,536	7,530	0.284
Atchison, Topeka and Santa Fe	90,289	6,720	0.074
land grant RR [f]	16,820	6,720	0.400
Northern Pacific	69,128	19,317	0.279
land grant RR [g]	44,589	19,317	0.433
Great Northern	78,492	8,962	0.114
land grant RR [h]	13,569	8,962	0.660
Canadian Pacific [i]	148,374	32,874	0.222

[a] Present value in year of first construction or purchase which begins the system.

[b] The ratio of the present value of net land grant revenues to the present value of investment expenditures.

[c] Central Pacific, Southern Pacific of California, and California and Oregon.

[d] Union Pacific, Kansas Pacific, and Denver Pacific. Because the Kansas Pacific and Denver Pacific did not join the system until 1880, the value of net land grant revenue for the included land grant railroads is greater than that for the system. Also, the present value of investment expenditures for the aided railroads considered separately exceeds the value for the system, because of the difference in timing of expenditures for the railroads compared to the system.

[e] Texas and Pacific Railroad. Land grant includes some acreage originally granted to the Southern Pacific Railroad Company and the Memphis, El Paso and Pacific Railroad Company. The latter roads were purchased in 1872 and 1873, respectively, by the Texas and Pacific Railroad.

[f] Atchison, Topeka and Santa Fe and Western Division of the Atlantic and Pacific. Proceeds from the 73,894-acre land grant of the Leavenworth, Lawrence and Galveston are apparently included, but were never reported separately.

[g] Transcontinental line of the Northern Pacific and the St. Paul and Northern Pacific between Brainerd and Sauk Rapids, Minnesota. *Public Aids* II, p. 111 also lists the Taylor Falls and Lake Superior, the Stillwater and St. Paul, and the Lake Superior and Mississippi as land grant components of the Northern Pacific System. These are excluded here because they were all part of the St. Paul and Duluth (formerly the Lake Superior and Mississippi) as late as 1900.

[h] The Minneapolis and St. Cloud and the St. Paul and Pacific.

[i] Values for component roads are not calculated separately. The aid seems to have been intended for the system in this case.

TABLE III

Investment Expenditures and Loan Subsidy for the
Central Pacific and Union Pacific Systems and
Component Aided Railroads

System and railroads	Investment expenditure present value[a]	Loan subsidy present value	$\left(\dfrac{PV_{ls}}{PV_{ie}}\right)$[b]
Central Pacific	61,381	10,542	0.172
bond-aided RR[c]	31,222	10,542	0.338
Union Pacific	64,840	12,045	0.186
bond-aided RR[d]	66,808	12,045	0.180

[a] Present value in year of first construction for system.
[b] Ratio of the present value of loan subsidy to present value of investment expenditures.
[c] Central and Western Pacific Railroads.
[d] Union Pacific, Kansas Pacific, and Central Branch of the Union Pacific.

mated real market rate of return applicable to the Union Pacific System is 9.03% and is calculated as above for the Central Pacific System. Hypothesis A1 would be accepted only with terminal adjustment D. With any of the other terminal adjustments, the system was profitable without land grant aid, and hypothesis A1 is rejected. Again, the preferred terminal adjustment is C, for which the estimated unaided private rate is 11.6%, compared with an aided private rate of 13.1%. Land grant aid raised the private rate of return 1.5 percentage points or 13.2%. The land grant made a significant contribution to the firm's private profitability, but on an *ex post* basis this aid was quite unnecessary; the policy of land grant subsidy to the Union Pacific System was therefore not optimal, because an optimal subsidy was zero.

TABLE IV

Estimated Private Rates of Return: Union Pacific System

Terminal adjustment[a]	Unaided private rate (%)	Aided private rate (%)
A	13.7	14.9
B	11.8	13.3
C	11.6	13.1
D	8.9	11.1

[a] See text for definition of alternative terminal adjustments.

The 1864 present value (at a discount rate of 9.03%) of the system's real net land grant revenue is $12.378 million.[23] The present value of real gross investment expenditures through 1889 is $64.840 million for the Union Pacific System and $62.344 million for the system's land grant railroads through 1870.[24] The land grant was equivalent to an 1864 capital grant representing 19.9% of the present value of investment in the land-grant-aided railroads of the system and 19.1% of that of the entire system. Land grants did not pay for the aided railroads, but they did make a significant contribution.

The 1864 real present value of the loan subsidy for bond-aided railroads in the Union Pacific System is $12.045 million, making the total present value of land and loan subsidies $24.423 million. The 1864 present value of real investment expenditures for bond-aided railroads is $62.572 million, while that for bond- and land-grant-aided railroads together is $64.351 million. Neither land grant nor loan subsidy nor the two together paid for the investment in the system, let alone the aided railroads. The loan subsidy alone was equivalent to a capital grant in 1864 equal to 19.2% of the present value of investment expenditure in the bond-aided railroads. Together the land and loan subsidies represented an 1864 capital grant of 37.9% of the present value of investment expenditures in the aided railroads and 37.7% of that of the system. Unlike the Central Pacific case, the loan and land subsidies for the Union Pacific were of about equal value. Total subsidies relative to investment expenditures for aided railroads in the Union Pacific and Central Pacific Systems were virtually identical; however, relative to system investment expenditure, subsidies were 50% more important for the Union Pacific System. Again, the most important point is the very significant contribution of the bond subsidy.

The Great Northern System

Table A-12 in Appendix A presents estimated investment expenditures of the Great Northern System for the period 1879–1900. Estimated capital earnings of the system for the years 1880–1900 are given in Table B-6 in Appendix B. Net land grant receipt estimates for 1880–1827 are provided in Table C-6 of Appendix C. Alternative estimates of the unaided and aided private rates of return for the system are contained in Table V. The

---

[23] This includes the net land revenue of the Union Pacific, Denver Pacific, and Kansas Pacific Railroads through 1889, plus the value of unsold land carried on the Union Pacific Railway's books at the end of 1889.

[24] The land-grant-aided figure is for the Union Pacific, Kansas Pacific, and Denver Pacific railroads, and includes expenditures of 1870. It appears that the Kansas Pacific and Union Pacific railroads, like the Central Pacific, found it necessary to carry out considerable improvements on the main line immediately after it was completed. A substantial portion of the Denver Pacific was built in 1870.

TABLE V

Estimated Private Rates of Return: Great Northern System

Terminal adjustment[a]	Unaided private rate (%)	Aided private rate (%)
A	13.1	14.3
B	9.0	10.4
C	8.7	10.0
D	−1.5	1.1

[a] See text for definition of alternative terminal adjustments.

real market alternate rate of return estimated for the Great Northern is 6.33%. Since terminal adjustment C is the preferred adjustment, the estimates presented for the Great Northern lead us to reject hypothesis A1 for that system. Unless one were to accept terminal adjustment D, aid was not necessary for the private profitability of investment in the Great Northern System; the subsidy provided was therefore not optimal on an *ex post* basis, because an optimal subsidy was zero. The land grants acquired by the Great Northern, along with the older railroads, simply increased the rate of return on an already profitable investment by 1.3 percentage points or 15.3%.

The above conclusion should be moderated by the fact that the basic building block of the Great Northern System—the St. Paul and Pacific—was (at least financially) unsuccessful. Apparently aid was required even *ex post* for that railroad, but the aid provided was insufficient at the time to make the investment a success. However, the new company formed 22 years after the initial land grant was a success, and by the estimates made here would have been successful without the aid it received. In 1857 aid was required to get a substantial railroad built in Minnesota and too little was provided at the time to get the job done. In 1879 such aid was not required, and at that stage of development should not have been provided even by the back door. The government should have reclaimed the original grant to the St. Paul and Pacific. The aid provided to the Northern Pacific really resulted in the opening up of the territory in which the Great Northern System was later built. Allowing the latter system also to receive aid was superfluous.

The excessiveness of the land grant subsidy received by the Great Northern System is illustrated by examination of whether the subsidy paid for investment in the system or in the aided railroads. In terms of 1879 real present value, at a discount rate of 6.33%, system investment expenditures are $78.492 million, compared to $13.569 million for the land-grant-aided railroads and $8.962 million for net land grant revenue. The land subsidy was equivalent to a capital grant in 1879 representing 11.4% of the present value of investment expenditures in the system and 66.0% of the present value of investment expenditures in the aided railroads. For the aided roads this is the largest proportion among the systems studied. Although the subsidy did not pay for the system or the aided roads in a literal sense, it certainly represented a substantial contribution for the promoters of the St. Paul, Minneapolis and Manitoba, who received in present-value terms a subsidy equal to two-thirds of the cost of the aided roads.[25]

Subsidy Necessary but Inadequate

We turn next to the second *ex post* outcome with regard to the policy of subsidizing the land grant railroads: the subsidy was necessary, but the amount provided was inadequate. Two of the systems studied, the Texas and Pacific and the Santa Fe, fall into this category.

The Texas and Pacific

The Texas and Pacific System's estimated investment expenditures for the period 1872–1900 are given in Table A-6 of Appendix A. Capital earnings estimates for the system during 1872–1900 are listed in Table B-3 of Appendix B. The system's net land grant receipts accrued only during 1876–1887. Estimates of net land grant receipts for these years are shown in Table C-3 in Appendix C. Table VI presents the estimated private rates of return for the system, utilizing the earnings and investment expenditure data presented and the alternative terminal adjustments.

The estimated market rate for comparison with the Texas and Pacific rates of return is 7.74%. Thus, we accept hypothesis A1, with the terminal-adjustment-C-unaided private rate estimate of 2.2%. In fact, hypothesis A1 would be accepted with any of the terminal adjustments. In the case of the Texas and Pacific, we reject hypothesis A2 for the first time. Government aid was required for private profitability of the Texas and Pacific, but the amount forthcoming was insufficient to assure private profitability. With terminal adjustment C the private rate of return was raised 2.1 percentage points or 95%, but the aided private rate (4.3%) was significantly less than the market rate. This latter conclusion holds with

---

[25] The reader may object that the land grant was all the investors received in taking over the bankrupt St. Paul and Pacific. This would be a gross exaggeration, although it is apparently true that the 560 miles of railroad were not in the best condition and probably required significant additional investment after the initial purchase.

4. Private Rates of Return

TABLE VI

Estimated Private Rates of Return: Texas and Pacific System

Terminal adjustment[a]	Unaided private rate (%)	Aided private rate (%)
A	3.5	5.4
B	1.1	3.5
C	2.2	4.3
D	-3.9	-0.3

[a] See text for definition of alternative terminal adjustments.

any of the terminal adjustments. The subsidy policy with respect to the Texas and Pacific was not optimal, because insufficient subsidy was provided. For the Texas and Pacific to have been privately profitable, additional subsidy with a real value of $11.592 million in 1872 was required.[26]

The 1872 real present value (at a discount rate of 7.74%) of the Texas and Pacific Railway's investment expenditures through 1900 is $26.536 million, whereas the system's is $38.702 million and that of the land grant is $7.530 million.[27] In terms of 1872 present value the Texas and Pacific land grant was equivalent to a capital grant of 28.4% of the Texas and Pacific Railway's investment expenditures and 19.5% of those of the system.[28] Again we see that the subsidy paid for neither the aided railroad nor

---

[26] Where S^* is the present value of the required subsidy and NR_t is the unaided net receipts stream defined above with terminal adjustment C, the additional subsidy required is calculated from

$$S^* = \sum_{t=0}^{T} \frac{NR_t}{(1.0774)^t},$$

where t ranges from 0 to 28 (1872 to 1900). The calculated S^* will be negative with too little subsidy and positive with too much subsidy, given the market rate of return (value of r) used in the calculation.

[27] Of the net land grant total, $19.763 million is the estimated value (in 1869 dollars) of the sale of the remaining land grant to a land trust in 1887, which was set up as part of the reorganization of the company following its failure to pay the interest due on mortgage bonds.

[28] As estimated in this study, the present value of the Texas and Pacific land grant in the initial construction year exceeded that of the Central Pacific System. Notice, however, that a subsidy whose present value was more than two and one-half times as large as the actual subsidy was necessary for private profitability, i.e., the required subsidy was $19.122 million, compared to the actual subsidy of $7.530 million. The required subsidy for the Texas and Pacific System was larger than the actual land grant subsidy for any of the United States systems included here, except the Northern Pacific.

the system, although it represented a significant contribution to both. The Texas and Pacific received much less aid relative to its investment expenditures in either aided railroads or the system than did the Central Pacific and Union Pacific systems.

Examination of the Central Pacific and Union Pacific subsidies indicates that the bond subsidy played a very significant role for those railroads. Despite strenuous efforts in Congress in 1874–1878, the Texas and Pacific did not receive such aid. It appears that the absence of a government loan is a major part of the explanation for the Texas and Pacific System's failure compared to the Central Pacific and Union Pacific Systems.

The Atchison, Topeka and Santa Fe System

Investment expenditure estimates for the Atchison, Topeka and Santa Fe System over the period 1869–1900 are presented in Table A-8 of Appendix A. Table B-4 in Appendix B shows estimated capital earnings of the system for 1870–1900. Table C-4 of Appendix C gives the estimated net land grant earnings for the system during 1870–1927. Three land grant railroads are included in the system as defined here. Besides the original Atchison, Topeka and Santa Fe Railroad in Kansas, land grants were given to the Leavenworth, Lawrence and Galveston, and to the Atlantic and Pacific, whose western division formed a major part of the Santa Fe transcontinental line.

Estimated private rates of return on the investment in the Santa Fe System are shown in Table VII. The estimated market alternative for the Santa Fe System is 7.86%. On the basis of the terminal adjustment C estimate of 6.1%, we accept hypothesis A1 for the Santa Fe system. However, as in the case of the Texas and Pacific, the subsidization policy was not optimal, because although land grant subsidy raised the private rate of return 1 percentage point or 16%, the terminal adjustment C estimate of the aided private rate (7.1%) is less than the estimated market rate

TABLE VII

Estimated Private Rates of Return: Atchison, Topeka and Santa Fe System

Terminal adjustment[a]	Unaided private rate (%)	Aided private rate (%)
A	8.1	9.0
B	5.0	6.0
C	6.1	7.1
D	−4.2	−2.3

[a] See text for definition of alternative terminal adjustments.

of 7.86%. For private profitability an additional subsidy with an 1869 present value of $4.027 million was required.[29]

The conclusion here regarding the land grant subsidy refers to the system in each case. For systems like the Santa Fe, in which there was a very substantial investment beyond the original railroad receiving the land grant, the unprofitability of the expanded firm with aid does not necessarily reflect a mistake in policy *ex ante*. The subsidy may have led the entrepreneurs to expand their investment beyond an efficient level. Government aid may have induced overexpansion of subsidized systems. We will examine this hypothesis in Chapter 6.

At a discount rate of 7.86%, the 1869 present value of real net land grant revenue is $6.720 million, compared to $16.820 million for the real investment expenditures of the included land grant railroads and $90.289 million for the system.[30] Again the land grant did not pay for the investment in either the land grant railroads or the system. For the land grant railroads, the subsidy was substantial compared to investment expenditures. It was equivalent to an 1869 capital grant worth 39.9% of the 1869 present value of the investment expenditures of the land grant railroads. With respect to the system, the subsidy was the smallest, when related to investment expenditure, of any system encompassed by this study. Net land grant revenues represented an 1869 capital grant equivalent to only 7.4% of the 1869 present value of investment expenditures in the system through 1900. For this system the land grant subsidy was indeed a tiny fraction of investment expenditures.

Subsidy Necessary and Adequate

The third *ex post* outcome for land grant policy includes those railroads for which subsidy was necessary and the amount provided raised the private rate of return to at least the level of the average opportunity cost of capital. Two of the systems reviewed in this study (the Northern Pacific and the Canadian Pacific) fall in this category.

The Northern Pacific System

In absolute terms, measured either in acreage or dollar value of receipts, the system receiving the most land grant aid was the Northern Pacific.[31] Table A-10 in Appendix A contains the estimates of investment

---

[29] At a discount rate of 7.86%. See footnote 26.
[30] The Leavenworth, Lawrence and Galveston is not included in investment expenditures for land grant railroads of the Santa Fe System, nor is any net land grant revenue received by it prior to 1880 included in the land grant subsidy figures given.
[31] See *Public Aids*, II, 107-115.

expenditure for this system over the period 1870–1900. Estimated capital earnings are presented for the years 1872–1900 in Table B-5, Appendix B. Annual net land grant receipts estimates are listed in Table C-5 of Appendix C. Along with the alternate terminal adjustments, these revenue and investment streams provide the basis for the estimated private rates of return in Table VIII.

Because the same years are included, the estimated market alternative rate is 7.86% for the Northern Pacific, as it is for the Santa Fe System. In the case of the Northern Pacific, we finally come to an instance in which we accept both hypotheses A1 and A2. The Northern Pacific System was unprofitable without the land subsidy, but profitable with it. The subsidy was necessary (*ex post*) and adequate for private profitability. In fact, we observe that the subsidy on an *ex post* basis was too generous. The policy was not optimal, because excessive subsidy was provided. The 1870 present value of the excess subsidy to the Northern Pacific System was $9.142 million (at a discount rate of 7.86%). Society would have been better served by a substantially smaller subsidy to the Northern Pacific.

At a discount rate of 7.86%, the 1870 real present value of the Northern Pacific's land grant subsidy is $19.317 million, whereas that of investment expenditure is $69.128 million for the system and $44.589 million for the land grant railroads. For the land grant railroads of the Northern Pacific System, the land grant subsidy was the same as an 1870 capital grant (at a discount rate of 7.86%) equal to 43.3% of the present value of their investment expenditure. On the same basis the land grant represented 27.9% of the investment expenditure in the system. The land grant did not pay for investment in the land grant railroads or in the system, but it did make a very significant contribution, and was substantially larger than necessary on grounds of efficiency.

TABLE VIII

Estimated Private Rates of Return: Northern Pacific System

Terminal adjustment[a]	Unaided private rate (%)	Aided private rate (%)
A	8.8	11.1
B	6.5	9.3
C	6.3	9.2
D	2.5	6.7

[a] See text for definition of alternative terminal adjustments.

4. Private Rates of Return

The Canadian Pacific System

The Canadian Pacific Railroad was truly a pioneer railroad, built almost 3,000 miles through lands that were virtually uninhabited. Because of this circumstance, as well as military and political considerations, the Canadian Pacific was the most heavily subsidized of the systems included in this study. The private rate of return estimates presented here provide both an alternative for and an extension of those in Peter J. George's earlier study.[32] These estimates are an alternative to George's because the internal rate of return method, rather than the gross profitability ratio, is used to compute rates of return. They are an extension of George's earlier estimates because the private rates of return with various subsidies and with *all* subsidies are considered, rather than simply the rate of return with some subsidies.[33] The question of the optimality of the subsidies to the Canadian Pacific and the issue of the magnitude of any excess subsidy is also considered in some detail below.

The procedure employed here to estimate gross investment expenditures for the Canadian Pacific System basically follows George's technique and relies on the same data sources. Rather than George's decade of 1886–1895, the time period covered by this study is 1881–1900. The adjustment to 1871–1880 government expenditures made by George is used here.[34] The use of Michell's Canadian wholesale price index with 1900 = 100 results in some slight difference in annual constant dollar values of investment expenditures and other data.[35] Another difference from George's investment series is the addition of expenditures in 1890–1893 on the Canadian Pacific Company's China and Japan steamships, whose revenues cannot be separated from the railroad revenues of the firm.[36] Current dollar capital earnings calculated for this study are identical (over the same years) to the net earnings presented by George.

Table A-14 in Appendix A presents both total investment expenditure and investment expenditure by the Canadian Pacific Company during the period 1881–1900. Total investment expenditure is the sum of expenditures by the dominion government and the Canadian Pacific Company,

---

[32] Peter J. George, *op. cit.*, pp. 760–762.

[33] For an earlier critique of the George estimates, see Lloyd J. Mercer, "Rates of Return and Government Subsidization of the Canadian Pacific Railway: An Alternate View," *Canadian Journal of Economics*, VI, 3 (August 1973), 428–437.

[34] *Ibid.*, p. 745.

[35] The index used is the all-commodity index from K. W. Taylor and H. Mitchell, *Statistical Contributions to Canadian Economic History* (Toronto: Macmillan of Canada, 1931), 11, 56. George also made calculations with this index and found essentially no difference in results from the index he selected.

[36] George apparently does not recognize this, and excludes the steamship expenditures from the investment stream.

and includes over $14 million spent by the government prior to 1881. Annual capital earnings for the period 1881–1900 are listed in Table B-7 in Appendix B, along with the annual real cash subsidy. Net land grant receipts for the years 1882–1917 are presented in Table C-7 of Appendix C.

The alternative estimated private rates of return for the Canadian Pacific System, based on the data discussed, are shown in Table IX. The estimated real market alternative rate of return for the Canadian Pacific is 6.75%. The estimated "unaided" private rates of return on a total cost basis indicate that the Canadian Pacific was privately unprofitable without subsidy. Hypothesis A1 is accepted for the Canadian Pacific on a total cost basis. It must be recognized that the actual *unaided* private rate of return is less than the estimates cited, because several unmeasured subsidies are included in the unaided rates of return estimated here, although their effect is probably not significant.[37]

Government construction of several hundred miles of railroad, which was then given to the Canadian Pacific, was a significant subsidy to the private owners of the Canadian Pacific. Estimation of the unaided private rate of return, using company investment expenditures (and value of leased lines) rather than total expenditures in the net receipts stream, takes account of this subsidy and results in estimated rates of return less than 6.75%, regardless of the terminal adjustment used. On this private cost basis, hypotheses A1 is also accepted for the Canadian Pacific.

If we evaluate private profitability with aid, using the total cost of the system (government plus company expenditures) as George does, we

---

[37] The Canadian Pacific received numerous subsidies. Many of these are included in the estimate of unaided private rates, although their total impact is relatively small. The subsidies that George cites are: the value of the railroad from Thunder Bay to Selkirk, and from Kamloops to Port Moody; the cash grants; the land grant; duty-free importation of construction materials; freedom from taxation of the capital stock and equipment of the company; tax exemption for the land grant for 20 years after its location; right-of-way and roadbed concessions; permission to take construction material from crown lands; prohibition of construction of any railway south of the Canadian Pacific mainline in the West within 15 miles of the American border for 20 years; and restriction on the authority of the government to regulate railway rates (see George, *op. cit.*, pp. 753–754). This is an impressive list, of which apparently only three items are included here; however, the impact of all these subsidies is included in the estimated rates of return presented. The railroad, cash, and land grant subsidies are explicitly included. All the other items have the effect of making the estimated net receipts stream larger than it would have been otherwise, either by raising gross revenue or lowering operating expenses so that gross capital earnings are larger, or by making investment expenditures smaller than they would have been in the absence of the cited provisions. As a result, the effect of these subsidies is implicitly included in the present estimate. George's private rate of return is the rate of return on *total* cost, thus excluding the railroad subsidy but *including* all others except the land grant and cash subsidies.

TABLE IX

Estimated Private Rates of Return: Canadian Pacific System

Rate of return	Terminal adjustment[a] (%)			
	A	B	C	D
Unaided private[b]				
Total cost	2.8	−2.7	2.4	−14.0
Company	4.4	−1.3	3.9	−12.7
Aided private				
Total cost				
Land grant	5.1	1.2	4.7	−2.9
Cash subsidy	4.0	−1.4	3.5	−11.4
Land grant and cash subsidy	6.4	2.6	6.1	−1.4
Company cost				
Land grant	6.9	3.0	6.6	−1.2
Cash subsidy	5.9	0.4	5.5	−9.8
Land grant and cash subsidy	8.8	4.8	8.4	0.8

[a] See text for definition of terminal adjustments.
[b] Includes unmeasured subsidies.
[c] Includes unmeasured subsidies and the measured subsidies indicated.

again find that the aided private rate of return was less than 6.75%, regardless of the terminal adjustment used, even counting *all* subsidies. Thus, on a total cost basis, hypothesis A2 is rejected.

If the cost basis is company expenditures rather than total expenditures, a different picture emerges. Moreover, because the company cost basis reflects the rate of return the private owners actually received, this is the correct basis upon which to view the *ex post* private profitability of the Canadian Pacific System. We previously observed that hypothesis A1 is accepted on this basis. The present estimates indicate three cases in which the Canadian Pacific System was privately profitable on the company cost basis with subsidy. These are: (1) with terminal adjustment A, including all subsidies except cash (6.9%), (2) with terminal adjustment A and all subsidies (8.8%), and (3) with terminal adjustment C (8.4%) and all subsidies. Because the preferred terminal adjustment is terminal adjustment C, the Canadian Pacific System was privately profitable with *all* subsidies. Hypothesis A2 is accepted on this basis. However, notice that it would be rejected if we considered the land grant aid alone. The private rate of return with terminal adjustment C and the land grant aid alone (on a company cost basis) is 6.6%, and is thus slightly less than the estimated market alternative. As we noted earlier, this rate of return also includes the effect of several minor subsidies and, since it is on a company cost basis, one major subsidy: the construction cost subsidy. On the company cost basis with the cash subsidy, but without the land grant, the private rate of return estimate (5.5%) is also less than the estimated market rate.

On a company (private) cost basis, the rate of return estimates of this study indicate that the Canadian Pacific System was privately unprofitable without aid, but privately profitable with *all* subsidies considered. In this case the subsidies came as a package and must be considered together rather than separately. Both hypotheses A1 and A2 are accepted for the Canadian Pacific. Subsidy was necessary for private profitability and adequate for that purpose. Since the cash and land grant subsidies more than double the rate of return based on company cost, it is clear that these subsidies played a major role in paying for the private investment in the Canadian Pacific System. Table II lists the 1881 real present value of investment and the land grant subsidy, while Table X shows those for the cash and railroad (construction cost) subsidies. In absolute value the land grant is the most important subsidy. However, when the subsidy streams are placed in terms of 1881 present value, the land grant's relative importance is much reduced because of the longer time it took to realize it. The 1881 real present value of the company's investment expenditures over the period 1881–1900 (at a discount rate of 6.75%) is $148.374 million, compared to $86.110 million for the three subsidies. Together, the subsidies were equivalent to a capital grant, equal to 58% of the 1881 present value of private investment expenditures. Although the subsidies did not literally pay for the investment in the railroad, they did make a very substantial contribution.

TABLE X

Investment Expenditure, Cash and Railroad Subsidies for the Canadian Pacific System

Item	Present value [a] (thousand 1900 $)	$\left(\dfrac{PV_s}{PV_{ie}}\right)$ [b]
Investment expenditures [c]	148,374	—
Cash subsidy	21,148	0.143
Railroad subsidy [d]	32,088	0.216

[a] Present value in 1881.
[b] Ratio of the present value of specific subsidy to the present value of investment expenditures.
[c] Private (company) expenditures.
[d] Investment expenditures by the dominion government.

4. Private Rates of Return

From the foregoing discussion it is obvious that (*ex post* and presumably *ex ante*) the Canadian Pacific System required subsidization for private investors to undertake the project. Given the estimates accepted here, it is also clear that based on private investment expenditures the Canadian Pacific System received (*ex post*) more subsidy than necessary on grounds of efficiency.[38] How large was this excess subsidy?

George's estimate of "required" subsidy ($\bar{L}$) in 1885 is calculated as[39]

$$\frac{1}{T} \sum_{t=1}^{10} L_t = \frac{1}{T} \sum_{t=1}^{10} \left(K_t - \frac{R_t}{r} \right)$$

$$= \sum_{t=1}^{10} \frac{K}{T} - \frac{1}{r} \sum_{t=1}^{10} R_t \frac{1}{T},$$

$$\bar{L} = \bar{K} - \frac{1}{r}\bar{R}. \tag{1}$$

George defines K_t as the 1885 present value of the capital base—the cumulative cost of construction and equipment—through year t. Reproduction of George's results shows that his K_t includes both government and private investment expenditure. R_t is defined as the 1885 present value of company net earnings in year t, while r is the assumed normal rate of return, $T = 10$, and L_t is the estimated 1885 present value of the "required" capital grant in year t that would allow reported company net earnings to yield the normal rate of return on privately contributed capital in year t.

In order to illustrate the computations included, let us rewrite George's equation as:

$$RS = \frac{1}{T} \sum_{t=1}^{10} \frac{SGI_t}{(1+r)^t} - \frac{1}{rT} \sum_{t=1}^{10} \frac{NE_t}{(1+r)^t}, \tag{2}$$

where

RS = required subsidy as defined by George,
SGI = the sum of gross investment expenditures (government plus private) from 1871 through year t,
NE = net earnings as defined by George,

---

[38] This is the case so long as one views the normal rate of return on investment in Canada during the period 1881–1900 as being less than 8.4%. If it was 8.4%, the system received just the right amount of subsidy, while if the normal rate of return was more than 8.4%, the system did not receive sufficient subsidy and was privately unprofitable with all subsidies.

[39] George, *op. cit.*, note to Table V, p. 760. This is the required subsidy in the sense that it is intended to be the capital grant in 1885 necessary to allow private capital in the project to earn the normal rate of return.

t = year subscript varying from 1 in 1886 to 10 in 1895,
r = the assumed normal rate of return,
$T = 10$.

Label the "accumulated costs" and "earnings" components of required subsidy computed by the above as X and Y, respectively. Then

$$RS = X - Y. \tag{3}$$

George computes required subsidy for assumed normal rates of return of 6, 8, and 10%. Total subsidy TS minus required subsidy RS equals excess subsidy ES, i.e.,

$$ES = TS - RS.[40] \tag{4}$$

Substituting (3) into (4) we have:

$$ES = TS - (X - Y). \tag{5}$$

From (5) it is clear that excess subsidy is overstated if TS is overstated, X is understated, or Y is overstated.

With George's technique the estimates of excess subsidy at each assumed normal rate of return are overstated. Several factors are responsible for the overstatement of excess subsidy. One is that NE_t includes the earnings of both the privately built railway *and* the government built railway. Thus, Y is overstated because the net earnings on the government built railroad are included in Y.

A second component of George's overstatement of excess subsidy results from inclusion of the 1885 present value of the tax exemption in TS, even though its effect is already included in NE_t, which is larger than it would otherwise have been (by the amount of the tax exemption). In effect, Y is overstated by this procedure.

A third source of overstatement of excess subsidy results from the way in which investment expenditures (private and government) are treated in calculation of RS compared to the evaluation of government investment expenditures in TS. In RS (X) they are simply summed from 1871 to year t. However, in calculating the value of the government construction expenditure subsidy for inclusion in TS, expenditures occurring before the base year of 1885 are compounded, at the assumed normal rate of return, to arrive at their 1885 value.[41] By this procedure X is understated and excess subsidy overstated. For George's technique a better approximation to the true excess subsidy will result if investment expenditures before 1885 are

---
[40] *Ibid.*, p. 758.
[41] *Ibid.*, p. 754, footnote 37.

4. Private Rates of Return

also compounded in calculation of RS, as one must then also do with the net earnings component of RS.

Finally, excess subsidy is overstated because the 1885 value of the remission of duties on materials imported for construction of the railway is already reflected in a lower value for RS. This is because George's $\overline{K}$ is smaller than it would have been without the duty remission, and X is in effect understated, given George's value for TS. This treatment double-counts the subsidy. This can be corrected by adding the 1885 present value of the subsidy to $\overline{K}$ or subtracting it from TS.

Given George's technique, the value of excess subsidy is recomputed with the adjustments suggested and shown in Table XI for his assumed

TABLE XI

Recalculation of Excess Subsidy (Millions of Current Dollars and 1885 Dollars) Using George's Technique with Adjustments

	Assumed normal rate					
	6%		8%		10%	
	Current	1885	Current	1885	Current	1885
$\overline{K}$	157.8	146.4	149.3	138.1	142.2	131.1
$\overline{R}_u$	95.1	94.2	66.3	65.4	49.5	48.9
$\overline{G}$	19.8	18.9	14.0	14.2	10.8	10.8
$\overline{T}$	8.4	8.3	5.8	5.7	4.4	4.4
$\overline{R}_a$	66.9	67.0	46.5	45.5	34.3	33.7
$\overline{RS}_m$	90.9	79.4	102.8	92.6	107.9	97.4
TS	145.6	120.2	126.9	110.3	121.1	107.6
ES_m	54.7	40.8	24.1	17.7	13.2	10.2
ES_g	77.3	61.0	48.0	39.8	40.2	34.1

$\overline{K}$ = George's $\overline{K}$ adjusted by (a) compounding expenditures before 1885 and (b) adding 1885 value of remission of tariff duties on construction materials.

$\overline{R}_u$ = George's R adjusted by addition of company net earnings 1881–1885, with those prior to 1885 compounded.

$\overline{G}$ = 1885 present value of earnings on government capital calculated annually as (sum of government investment expenditures) (net earnings/sum of investment expenditure).

$\overline{T}$ = 1885 present value of tax exemption over 1881–1895.

$\overline{R}_a = \overline{R}_u - (\overline{G} + \overline{T})$.

$RS = \overline{K} - \overline{R}_a$.

TS = George's total value of subsidies.

$ES_m = TS - RS_m$, i.e., excess subsidy.

ES_g = George's estimate of excess subsidy.

interest rates. These calculations show that George's estimates of excess subsidy are rather considerable overstatements.

Estimating excess subsidy with George's technique is unsatisfactory in the same sense that his technique for calculating the private rate of return is unsatisfactory. Fortunately, this is easily corrected with the internal rate of return technique. The 1881 present value of the total excess subsidy can be computed very simply from

$$S^* = \sum_{t=0}^{T} \frac{NR_t}{(1 + r)^t},$$

where t ranges from 0 to 19 (1881 to 1900), S^* is the excess subsidy (or subsidy shortage) at the given normal rate of return r, which is estimated to be 6.75%, and NR_t is net receipts (earnings plus subsidies less operating expenses and investment expenditure plus the terminal adjustment). The estimated 1881 present value of the excess subsidy in 1990 dollars is $19.767 million, with terminal adjustment C used in the net receipts stream based on private investment expenditures. The 1881 present value of the separate components in this estimate of excess subsidy is shown in Table XII.

The reader may object that Table XII does not list government investment expenditures, whose 1881 present value at a 6.75% discount rate is $32.088 million, as a subsidy. Those expenditures were, of course, a subsidy, but as noted with respect to George's estimates, their effect is already included in two items. One is the 1881 present value of capital earnings and terminal adjustment C. Earnings attributable to that portion of the firm's capital stock financed by government investment expenditure

TABLE XII

New Excess Subsidy Estimate

Item	1881 present value at 6.75% (thousand 1900 $)
Capital earnings[a]	114,119
Cash subsidy	21,148
Net land grant revenue	32,874
Private investment expenditure[b]	148,374
Excess subsidy[c]	19,767

[a] Includes terminal adjustment C.
[b] Includes value of leased lines.
[c] The sum of capital earnings, cash subsidy, and net land grant revenue minus private investment expenditure.

4. Private Rates of Return

are included in capital earnings, whereas the 1900 value of capital stock also includes the government financed portion. The 1881 present value of investment expenditures includes only private expenditures, which is thus the second item reflecting the impact of the subsidy provided by the government investment expenditures. The value of $19.767 million is the 1881 real present value of the excess subsidy to the *private* owners, given the value of their investment in the system. This is about one-third of the implicit excess subsidy at a discount rate of 6.75%, based on George's figures.[42]

Summary

This evaluation of hypotheses A1 and A2 gets us only part of the way to a test of the economic rationality of land grant policy. We have seen that the *ex post* results with respect to private profitability of the land grant systems studied are quite mixed, and range across the spectrum of possibilities from aid necessary, to aid unnecessary, *and* from too little aid to too much aid. The fundamental test of land grant policy's contribution to society rests on evaluation of hypotheses B1 and B2. We now turn to this task.

---

[42] *Ibid.*, see Table VI, p. 961. The approximate constant dollar excess subsidy at a 6.75% rate of interest based on George's figures is $53 million.

Chapter 5

Social Rates of Return

Estimates of the social rates of return for use in evaluation of hypotheses B1 and B2 are presented in this chapter. Calculation of these social rates of return depends on the estimation of the stream of externalities resulting from the operation of each railroad system.

The private and social rates of return for an investment project diverge only if there are externalities (external benefits and/or external costs) associated with the project. Benefits derived from improved transportation facilities are mainly reflected in reduced costs for moving goods and people. External benefits are the favorable effects produced by an economic agent (e.g., a firm) which accrue to other economic agents that do not pay for those benefits. As we noted earlier, such externalities are often termed "unpaid benefits." The creation of unpaid benefits by the railroad firm is the result of the firm's internal economies, which result from the high degree of indivisibility of its capital. When the railroad is unable to charge for all the benefits it produces, i.e., to internalize unpaid benefits, the cost or utility functions of other economic agents are shifted in a favorable direction. The unpaid benefits defined here are labeled pecuniary external benefits and are primarily transmitted through the price system in the form of lower input prices for transportation. In the short run, as a result of these pecuniary external economies the profits of producers external to the railroad firm are a function not only of their own inputs and outputs but also of the inputs and output of the railroad firm.[1]

---

[1] The definition of pecuniary external economies used here follows that originally suggested by Tibor Scitovsky in "Two Concepts of External Economies," *The Journal of*

5. Social Rates of Return

External benefits produced by the railroad can be separated into three distinct categories reflecting different classes of users of railroad transportation. For reference convenience these are labeled intraregional, interregional, and passenger external benefits. These in turn reflect the unpaid benefits received by producers within the region served by the railroad, shippers involved in interregional trade, and passengers who travel both within the region and between regions.

Intraregional Benefits

Intraregional benefits are reflected in an increase in income and output in the region in which the railroad operates. This rise in income and output is a function of the operation of the railroad. However, because the increased income consists of unpaid benefits, it is not captured in the railroad's revenues. Intraregional benefits are estimated here only for agricultural producers. The theory of rent provides the theoretical basis for the estimate. Although unpaid benefits to other producers within the region are ignored, the resulting understatement of the social returns (externality) stream is probably slight. Construction and operation of a railroad that lowered the cost of transporting output from farms to markets within a region would result both in new lands being brought into commercial agriculture and lands previously farmed being used more intensively, i.e., more units of labor and capital would be employed per unit of land. In short, as a result of lowered transport costs upon construction and operation of the railroad, both the extensive and the intensive margins would expand. Capital and labor employed in this expansion of production would receive their opportunity cost. Additional land located away from transportation facilities would be brought into production so long as the rent accruing to it was at least zero. On land within the extensive margin, additional units of capital and labor would be used per unit of land until the return from the last "dose" of capital and labor equaled the opportunity cost of that capital and labor. The external benefits (producers' surplus) received by agricultural producers as a result of this expansion of production would accrue to land as rent because of its relative inelasticity of supply.[2] The incremental rent to land within the extensive margin following a railroad's initial operation (and the resultant lowering of farm-to-market transport costs within the region) is a measure of the intraregional external benefits to agricultural producers resulting from

---

Political Economy, LXII, (April 1954), 143–151. As Scitovsky points out, his definition of pecuniary external economies includes not only interdependence among producers through the market mechanism, but also direct interdependence among producers.

[2] While its supply elasticity may not be zero, land would have the most inelastic supply of any factor and as a result would capture the unpaid benefits.

the operation of the specific railroad. Since the value of land is the capitalization (at the market rate of interest) of its rent, incremental land value would also serve as a measure of intraregional benefits. In this study, intraregional benefits are estimated on the basis of incremental land value.

Estimation of the intraregional external benefits on the basis of the increment in land values following the start of a railroad's operation requires four additional pieces of information. The first is the straight-line distance of the extensive margin from the railroad.[3]

The second piece of information is an estimate of the change in farm values that would have occurred without the railroad. The increment in farm values reported by the census (following construction and operation of the railroad) for the counties at least partially within the estimated extensive margin is adjusted downward to allow for the rise in farm values that it is assumed would have occurred without the railroad.

Third, because farm values include both land and capital values they must be partitioned into capital and "pure" land values. An estimate is required (by county) of the capital value included in farm values reported in the census.

Finally, other railroads may also influence land values in counties where land values are affected by the operation of a particular railroad. Estimated intraregional benefits are attributed to a particular railroad in proportion to its share of total ton-miles of agricultural goods transported within the region it serves.[4]

Interregional Benefits

Interregional external benefits depend on two pieces of data: (1) the volume of interregional shipments on the railroad, and (2) the saving per unit compared to the next best alternative. One way to obtain the first of these is to assume that the same tonnage would be shipped with or without the railroad. The estimate is then the product of the tonnage shipped to interregional trade with the railroad and the differential in total transport cost per unit (counting both direct and indirect costs) between rail and the next best alternative shipment means.

The well known difficulty with this estimate of interregional benefits is that it will always overstate the quantity shipped in the absence of the railroad if the total unit cost of rail shipment is less than the least-cost

---

[3] Appendix D contains the details of this estimate for the systems in the United States. A different technique than that described here is necessary in the case of the Canadian Pacific System. See Appendix E.

[4] Details of the estimates of intraregional benefits by system are contained in Appendix E. This includes the second, third, and fourth steps just described.

5. Social Rates of Return

alternative. This follows from the law of demand and the consequent fact that under this circumstance more tonnage will be involved in interregional trade with the railroad than in its absence. Reduced transport costs within the region, after the railroad begins operation, lead to both an outward shift of the extensive margin (zero rent perimeter) and an upward shift of the intensive margin. More land, labor, and capital are employed within the region, and regional income and output grow. At least the quantity of interregional transport services demanded (if not the demand for interregional transport services) must increase in this case. Since tonnage shipped with the railroad exceeds that shipped without the railroad, interregional benefits are overstated by the calculation discussed.

The external benefits received by shippers in interregional trade can be viewed as the increase in consumer surplus to these shippers, as buyers of transport services, that results from a decline in transport costs. Based on shipments with the railroad, interregional benefits per time unit would be estimated as the area $rBCr'$ in Fig. 1, where r is the transport cost per unit with the next best alternative in the absence of the railroad, r' is the cost with the railroad, Q is the tonnage shipped with the next best alternative to the railroad, and Q' is the tonnage shipped with the railroad. This is an overstatement, because, with demand constant, interregional benefits per time unit are actually the area $rACr'$ in Fig. 1. If demand curves are assumed to be linear, interregional benefits per time unit can be estimated by a simple calculation. With reference to Fig. 1, we have

$$IR_t = r_t^* Q_t + \frac{r_t^*}{2}(Q_t' - Q_t), \tag{1}$$

where IR is the estimate of interregional benefits during time period t, $r^* = r - r'$, r is the transport cost with the next best alternative to the railroad, r' is the transport cost with the railroad, Q_t' is tonnage shipped with the railroad in period t, and Q_t is the tonnage that would have been shipped during period t in the absence of the railroad.

So far it has been assumed that interregional benefits are being measured at a point in time. For the purposes of this study, however, what is needed is an estimate of a stream of interregional benefits over time. If the estimation procedure suggested is used, a new theoretical problem appears. The curve DD in Fig. 1 is the net excess supply curve for good X. Assume good X is an agricultural good produced in the region served by a particular railroad. The horizontal axis of Fig. 1 shows the *amount* of X shipped in interregional trade per time period. Following the beginning of operation of the railroad in a particular region, two sets of forces would work to shift DD to the right. One is the extension of the extensive and intensive margins in the region as transport costs fall with the railroad.

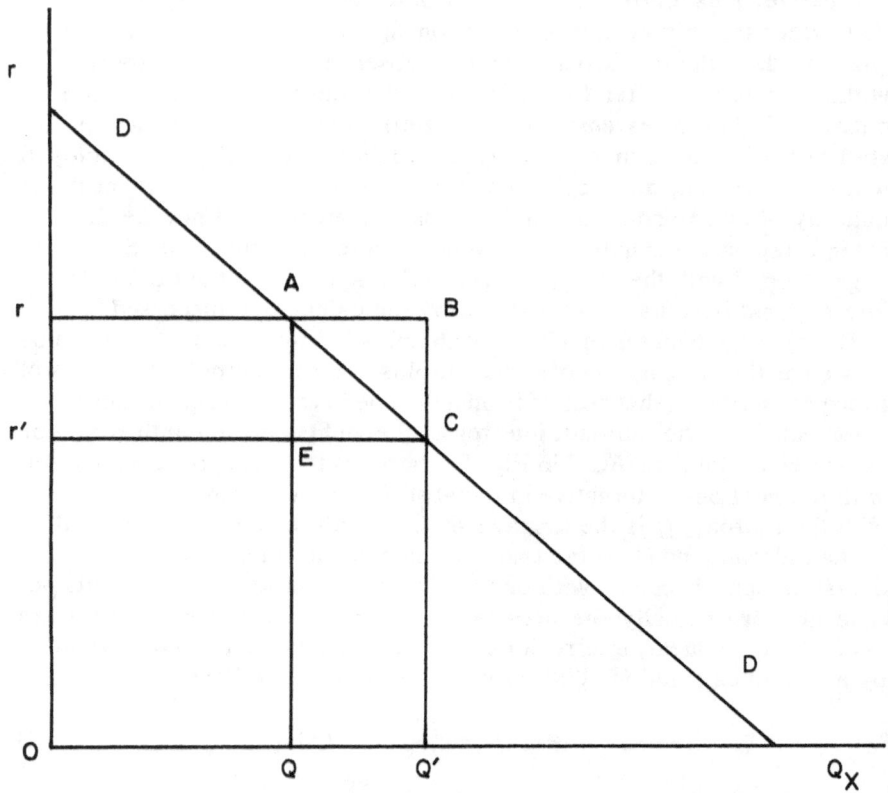

Fig. 1. Calculation of interregional external benefits.

This would shift the positive excess supply curve of the "surplus" region (the region with the newly introduced railroad) to the right. At the same time, both economic growth and population growth would shift the negative excess supply curve of the "deficit" region to the right. This is illustrated in Fig. 2 with the new net excess supply curve D_2D_2, where region 1 is the "surplus" region and region 2 is the deficit region. Now the points rQ with the next best alternative to the railroad in its absence and $r'Q'$ with the railroad are on different demand curves.

Figure 3 illustrates the problem suggested, with demand assumed to increase from D_1D_1 to D_2D_2.[5] The observation of price and quantity with

---

[5] It has been suggested that the legitimacy of partial equilibrium analysis disappears once shifts in demand become a function of railroad investment in the manner suggested here (see Peter D. McClelland, "Social Rates of Return on American Railroads in the Nineteenth Century," *Economic History Review*, Second Series, 25, 3 (August 1972), 484). There is no

5. Social Rates of Return

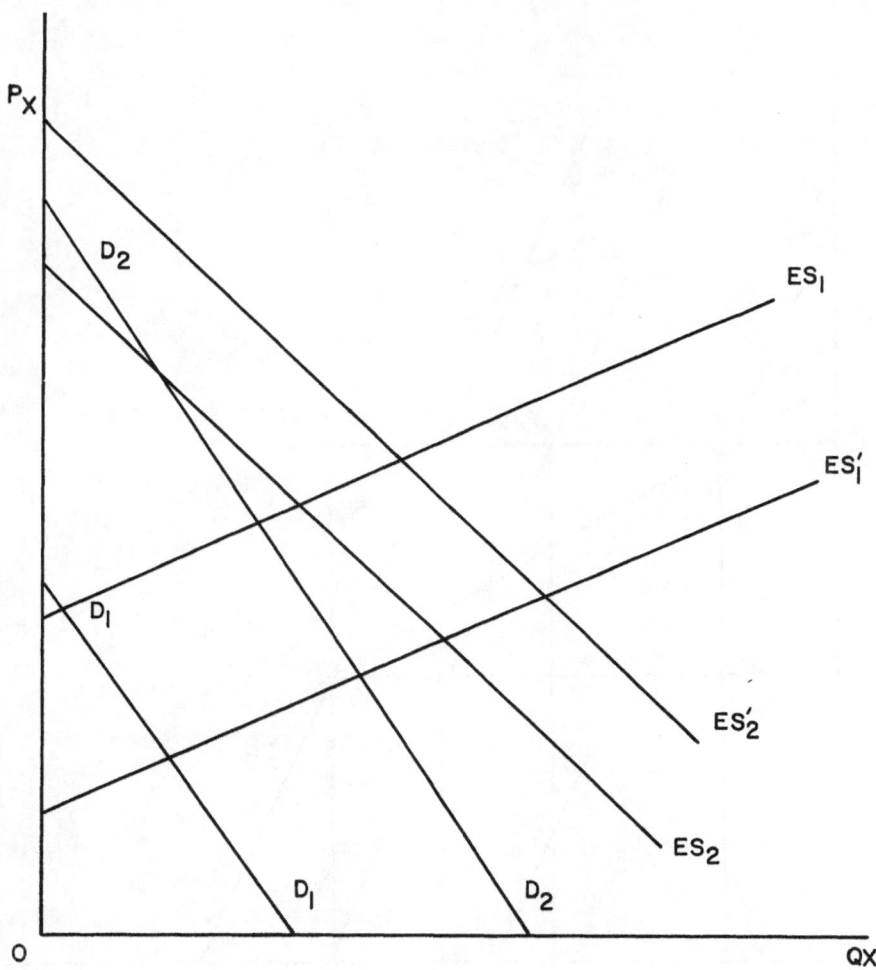

Fig. 2. Increasing net excess demand.

doubt that, as with all analyses of this kind, partial equilibrium analysis is somewhat incomplete. The question is, how incomplete? For the problem at hand, the error introduced by use of partial rather than general equilibrium analysis appears likely to be insignificant. The area under the demand curve for transport services measures the net gain (social payoff) to both regions from the trade considered [cf. Paul A. Samuelson, "Spatial Price Equilibrium and Linear Programming," *The American Economic Review*, XLII, 3 (June 1952), 288]. The shift in that demand curve because of the entrance of the railroad would thus indicate the increment of net gain to both regions because of the railroad's operation in the exporting region. This increment is exactly what we want to measure.

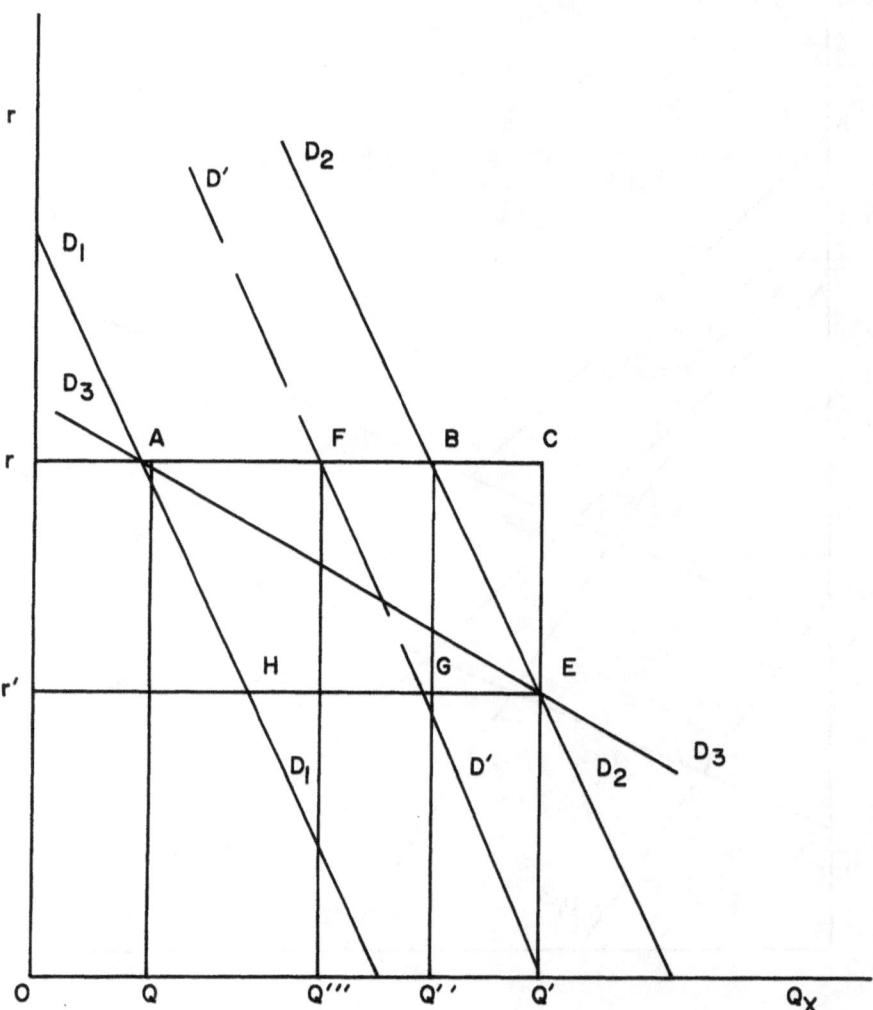

Fig. 3. Calculation of interregional external benefits with an increase in demand.

the next best alternative to the railroad is rQ, whereas that with the railroad is $r'Q'$. The correct estimate of interregional benefits would be that of Eq. (1). It might be argued that this is an underestimate of the true interregional benefits, which are

$$IR_t = r_t^* Q_t'' + \frac{r_t^*}{2}(Q_t'' - Q_t'). \qquad (2)$$

5. Social Rates of Return

Note that this is not the case. The point rQ' was not observed in the absence of the railroad because D_2D_2 includes the effect of the extension of the extensive and intensive margins following the lowering of transport costs with the railroad. Thus, rQ' is not relevant to the estimate of interregional benefits.[6]

It is entirely possible that demand could have shifted in the absence of the railroad, say, from ES_2 to ES_2' in Fig. 2. In this case the net excess demand curve would have shifted to the right, say to $D'D'$ in Fig. 3, in the absence of the railroad. The relevant observation without the railroad becomes rQ'''. The correct estimate of interregional benefits is

$$IR_t = r_t^* Q_t''' + \frac{r_t^*}{2}(Q_t' - Q_t'''). \qquad (3)$$

This estimate is larger than the one that results when the price–quantity situation in the absence of the railroad is always assumed to be rQ. Thus, the interregional benefits estimate made here will be understated slightly as long as demand in the "deficit" region increases over time.[7]

Appendix F contains the details on the interregional benefits estimate made here. This component of the social returns stream is estimated only for the Central Pacific System in this study because of data limitations and the apparently trivial impact of this category of external benefits.[8]

Passenger Benefits

Passenger external benefits include both a direct and an indirect component. Direct benefits result from the lower cost of rail travel compared to alternatives. Indirect benefits occur because time is saved in travel by rail compared with alternatives.

Direct benefits to passengers could be estimated as the area $pBCp'$ in Fig. 4. Although this calculation has been used by other researchers, it is

---

[6] McClelland, *op. cit.*, maintains that the area $rr'EB$ is the correct measure of the gain in consumer surplus. This is true only if the demand curve at this latter point in time without the railroad would be D_2D_2. It is again clear that this would not be the case, but that the demand curve would lie somewhere between D_1D_1 and D_2D_2. Since this position is not known, the present estimate of the increment to consumers' surplus resulting from increased demand (which is appropriate to the hypothesis test employed here) is the downward-biased area under D_3D_3 at each point in time.

[7] And as long as demand curves are linear. The estimate of Eq. (1) is the true estimate of interregional benefits, given that shifts in demand do occur over time, if the relevant demand curve is some curve like D_3D_3 in Fig. 3. Actually, D_3D_3 is simply a locus of equilibrium points, although it might be thought of as the long-run demand or supply curve. The observations that trace out D_3D_3 are used here to estimate interregional benefits.

[8] Exclusion of interregional benefits reduces the Central Pacific social rates of return by 0.1% or less.

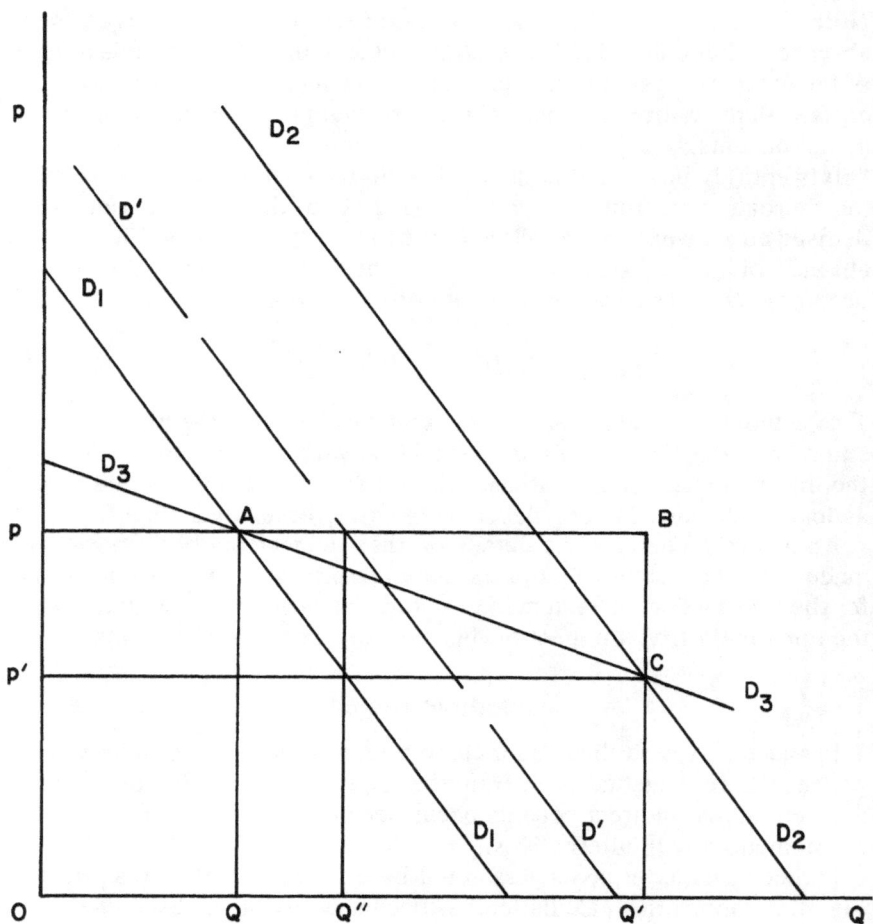

Fig. 4. Calculation of direct external benefits to passengers.

clear that passenger benefits are thereby overstated, because it is assumed that the same amount of passenger miles would be demanded with and without the railroad.[9] With reference to Fig. 4, the calculation of direct benefits (with demand assumed to increase from D_1D_1 to D_2D_2) is

$$DB_t = p_t^* Q_t + \frac{p_t^*}{2}(Q_t' - Q_t), \qquad (4)$$

[9] Cf. Albert Fishlow, *American Railroads and the Transformation of the Ante-Bellum Economy* (Cambridge, Mass.: Harvard Univ. Press, 1965), pp. 90–92.

where DB_t is direct passenger benefits in period t, p^* is $p - p'$, Q is passenger miles in period t with the next best alternative in the absence of the railroad, and Q' is passenger miles in period t with the railroad.

If demand for passenger travel would have increased in the absence of the railroad, with cost per unit unchanged, direct benefits as in Fig. 4 (demand having increased from D_1D_1 to $D'D'$) would be

$$DB_t = p_t^* Q_t'' + \frac{p_t^*}{2}(Q_t' - Q_t''). \tag{5}$$

The estimate of Eq. (5) is clearly larger than that of Eq. (4); however, the Eq. (4) estimate is used here.[10] Details of the estimates of passenger benefits are contained in Appendix G.

The estimation of indirect benefits requires valuation of the opportunity cost of time saved by rail travel. So far as the time saving represents labor put to productive use, the result is an increase in real output (income) for both individuals and society, which should be included in evaluating the social rate of return on investment in the railroads that made it possible.

The Social Returns Stream

The social returns stream used here to calculate the social rate of return is the sum of the estimated flows of intraregional, interregional, and passenger external benefits. The only social cost estimated for this study is the cost to society of the federal government construction loans to railroads included in the Central Pacific and Union Pacific Systems. Besides the original construction loan, the government in effect made a second (interest-free) loan by not requiring payment of the annual interest charge on the first loan until after it was due. Extension of the payment period for the original loan and accumulated interest when they fell due constituted a third loan. These loans involved an opportunity cost to society, because the railroads paid less than they would have been required to pay private lenders for the same funds.[11] The stream of social returns minus social costs is added to the unaided private net receipts stream of each system to calculate the social rate of return by the internal rate of return algorithm.[12]

---

[10] This is the case when an early observation of passenger miles on the railroad is used continuously for the value of Q as we do here.

[11] See Appendix H for a discussion of this point and the estimates of the loan subsidy cost for the individual systems.

[12] The social returns stream discussed here is based, as noted in footnote 5, on partial equilibrium analysis. This partial, rather than general, equilibrium approach results in a somewhat limited definition of social returns. In particular, indirect or second-round effects are ignored. These include (1) the full general equilibrium comparative static resource reallo-

Tests of Hypotheses B1 and B2

The Central Pacific System

The placement of intraregional benefits, as estimated here, in the social returns stream has a significant effect on the calculated internal rate of return. The estimated intraregional benefits between two successive census years could be placed in the social returns stream with a lag of 1 to 10 years from the initial census year for each pair of census years. The sensitivity of the social rate of return to these alternative lags is illustrated here for each system. In addition, two other alternatives are presented. One is the social rate of return, excluding the estimate of intraregional benefits. The second involves the use of a uniform distribution in entering intraregional benefits into the social returns stream. With the latter method, the estimated incremental pure land value between two censuses for each county is distributed by placing one-tenth of the total increment in each of the 10 years between successive censuses.[13]

As is the case with the private rates of return, the terminal adjustment used in the net receipts stream has a substantial effect on the computed internal rate of return. The alternative terminal adjustment methods presented in Chapter 4 are also utilized in the calculation of the social rates of return.

---

cation effects, (2) dynamic effects, including impacts on technical change, scale of plant, and immigration, and (3) inducement of more rapid capital accumulation. For a discussion of these points, see Jeffrey G. Williamson, *Late Nineteenth Century American Development: A General Equilibrium History* (New York: Cambridge Univ. Press, 1974), pp. 184–187. Williamson applies a general equilibrium model that takes second-round effects into account to estimate railroad social savings in 1890. His estimate of social savings in 1890 is 21% of GNP (p. 194). This is several times larger than Fogel's partial equilibrium estimate of 1890 social savings. Since we are dealing here with individual railroad systems rather than the entire national system, the general versus partial equilibrium problem is greatly reduced compared to that faced by Fogel and Fishlow. Still, comparison of the Williamson estimate of social savings with Fogel's indicates that the estimates of social rates here are probably understated. For the hypothesis tests at hand, this is the bias we want, provided it is not overwhelming. For individual railroad systems this does not appear likely to be the case.

[13] Thus, for a county that was within the extensive margin by 1870, one-tenth of the estimated incremental pure land value between 1870 and 1880 is placed in each year from 1871 through 1880. A county that was first within the extensive margin between census years—1876, for example—would be treated in the same way except that one-tenth of the 1870–1880 incremental land value would be placed in the social returns stream for 1877 through 1880. Thus, only four-tenths of estimated incremental land value would be used in the social returns stream for the county in question. The underlying assumption here is that total "pure" land value in a county between census observations increases at a decreasing rate with respect to time—i.e., $\partial^2 PLV_i / \partial t^2 < 0$ where PLV = total pure land value in county i, t = time.

TABLE XIII

Alternative Estimates of the Social Rate of Return for the Central Pacific System

Years of lag on intraregional benefits	Alternative terminal adjustment methods[a] (%)			
	A	B	C	D
No intraregional benefits	15.7	14.4	14.0	12.7
10	19.0	18.3	18.1	17.6
9	19.5	18.9	18.7	18.2
8	20.3	19.8	19.6	19.2
7	21.1	20.5	20.4	20.0
6	21.9	21.5	21.4	21.0
5	23.2	22.8	22.7	22.4
4	24.8	24.5	24.4	24.2
3	26.8	26.5	26.4	26.2
2	29.3	29.1	29.1	28.9
1	33.1	32.9	32.9	32.9
Uniform distribution	23.7	23.3	23.2	22.9

[a] See text for definition of alternative terminal adjustments.

Table XIII presents the estimated *ex post* social rates of return for the Central Pacific System, with alternative lags on intraregional benefits (including the alternative of taking no account of these benefits) and the alternative terminal adjustments as defined in Chapter 4. The range of the estimated social rate of return for the Central Pacific System is 33.1 to 12.7%.

The direction of net bias in the estimated social rates of return in this study cannot be determined with certainty, but they are probably understated because of the exclusion of indirect effects in the social returns stream (see footnote 12). In addition it should be noted that two of the external benefit streams estimated here are probably understated, so that the present value of the social net receipts (private net receipts plus social returns minus social costs) is probably understated at each rate of discount.[14] One of the understatements is the result of the exclusion of interregional benefits from the social returns stream for all systems (except the Central Pacific) because of the lack of data. Even in the case of the Central Pacific, the lack of data relating to the indirect costs of water transport reduces the value of interregional benefits estimates, because r^* is smaller

---

[14] The higher the absolute value of the net receipts stream, the higher the discount rate required to make the present value of that stream zero.

than it should be.¹⁵ The fact that external benefits for each system are estimated only to the terminal year also results in understatement of the true social returns stream attributable to the capital stock included in the net receipts stream.

Various writers have criticized computations of the type presented here on several grounds, including: (a) the use of prices rather than marginal cost, (b) the assumption that the alternative mode of transport is available at constant unit cost, and (c) the assumption that the price elasticity of demand for transportable goods is zero.¹⁶ The use of prices rather than marginal cost results in understatement of the benefits attributed to the railroad by these computations.¹⁷ For this reason the social rates here are biased downward. The same bias results from the assumption of constant unit cost for alternative modes of transportation.¹⁸ Since this bias works against acceptance of the hypothesis that the land grant policy was beneficial, it strengthens the test of that hypothesis. The computational procedure here has taken account (although imperfectly) of the fact that the absolute value of the price elasticity of demand for transportable goods is greater than zero. Significant upward bias in the estimated social rates of return from this source appears unlikely.

Consideration of these points leads to the conclusion that the computational procedures employed here most likely result in a general downward bias to the estimated social rates of return, given a specific lag on intraregional external benefits and a specific terminal adjustment.

A wide choice of estimates has been presented for the social rate of return of the Central Pacific System. The choice of one estimate out of these as *the* estimate of the social rate of return is neither obvious nor easy. The choice here is determined by the terminal adjustment method and procedure for placing intraregional benefits in the social return stream that appear most reasonable. Since the basic menu has been presented, others may select their favorite if they find another method more to their taste. Terminal adjustment C is preferred, as before. The uniform distribution appears most reasonable as a way of placing the intraregional benefits in the social returns stream. Thus, the social rate of return accepted here for the Central Pacific System is 23.2%. Hypothesis B1 is accepted for the

---

¹⁵ The neglected indirect costs are the extra cost of cargo losses in water shipment, transhipping costs, additional inventory costs, neglected capital costs, and supplementary wagon haulage.

¹⁶ Cf. Peter D. McClelland, "Railroads, American Growth and the New Economic History: A Critique," *The Journal of Economic History*, XXVIII (March 1968), 102–123.

¹⁷ *Ibid.*, 114.

¹⁸ Provided one assumes unit costs would rise in the absence of the railroad. For the opposite conclusion it would be necessary that unit costs fall for alternatives in the absence of the railroad, which seems unlikely.

5. Social Rates of Return

Central Pacific System, for which the estimated average opportunity cost is 9.03%.

Since we do not have (and cannot obtain) estimates of the *ex post* social rates of return on those projects abandoned because capital was diverted to the Central Pacific System or any other system included in this study, hypothesis B2 can be dealt with only in a probabilistic sense. It is highly unlikely that there were projects of comparable total size that would have had *ex post* social rates of return as high as or higher than 23.2% and that were not undertaken or were reduced because of the land grants to the Central Pacific System. On this basis hypothesis B2 can be accepted, and it can be concluded that the land grant policy with respect to the Central Pacific System was beneficial to society. This rests on the further assumption that land grant policy hastened construction of the system.[19]

But what if one does not agree with the stated choice among the alternative social rates presented? The likelihood that hypotheses B1 and B2 are false appears to be relatively small regardless of the choice of terminal adjustment method or length of lag on intraregional benefits in the social returns stream. Even when no terminal adjustment is made and no intraregional benefits are included, the social rate is more than 40% greater than the (upward biased) market rate of 9.03% with the Central Pacific System. These latter specifications of the terminal adjustment and intraregional benefits are clearly unreasonable. However, even with those conditions it is not obvious that hypotheses B1 and B2 are false. Indeed, it is quite likely that they are true. With the maximum lag of 10 years on intraregional benefits, the estimated social rate is about double the market rate. The likelihood that hypotheses B1 and B2 are true is further increased as the lag on intraregional benefits becomes shorter, regardless of the terminal adjustment method adopted.

The evidence reported here offers strong support for the conclusion that land grant policy was beneficial to society with respect to the Central Pacific System, and made a positive contribution to nineteenth century economic growth in the United States.

The Union Pacific System

Alternative estimates of the *ex post* social rate of return for the Union Pacific System are contained in Table XIV. The range again is wide, from a high of 24 to a low of 12.9%, but not as great as that for the Central Pacific System. Adopting the same selection rule as before, the preferred

---

[19] It has been suggested that the acceleration of construction was 10 to 15 years at most (cf. Robert Edgar Riegel, *The Story of Western Railroads*, p. 43). As Engerman has pointed out, this is clearly only an educated impression rather than the specific result of the testing of any hypothesis (Stanley L. Engerman, "Some Economic Issues Relating to Railroad Subsidies and the Evaluation of Land Grants," p. 458).

TABLE XIV

Alternative Estimates of the Social Rate of Return for the Union Pacific System

Years of lag on intraregional benefits	Alternative terminal adjustment methods [a] (%)			
	A	B	C	D
No intraregional benefits	16.1	14.7	14.6	12.9
10	17.9	16.9	16.9	15.9
9	18.2	17.3	17.2	16.3
8	18.5	17.7	17.6	16.7
7	18.9	18.1	18.1	17.3
6	19.4	18.6	18.6	17.8
5	19.9	19.2	19.2	18.5
4	20.7	20.0	20.0	19.4
3	21.5	20.9	20.9	20.3
2	22.5	22.0	22.0	21.4
1	24.0	23.6	23.6	23.1
Uniform distribution	20.5	19.8	19.8	19.1

[a] See text for definition of alternative terminal adjustments.

estimate is 19.8%, with the uniform distribution of intraregional benefits and terminal adjustment C. For the Union Pacific, as in the case of the Central Pacific, no intraregional benefits are included in the social returns stream before 1870. Thus, given the estimation technique used, the social rate estimate is further biased downward for all instances in which intraregional benefits are included in the social returns stream.

On the basis previously discussed, hypotheses B1 and B2 are accepted for the Union Pacific System. Even without taking account of intraregional benefits, the estimated social rate of return ranges from 12.9 to 16.1%. The former value includes no terminal adjustment as well as no intraregional benefits, but is still more than 40% greater than the estimated market rate (average opportunity cost of capital) of 9.03%. Given the techniques used, this is certainly a lower-bound estimate. It again appears unlikely that capital diverted to the Union Pacific by the land grant subsidy (and for that matter, the loan subsidy) would have had an opportunity cost to society of 12.9% or more. This, of course, is even more unlikely for the preferred estimate of 19.8%.

The Texas and Pacific System

The estimates of the social rate of return in Table XV cover a narrower range for the Texas and Pacific System than was the case for the Union Pacific. Here the highest estimate is 10.8% and the lowest only 2.6%. The

TABLE XV

Alternative Estimates of the Social Rate of Return for the Texas and Pacific System

Years of lag on intraregional benefits	Alternative terminal adjustment methods[a] (%)			
	A	B	C	D
No intraregional benefits	6.6	5.1	5.7	2.6
10	7.7	6.5	7.0	4.7
9	7.8	6.5	7.0	4.8
8	8.1	6.9	7.4	5.3
7	8.7	7.6	8.0	6.0
6	8.9	7.8	8.2	6.2
5	9.1	8.0	8.4	6.4
4	9.6	8.5	8.9	6.9
3	9.9	8.8	9.2	7.2
2	10.3	9.2	9.6	7.6
1	10.8	9.6	10.1	8.1
Uniform distribution	9.0	7.8	8.3	6.2

[a] See text for definition of alternative terminal adjustments.

preferred estimate of the social rate of return over the initial investment period for the Texas and Pacific is only 8.3%, while the estimated average opportunity cost of capital over the same time period is 7.74%. Hypothesis B1 is accepted for the Texas and Pacific System.

Hypothesis B2 is rejected for the Texas and Pacific System. This rejection is obvious for the case of the social returns stream with no intraregional benefits, because the range is 2.7 to 6.6% with the terminal adjustment methods used. It is less obvious with the preferred estimate of 8.3%. However, this latter estimate is only 7% higher than the estimated average opportunity cost of capital. It is quite likely that capital diverted to the Texas and Pacific could have found more socially profitable use elsewhere in the economy, i.e., the marginal opportunity cost of capital was most likely higher than 8.3%. Thus, while the Texas and Pacific required a larger land grant (than the one it received) for private profitability, the optimal subsidy from society's point of view, based on the *ex post* social rate of return estimated in this study, is in fact smaller than provided, namely, zero.

The Atchison, Topeka and Santa Fe System

Estimates of the *ex post* social rate of return for the Atchison, Topeka and Santa Fe System are shown in Table XVI. The range for this system is the second widest among the systems considered here, running from 47.4

TABLE XVI

Alternative Estimates of the Social Rate of Return for the Santa Fe System

Years of lag on intraregional benefits	Alternative terminal adjustment methods[a] (%)			
	A	B	C	D
No intraregional benefits	13.3	11.6	12.1	8.7
10	15.0	13.7	14.1	11.9
9	15.8	14.6	15.0	11.9
8	16.7	15.6	16.0	14.1
7	17.3	16.3	16.6	14.9
6	18.0	17.1	17.4	15.8
5	19.2	18.3	18.6	17.2
4	21.0	20.3	20.5	19.4
3	23.8	23.3	23.5	22.7
2	28.7	28.4	28.5	28.0
1	47.4	47.4	47.4	47.4
Uniform distribution	19.6	18.8	19.0	17.6

[a] See text for definition of alternative adjustments.

to 8.7%. The preferred estimate of 19% is almost two and one-half times the estimated average opportunity cost of capital of 7.86%. This comparison suggests that hypotheses B1 and B2 should be accepted for the Santa Fe System. If one made the judgment regarding hypothesis B2 on the basis of the estimate with no intraregional benefits and terminal adjustment D, hypothesis B2 would be rejected, because the social rate then would be only about 11% above the estimated average opportunity cost of capital. However, with no intraregional benefits and terminal adjustment C the estimated social rate is more than 50% above the market rate. Since this is a more reasonable lower-bound estimate than that with terminal adjustment D and no intraregional benefits, hypotheses B1 and B2 are accepted for the Santa Fe System.

The Northern Pacific System

Table XVII contains the estimated *ex post* social rates of return for the Northern Pacific System. The range of estimates for this system is relatively narrow, with the highest being 16% and the lowest only 7.3%. The preferred estimate is that with the uniform distribution of intraregional benefits and terminal adjustment C, which in this case is 12.5%.

The estimate average opportunity cost of capital for the initial investment period in the Northern Pacific is identical to that for the Santa Fe—7.86%. While the margin is not so substantial as with the Santa Fe,

TABLE XVII

Alternative Estimates of the Social Rate of Return for the Northern Pacific System

Years of lag on intraregional benefits	Alternative terminal adjustment methods[a] (%)			
	A	B	C	D
No intraregional benefits	11.0	9.5	9.4	7.3
10	11.9	10.6	10.5	9.1
9	12.3	11.1	11.0	9.6
8	12.5	11.3	11.2	9.9
7	13.0	11.9	11.9	10.7
6	13.4	12.3	12.3	11.1
5	13.7	12.7	12.7	11.6
4	14.1	13.1	13.1	12.0
3	14.8	13.8	13.8	12.8
2	15.3	14.5	14.4	13.5
1	16.0	15.2	15.2	14.3
Uniform distribution	13.6	12.6	12.5	11.4

[a] See text for definition of alternative adjustments.

hypotheses B1 and B2 are accepted for the Northern Pacific, with the preferred estimate of the social rate of return being almost 60% higher than the market rate. On the basis of terminal adjustment D, with no intraregional benefits, hypotheses B1 and B2 would be rejected for the Northern Pacific. With terminal adjustment C and no intraregional benefits, hypotheses B1 and B2 would be accepted, although since the social rate of return is only 20% above the market rate the case for acceptance of hypotheses B2 is not strong. Thus, the lower-bound estimates do not provide the strong support for acceptance of hypothesis B2 that is present for the Central Pacific and the Union Pacific. Nevertheless, hypotheses B1 and B2 are accepted for the Northern Pacific on the basis of the preferred estimate of the social rate.

The Great Northern System

The Great Northern System, as pointed out earlier, was not a land grant railroad except for the circumstance of taking over grants made initially to other railroads. There was no conscious subsidy policy followed with respect to the Great Northern by the governments involved in grants obtained by the Great Northern, unless one wishes to call the provision allowing the land grant to pass to the new owners under foreclosure a conscious subsidy policy. In this sense hypotheses B1 and B2 (like hypotheses A1 and A2) are really not applicable to the Great Northern.

TABLE XVIII

Alternative Estimates of the Social Rate of Return for the Great Northern System

Years of lag on intraregional benefits	Alternative terminal adjustment methods[a] (%)			
	A	B	C	D
No intraregional benefits	18.7	15.6	15.3	9.4
10	20.6	18.2	18.0	14.5
9	21.7	19.5	19.4	16.2
8	22.9	21.0	20.9	18.2
7	24.0	22.3	22.2	19.8
6	25.3	23.7	23.6	21.5
5	27.1	25.7	25.6	23.8
4	29.8	28.6	28.6	27.2
3	34.2	33.5	33.4	32.6
2	42.2	41.9	41.9	41.6
1	58.0	57.9	57.9	57.8
Uniform distribution	28.3	26.9	26.8	25.1

[a] See text for definition of alternative adjustments.

Despite these considerations it is of interest to consider the test of the hypotheses for the system.

The range of estimated *ex post* social rates of return (58.0 to 9.4%) is wider for the Great Northern than for any other system considered here. Table XVIII presents the alternative estimates of the social rate of return. The preferred estimate of the social rate (26.8%) is almost four times higher than the market rate estimate (6.33%).[20] Hypotheses B1 and B2 are accepted for the Great Northern on this basis. Even the relevant lower-bound estimates (those with terminal adjustments C or D and no intraregional benefits) are sufficiently high, relative to the estimated opportunity cost of capital, to allow acceptance of hypotheses B1 and B2 in this case.

The Canadian Pacific System

The alternative estimates of the *ex post* social rate of return for the Canadian Pacific System are presented in Table XIX. The range is from

---

[20] The relatively high social (and private) rates of return for the Great Northern System appear to be the result of what Albert Fishlow (*op. cit.*, pp. 196–204) called anticipatory settlement. The long operation period of the Great Northern System's predecessor railroads in Minnesota resulted in a substantial base of settlement and development in the area by the start of the time period considered here for the Great Northern System. As a result, the benefits (both social and private) of railroad operations were realized at an earlier point in the Great Northern System's existence than was the case for some of the other systems.

TABLE XIX

Alternative Estimates of the Social Rate of Return for the Canadian Pacific System

Years of lag on intraregional benefits	Alternative terminal adjustment methods[a] (%)			
	A	B	C	D
No intraregional benefits	7.3	4.0	7.0	0.8
10	9.6	7.4	9.4	5.7
9	9.9	7.7	9.6	5.9
8	10.6	8.5	10.4	6.9
7	11.8	9.9	11.6	8.4
6	13.1	11.4	12.9	10.1
5	14.0	12.4	13.9	11.2
4	14.9	13.2	14.7	12.0
3	16.0	14.5	15.9	13.3
2	17.8	16.2	17.6	15.1
1	20.3	18.9	20.2	17.8
Uniform distribution	13.3	11.4	13.1	10.0

[a] See text for definition of alternative adjustments.

20.3 to 0.8%, with the preferred estimate being 13.1%. The estimated average opportunity cost of capital is 6.75%. Thus, the preferred social rate of return estimate is almost double the market rate, and hypotheses B1 and B2 are accepted. In this case again, the social rate of return estimated with terminal adjustment D and no intraregional benefits does not support acceptance of hypotheses B1 and B2. Regardless of terminal adjustment, intraregional benefits are necessary for a judgment that hypothesis B2 should be accepted, since the range of estimates without intraregional benefits is from 7.3 to 0.8%.

Considerations of national defense and political unification played a role in the initial decisions for subsidization of the pioneer railroads included in this study. No value is attached here to these factors in estimating social rates of return. For the United States systems, it appears reasonable to conclude that the national defense and political unification values were sufficiently small to be ignored by the time the roads were built. This is less obvious in the case of the Canadian Pacific. It can be argued that a rather substantial value should be included in the estimation of the social returns stream for the latter road. This value is illustrated by the relative speed with which the second Riel Rebellion was suppressed in 1885. With the railroad, troops were transported from Ottawa to Qu'Appelle in less than 2 weeks. The 1885 rebellion, which was better organized and more widespread than that of 1870, was put down in less than 3 months; in 1870 it had taken almost 6 months just to move the troops from east to west.[21] Without the railroad, it appears that the history of western Canada, and the nation, could easily have been quite different. This historical consideration (and its economic implications) adds significantly to our confidence in accepting hypotheses B1 and B2 for the Canadian Pacific System.

---

[21] John Murray Gibbon, *The Romantic History of the Canadian Pacific* (New York: Tudor, 1937), pp. 284–288.

Chapter 6

Building Ahead of Demand

The proposition that American railroads were typically built "ahead of traffic" or "ahead of demand" has found wide acceptance in the literature even though few empirical tests have been attempted. While we have seen that building ahead of demand does not by itself justify governmental subsidization of private ventures, the concept does suggest a developmental role for pioneer railroads. For that reason it is a hypothesis worth evaluation. This chapter presents tests of the hypothesis of construction ahead of demand for the land grant railroad systems included in this study. A by-product of these tests is an evaluation of Albert Fishlow's specification of the hypothesis of building ahead of demand.[1]

Test of the Fishlow Hypothesis for the Land Grant Systems

The only previous thorough general analysis of the hypothesis of building ahead of demand, with specific application to railroad construction in the ante-bellum American West, is Albert Fishlow's. His rigorous specification and testing (for the ante-bellum West) of this proposition has been praised by Robert Fogel and Meghnad Desai in separate articles that discuss the specification and identification problems in economic (or, if

---

[1] Albert Fishlow, *American Railroads and the Transformation of the Ante-Bellum Economy* (Cambridge, Mass.: Harvard Univ. Press, 1965), ch. IV.

you prefer, econometric) history.² Fishlow suggests that a meaningful definition of building ahead of demand must involve the notion of an initial disequilibrium in which the demand curve facing the railroad lies to the left of the firm's average cost curve, but in time shifts rightward so that average revenues exceed average cost.³ Two testable hypotheses are derived from this definition.⁴ One hypothesis is that for the railroad built ahead of demand the rate of profit in its early years will be less than that for alternative investments. The second is that there should be a positive correlation between the firm's profit rate and its age. On the basis of statistical tests that contradict both implications Fishlow rejects the hypothesis of construction ahead of demand for railroads in the ante-bellum West. However, he suggests in a footnote that

> a similar set of criteria casually applied to post-Civil War railroad construction in states farther west suggest that this constituted a true episode of building before demand.⁵

The annual series of estimated real accounting rates of profit and the estimated real opportunity cost of capital for the seven systems of this study are presented in Table XX.⁶ The annual accounting rate of profit estimated here is the net profitability ratio, i.e., the ratio of net capital earnings to capital stock.⁷ The earnings/price ratio for all common stock on the New York Stock Exchange, adjusted from a money rate to a real rate using the conventional approximation for the relationship between the two, is used again as the proxy for the opportunity cost of capital.⁸ While the period to be included in the early years for each system is not obvious, it is clear that for each system except the Great Northern it took several years of operation before the firm's annual rate of return exceeded the earnings/price ratio. In fact, the Texas and Pacific and Canadian Pacific rates of return are less than the earnings/price ratio in almost every year included.

The Great Northern's rate of return exceeds the indicated alternative

---

² Robert W. Fogel, "The Specification Problem in Economic History," *Journal of Economic History*, XXVII, 3 (Sept. 1967), 296, and Meghnad Desai, "Some Issues in Econometric History," *Economic History Review*, Second Series, XXI, 2 (April 1968), 12.

³ Fishlow, *op. cit.*, p. 166.

⁴ *Ibid.*, pp. 177–189.

⁵ *Ibid.*, p. 204.

⁶ The period for each system is identical to that used elsewhere in this study, and is an approximation to the life of the original investment in the system.

⁷ The estimates of capital earnings for each system are developed in Appendix B. Estimation of the gross investment streams is presented in Appendix A. Capital stock is calculated by the perceptual inventory method in Appendix I. The double declining balance depreciation rates used are discussed in Chapter 4.

⁸ The earnings/price ratio is available only beginning with 1871.

TABLE XX

Real Accounting Rates of Return and Opportunity Cost of Capital by System (%)

Year	Central Pacific	Union Pacific	Texas and Pacific	Santa Fe	Northern Pacific	Great Northern	Canadian Pacific	U.S.	Canada
1864	1.3	—	—	—	—	—	—	—	—
1865	5.9	—	—	—	—	—	—	—	—
1866	7.4	4.3	—	—	—	—	—	—	—
1867	8.0	7.7	—	—	—	—	—	—	—
1868	2.7	2.1	—	—	—	—	—	—	—
1869	3.9	0.9	—	—	—	—	—	—	—
1870	2.0	2.6	—	2.7	—	—	—	—	—
1871	4.1	4.9	—	3.9	—	—	—	11.6	8.1
1872	7.5	5.2	10.5	3.3	−0.4	—	—	5.6	1.0
1873	10.0	8.3	0.9	2.3	−0.7	—	—	11.5	11.6
1874	10.4	10.3	2.3	4.2	−2.0	—	—	14.0	9.6
1875	12.2	13.9	4.6	5.0	−1.6	—	—	12.3	12.3
1876	8.7	15.0	3.7	8.2	−1.3	—	—	12.3	13.1
1877	8.9	13.9	4.7	5.2	−0.4	—	—	13.0	12.1
1878	10.3	16.6	3.4	14.1	−0.1	—	—	16.4	18.9
1879	9.6	16.0	−6.1	11.9	0.8	—	—	10.4	7.3
1880	11.8	16.7	−2.6	8.0	−0.5	15.2	—	2.9	0.9
1881	16.3	15.9	2.2	7.1	2.3	13.3	0.2	3.4	6.2
1882	14.4	15.4	1.8	8.9	2.8	17.2	0.2	4.9	2.7
1883	13.3	13.4	1.9	11.2	2.7	17.0	−0.8	9.2	11.9
1884	8.7	9.3	−0.2	9.6	6.1	13.9	−0.6	12.4	9.9
1885	12.1	9.4	0.7	9.5	5.6	13.4	0.5	8.4	14.5
1886	11.9	8.7	−0.8	7.1	6.1	10.3	0.6	7.4	9.8
1887	10.5	9.7	−1.2	4.4	5.6	6.6	0.3	5.2	1.2
1888	12.5	8.5	1.4	2.1	6.3	4.6	0.4	3.7	1.8
1889	11.0	9.5	2.5	3.1	6.9	3.1	1.7	6.9	6.6
1890	—	—	2.4	4.0	9.0	4.5	1.7	4.1	6.7
1891	—	—	2.6	4.6	9.1	6.0	2.5	8.0	5.4
1892	—	—	1.6	5.6	11.3	6.6	2.8	7.9	14.4
1893	—	—	3.4	4.4	10.5	5.8	2.3	6.8	2.7
1894	—	—	2.7	2.3	3.1	4.6	1.7	9.0	10.8
1895	—	—	2.7	2.0	4.0	5.6	2.5	3.9	9.5
1896	—	—	2.4	2.6	6.5	7.1	3.1	6.3	10.8
1897	—	—	4.6	3.4	5.3	6.4	4.4	5.5	3.9
1898	—	—	4.2	4.9	12.1	8.7	3.9	5.6	0.5
1899	—	—	5.0	6.9	12.1	8.9	4.7	2.2	6.8
1900	—	—	7.1	9.2	13.4	9.6	3.7	5.1	−1.1[a]

[a] This results from an 8.8% rise in the Michell price index in 1900 relative to 1899 and an earnings price ratio of 7.7%.

for the first 8 years of its operation. Expansion of the Great Northern was relatively slow in these years following the formation of the St. Paul, Minneapolis and Manitoba Railway out of the bankrupt St. Paul and Pacific, which had been operating several hundred miles of railroad for several years. The Great Northern exhibits rates of return lower than the alternative during and immediately after the beginning of its substantial expansion, which can be considered a new investment project. Thus, in perspective, each of the systems considered here was built ahead of demand according to the first implication of Fishlow's specification of the concept of building ahead of demand.

The second hypothesis derived from Fishlow's definition is that a positive correlation will exist between the rate of return and the age of the firm if the railroad was built ahead of demand. This is tested here by a simple Ordinary Least Squares (OLS) regression, with the rate of return as the dependent variable and time as the independent variable. The results of these regressions are presented in Table XXI.

Initial regressions over the entire sample period for the Texas and Pacific, Santa Fe, and Great Northern yield insignificant or negative coefficients on time. On the basis of these results one would reject the hy-

TABLE XXI

Regression Results by System[a]

System	α	β	R^2	df[b]
Central Pacific	.0318	.0036	.5272	24
	(2.67)	(5.17)		
Union Pacific	.0429	.0034	.2439	22
	(1.87)	(2.66)		
Texas and Pacific	−.0487	.0034	.6239	20
	(−4.11)	(5.87)		
Santa Fe	.0095	.0061	.5642	13
	(0.59)	(4.10)		
Northern Pacific	−.0386	.0047	.7539	27
	(−3.74)	(9.09)		
Great Northern	.0142	.0029	.4652	11
	(0.93)	(3.09)		
Canadian Pacific	−.0122	.0026	.8715	18
	(−4.00)	(11.05)		

[a] Regressions of the form $RR = \alpha + \beta\ Time$; where RR = annual real net profitability ratio and $Time$ represents the age of the project. The t value for each coefficient is shown in parentheses below the coefficient.

[b] Degrees of freedom.

pothesis of building ahead of demand for these three railroads. However, examination of the data suggests that these results occur because of a marked change in the investment project in each case, so that a test over the entire sample period is inadequate for the Texas and Pacific, Santa Fe, and Great Northern systems.

The Texas and Pacific began with the purchase of two small roads in eastern Texas and until 1880 undertook relatively slow expansion of its line in that area. In 1880 the Texas and Pacific undertook a crash program of building across western Texas in a race with the Southern Pacific. This marks the initiation of what was in essence a new investment project. Because of this circumstance, the regression reported in Table XXI for the Texas and Pacific covers the period 1880–1900.

The Santa Fe began an enormous continuing expansion in 1886 after completion of the transcontinental and considerable feeder lines. The regression reported for the Santa Fe in Table XXI covers the period 1870–1885 before this sharp expansion, and in effect includes the first investment period involving the construction of the basic systems. As noted previously, the Great Northern's expansion, which began in 1887, was essentially a new investment project. The regression reported in Table XXI for the Great Northern is for the period 1887–1900.

The value of β for the Union Pacific and Great Northern is significant at the .99 level of the t test, and β for the other five systems is highly significant at the .995 level. Thus one can conclude that the second implication of Fishlow's test is also met for all seven systems. Apparently one can conclude that all seven systems were built ahead of demand.

Estimation of Investment Demand

Building ahead of demand implies that the capacity put in place by these systems to move goods and people was excessive during their early lives, or during the early life of a substantial expansion. That is, we would expect to find substantial underutilization of capacity in these early years, and increasing capacity utilization over time. The usual hypothesis regarding building ahead of demand appears to imply such a movement of capacity utilization over time. It is this hypothesis that we will examine next. The capacity concept used here is the conventional economic concept related to cost, rather than an engineering notion of physical capacity. Thus, capacity output is defined as the output of minimum average total cost per unit, given the existing capital stock and resource prices.

Evaluation of the excess-capacity hypothesis requires an estimate of the investment demand function for each of the seven systems included in the study. Structural parameters from these functions are used to estimate annual economic capacity for each of the systems, following the procedure developed by Bert G. Hickman.[9] Calculation of the ratio of expected output to capacity output provides a capacity utilization series for each system.

The investment model applied here is a version of the stock adjustment model that has been commonly used in empirical studies of investment demand in recent years. The basic hypothesis is that the adjustment relation is

$$\frac{K_t}{K_{t-1}} = \left(\frac{K_t^*}{K_{t-1}}\right)^b, \quad 0 < b < 1. \tag{1}$$

Expressing (1) in logarithmic form we have

$$\log K_t - \log K_{t-1} = b(\log K_t^* - \log K_{t-1}), \quad 0 < b < 1. \tag{2}$$

In these relations K_t^* is the long-run equilibrium (desired) capital stock in year t, while K_{t-1} is the actual stock at the end of the preceding year. With the relation in the form of (2) the constant adjustment coefficient b represents the approximate proportion of the percentage gap between desired and actual stock that is closed during year t. The value of b is expected to be less than 1, reflecting the partial adjustment to the existence of a gap between desired and actual stock in any one year. Technical lags in financing, creating, and putting new capital in place, and the reluctance of businessmen to adjust production facilities immediately and fully to new demand or cost conditions, account for this partial adjustment to a divergence between desired and actual stock. The functional form adopted for the investment demand regressions in this study is that of Eq. (2).

Empirical application of Eq. (2) requires specification of the determinants of desired stock. Following the now-traditional neoclassical approach to this problem, the basic hypothesis applied here is that desired stock is a function of (1) expected output, (2) expected prices, and (3) the level of technology.

Given the state of technology, the demand for capital stock varies directly with output (Y). The price variable (C) used here is the cost of capital, i.e., an implicit rental price of capital, rather than relative price.[10]

---

[9] Bert G. Hickman, *Investment Demand and U.S. Economic Growth* (Washington, D.C.: The Brookings Institution, 1965).

[10] The formulation of capital cost used here is a simpler version of that originally suggested by Dale W. Jorgenson in "Capital Theory and Investment Behavior," *American Economic Review* (May 1963), pp. 247–259. During the period covered by this study, depreciation accounting was not used by railroads and was not necessary for tax purposes. Thus Jorgenson's complex formulation of "user cost" is not relevant. The real price of capital, $q(\delta + r)/P$, where P is a product price index, or the ratio of money wages (W) to the money price of

6. Building Ahead of Demand

The capital cost variables tried in the regressions are

$$c = q(\delta + r),$$
$$c = q(\delta + r) - \Delta q,$$
$$c = \frac{q(\delta + r)}{1 - u},$$

where q is the investment goods price index, δ is the annual depreciation rate, u is the effective tax rate, and r is an interest rate.[11] Three alternative variables are tested for the interest rate. One is the accounting rate of return, measured as the net profitability ratio, i.e., the annual ratio of system net capital earnings to midperiod capital stock.[12] A second is the railroad bond yield, and the third is the earnings/price ratio on railroad common stock.[13] Demand for capital varies inversely with capital cost. A time trend (T) is included to reflect the influence of technical progress on the efficiency of the capital stock. The sign on the trend is expected to be negative, indicating that less real capital in constant dollars is required to produce a unit of output in succeeding years ($t + 1, t + 2$, etc.) than in year t.[14]

Given the functional form and the specification of K^*, the relation for desired stock is

$$\log K_t^* = \log a_1 + a_2 \log Y_t' + a_3 \log C_t' + a_4 T, \qquad (2.1)$$

where primes represent expected long-term or "normal" levels of the variables.

The logarithmic form is especially convenient because the coefficients a_2 and a_3 represent the estimated long-run elasticity of desired capital stock with respect to output and capital cost, while a_4 is a measure of the net trend of desired capital stock in compound interest terms. The ex-

---

capital, $W/q(\delta + r)$, is often used as a determinant of desired capital stock representing, respectively, hypotheses of profit maximization and cost minimization. Unfortunately, relative price variables cannot be used here because of insufficient information to derive an index of either railroad money wages or product prices.

[11] The Snyder–Tucker price index is used for the U.S. systems and the Michell index for the Canadian Pacific.

[12] Estimates of the end-of-period and midperiod capital stock are presented in Appendix I.

[13] The bond yield used is that provided by Frederick R. Macaulay, *Some Theoretical Problems Suggested by the Movements of Interest Rates, Bond Yields, and Stock Prices in the United States Since 1856*. The railroad earnings/price ratio is from Alfred Cowles III and Associates, *Common-Stock Indexes 1871–1937*.

[14] The sign on the trend term could be positive if technical change were biased in the direction of increasing the capital/labor ratio, given a constant ratio of factor prices, and if the bias were large enough to offset the general tendency for technical change to reduce all unit factor requirements.

pected values of the coefficients are: $a_2 > 0$, $a_3 < 0$, and $a_4 < 0$, although $a_4 > 0$ is possible.[15]

Substitution of Eq. (2.1) into Eq. (2) yields

$$\log K_t - \log K_{t-1} = b \log a_1 + ba_2 \log Y'_t \\ + ba_3 \log C'_t + ba_4 T - b \log K_{t-1}. \quad (3)$$

The general form of the basic investment hypothesis is indicated by Eq. (3). The regressions reported below used this form, with the addition of a stochastic error term.

The structure of the normal or expected variables must be specified to fit the regressions using the form of Eq. (3). It could be assumed that current levels of output and capital cost are expected to continue indefinitely, so that desired stock depends only on current output and capital cost plus the trend term. In this event Eq. (3) could be fitted directly to the current data. This simple procedure has two implications that do not correspond with the existing evidence on investment. One is that the largest portion of the total long-term adjustment to a change in a determinant of desired stock takes place in the same year as the change in, say, output. The second is that entrepreneurs automatically accept the current level of output or capital cost as the continuing or "normal" value. Since neither of these implications may be correct, regressions of the form of Eq. (3) are tested using lagged as well as current output and capital cost, along with lags of 1, 2, or 3 years on the same terms as individual variables. In each case the equation and corresponding lag structure selected as best are those that produce superior overall results for each system, as judged by the usual statistical criteria. Where more than one output or cost variable is used in a final regression, the normal or expected variable is the weighted (geometric) mean of the individual current and/or lagged terms for the variable.

The best OLS regression for each railroad system is reported in Table XXII.[16] Capital cost enters significantly in six of the final seven equations. Since capital cost did not work in all cases, another determinant of desired stock is tried in all equations. This is the annual net profitability ratio for each system, relative to railroad bond yield (BR). In logarithmic form this becomes

$$\log R_t - \log BR_t$$

---

[15] Since we are dealing with one industry over essentially the same time period, the expected sign of the coefficient on time representing technological change should be the same for all firms, on the ground that the net effect of technological change would be the same for all firms in a specific industry over a similar long time period.

[16] Output is real dollar gross revenue for each system.

TABLE XXII

Regression Results for the Seven Systems with Normalized Variables[a]

Railroad system	Constant	log K_{t-1}	log Y'	log C'	(log R − log BR)'	T	R^2	DW	df
Central Pacific	5.7424 (20.85)	−0.6821 (−9.76)	0.1903 (3.34)	—	0.1062 (5.11)	—	.9763	1.56	17
Union Pacific	—	−0.1171 (−4.79)	0.1649 (5.60)	−0.0695[b] (−4.69)	—	−0.0106 (−5.21)	.8354	2.07	13
Texas and Pacific	0.4399 (0.70)	−0.6445 (−4.18)	0.7515 (3.33)	−0.0696[c] (−1.79)	—	−0.0158 (−2.31)	.7259	1.71	16
Santa Fe	3.4888 (8.54)	−0.8660 (−7.21)	0.6972 (5.88)	−0.2870[c] (−2.87)	—	—	.8050	2.06	25
Great Northern	—	−0.1675 (−4.11)	0.2797 (5.21)	−0.1890[c] (−3.25)	—	−0.0286 (−4.76)	.8093	1.84	11
Northern Pacific	3.3482 (4.85)	−0.3578 (−3.61)	0.1858 (3.45)	−0.2903[b] (−10.67)	—	−0.0237 (−6.30)	.9033	2.12	16
Canadian Pacific[d]	4.1184 (2.28)	−0.4190 (−2.19)	0.0980 (1.76)	−0.0136[b] (−2.04)	—	—	.8855	2.03	12

[a] Note: The dependent variable is (log K_t − log K_{t-1}). The general form of the equations is shown in Eqs. (3) and (4). The t value is shown in parentheses below each coefficient. DW is the Durbin–Watson statistic. df is degrees of freedom.
[b] $C = q(\delta + BR) - \Delta q$ where q = the investment deflator, BR = railroad bond yield and δ = annual depreciation rate.
[c] $C = (\delta + RR)$ where RR is net capital earnings divided by midperiod capital stock.
[d] Estimated using the Cochrane–Orcutt technique to adjust for serial correlation; $\rho = 0.368$.

for each year t. With this variable, Eq. (3) takes the form

$$\log K_t - \log K_{t-1} = b \log a_1 + ba_2 \log Y'_t$$
$$+ ba_3 (\log R_2 - \log BR_t)'$$
$$+ ba_4 T - b \log K_{t-1}; \qquad a_3 > 0. \quad (4)$$

The rationale for this variable is that, other things being equal, desired stock will vary directly with the profitability of the specific investment project relative to available alternatives. This variable is significant only in the case of the Central Pacific system, for which capital cost did not enter significantly.

Estimation indicates that more than one component enters significantly in the normal variables for only two systems. The underlying free-form equations for these two systems are presented in Table XXIII. For the other systems Y'_t is Y_t, except for the Union Pacific, where it is Y_{t-1}. The variable C'_t is C_t for the Union Pacific and the Santa Fe, C_{t-2} for the Texas and Pacific, and C_{t-3} for the Great Northern and Canadian Pacific.

TABLE XXIII

Free-Form Regression Results[a]

Railroad system	
Central Pacific	$5.7413 + 0.1902 \log Y_t + 0.0691 (\log RR_{t-3} - \log BR_{t-3})$ $(13.52)\quad (2.69)\qquad\qquad (2.44)$ $+ 0.0371 (\log RR_{t-4} - \log BR_{t-4}) - 0.6819 \log K_{t-1}$ $\quad (1.45) \qquad\qquad\qquad\qquad\qquad (-7.10)$ $R^2 = .9763 \qquad\qquad DW = 1.56 \qquad\qquad df = 16$
Northern Pacific	$3.3486 + 0.0422 \log Y_{t-2} + 0.1435 \log Y_{t-3} - 0.0281 \log C_t - 0.0468 \log C_{t-1}$ $(3.02)\quad (0.47)\qquad\qquad (1.90)\qquad\qquad (-1.31)\qquad\qquad (-2.13)$ $- 0.1010 \log C_{t-2} - 0.1145 \log C_{t-3} - 0.0237 T - 0.3578 \log K_{t-1}$ $\quad (-3.81)\qquad\qquad (-4.42)\qquad\qquad (-4.71)\qquad (-2.21)$ $R^2 = .9033 \qquad\qquad DW = 2.12 \qquad\qquad df = 12$

[a] Note: The dependent variable is $(\log K_t - \log K_{t-1})$. The t value is shown in parentheses below each coefficient.

By the usual statistical tests, the regressions of Tables XXII and XXIII are reasonably satisfactory. As measured by R^2, the regressions "explain" from 72.6 to 97.6% of the variance in the capital expansion ratio. Three of the seven explain 88% or more, while six of seven explain 80% or more, which can be considered excellent considering the data limitations involved. Most of the coefficients in Table XXII are significant at the .995 level of the t test. Only the constant for the Texas and Pacific and the output coefficient for the Canadian Pacific fall short of being significant at the .95 level of the t test. The Durbin–Watson test statistics indicate little cause for concern about serial correlation in the residuals of the reported equations.

These results demonstrate that the dominant determinant of long-run investment behavior for these systems is the acceleration principle. This is consistent with earlier studies using aggregative investment data for the entire United States railroad system during approximately the same time period.[17] The availability of retained profits and receipts from land and other subsidies were tried as an additional determinant of investment for

---

[17] Cf. Jan Kmenta and Jeffrey G. Williamson, "Determinants of Investment Behavior: United States Railroads, 1872–1941," *Review of Economics and Statistics*, XLVIII, 2 (May 1966), 172–181, and W. Douglas Morgan, "Investment Behavior by American Railroads: 1897–1914, A Comment," *Review of Economics and Statistics*, LIII, 3 (August 1971), 294–298.

all systems, but in all cases the coefficients were insignificant at the .90 level or of the wrong sign.[18]

Because of the expected importance of the accelerator mechanism as a determinant of investment demand it is necessary to select the sample period for the regressions with care. First, one would not expect an accelerator to explain the early substantial investment with little or no past or present output.[19] Second, for similar reasons it would be surprising if the accelerator mechanism explained merger very well.[20] Third, there are few years for which no information on gross investment is reported by the firms or derivable from existing records, although it is likely that there was gross investment during those years. Years that fall into these three categories are excluded from the sample period for the reported regressions. The years for which data are available and the sample period for the regression are listed by system in Table XXIV. The first year for which data are available in each case is the year construction or formation of the system began. The periods of data availability represent an approximation to the lifespan of the major original investment in the systems.

For the Central Pacific, a substantial merger occurred in 1876, which is thus deleted from the sample period. The years 1876 and 1880 are excluded for the same reason for the Union Pacific. For the Texas and Pacific 1881 is not included, because several hundred miles of railroad were built or acquired by merger in the completion of the main line in that year. No gross investment is reported in 1877, 1882, and 1885–1886 for the Texas and Pacific. For 1877 and 1882 the zero gross investment figures may be the result of errors in estimation of the investment stream (due to the extreme paucity of data), while 1885–1886 includes the period of financial reorganization of the firm, during which it reported a minimum of information. The years 1887 and 1897 are removed from the sample period for the

---

[18] Thus governmental interference appears to have played no major role in the *long-run* investment decisions for these railroads. It would seem that this by itself is strong evidence that governmental subsidies did not induce incorrect investment decisions with respect to long-run capital stock. In general one would expect that subsidy receipts or retained profits would affect only the timing of investment. As a test, regressions were also run with subsidy receipts or retained profits in place of output. The results were very poor.

[19] The prime exception here is the Santa Fe, which got off to a rather slow start in the 1870s (the railroad being only 508 miles long after 5 years), so that the best results are obtained by starting with the second year in the overall sample period of 1869–1900.

[20] The Canadian Pacific is an exception here. Regressions fitted including merger years are much better than those excluding mergers. The reason for this appears to be the very substantial and continuous part which mergers (and leases) played in the formation of the Canadian Pacific system. These account for 25% of the total estimated current dollar bross investment during the sample period.

TABLE XXIV

Years for Which Data Are Available and the Regressions Are Fitted for the Seven Systems

Railroad	Data available	Regression sample period
Central Pacific[a]	1863–1889	1868–1875, 1877–1889
Union Pacific[a]	1864–1889	1871–1875, 1877–1879, 1881–1889
Texas and Pacific[a]	1872–1900	1874–1876, 1878–1880, 1883–1884, 1887–1899
Santa Fe[a]	1869–1900	1870–1886, 1888–1896, 1898–1900
Great Northern[b]	1879–1900	1883–1886, 1889–1892, 1894–1900
Northern Pacific[b]	1870–1900	1877–1893, 1897–1900
Canadian Pacific[a]	1881–1900	1884–1900

[a] Calendar years.
[b] June 30 fiscal years.

Santa Fe because of the substantial mergers in those years. The deleted years for the Great Northern are ones in which unusually high investment occurred as a result both of mergers and accelerated construction to get to the West Coast. Because no gross investment was reported during the period the Northern Pacific was in receivership, the years 1894–1896 are excluded from the sample period for that system, again because it seems very unlikely that this is the true situation.

The adjustment speeds reported range from the relatively slow rate of the Union Pacific and Great Northern to the quite rapid rates of the Central Pacific, Texas and Pacific, and Santa Fe. The adjustment speeds of the Northern Pacific and Canadian Pacific are more moderate. There is no ready economic explanation for the relatively low adjustment coefficients in the case of the Union Pacific and Great Northern nor any apparent economic grounds for rejecting either these or the high coefficients for the Central Pacific, Texas and Pacific, and Santa Fe. One can speculate that the difference in adjustment speeds may result in part from variations in the composition of capital stock for the various systems, reflecting differences in the nature of demand faced by the individual systems or geographic differences, e.g., mountains vs. plains.

The adjustment speeds do allow the calculation of the long-run elasticity of capital with respect to output, capital price, and relative profitability; the results are given in Table XXV. The long-term capital output

TABLE XXV

Long-Term Elasticities of Capital Stock with Respect to Output, Price, and Relative Profitability

Railroad system	Output	Capital price	Relative profitability
Central Pacific	0.2790	—	0.1557
Union Pacific	1.4082	0.5935	—
Texas and Pacific	1.1660	0.1080	—
Santa Fe	0.8051	0.3314	—
Great Northern	1.6698	1.1284	—
Northern Pacific	0.5193	0.8113	—
Canadian Pacific	0.2339	0.0325	—

elasticities for the Central Pacific, Santa Fe, Northern Pacific, and Canadian Pacific are less than 1, indicating that these roads were subject to increasing returns to scale during the period covered. With capital output elasticities greater than 1 the indication is that the other three systems were subject to decreasing returns to scale. Since the systems studied were generally built in relatively undeveloped areas, and indivisibilities in the production function for railroad services appear plausible over at least some initial range of output, increasing returns to scale for these railroads are not surprising on economic grounds. Decreasing returns to scale are unexpected. The Great Northern is the exception to the last point. Because of the late period of its formation, the Great Northern began operation in what was probably the most developed area of any of the systems studied.

To evaluate the validity of the results regarding returns to scale, new regressions are tried in which a value of 1 is imposed on the elasticity of capital stock with respect to output. This, of course, implies constant returns to scale. The restriction on the coefficients for output and capital stock is

$$\frac{ba_2 + ba_3}{b} = 1,$$

where

$$\log K_t - \log K_{t-1} = b \log a_1 + ba_2 \log Y_t \\ + ba_3 \log Y_{t-1} + ba_4 \log C_t \\ + ba_5 T - b \log K_{t-1}. \quad (5)$$

When $ba_2 + ba_3$ is substituted for b in Eq. (5), the result is

$$\log K_t - \log K_{t-1} = b \log a_1 + ba_2 (\log Y_t - \log K_{t-1})$$
$$+ ba_3 (\log Y_{t-1} - \log K_{t-1})$$
$$+ ba_4 \log C_t + ba_5 T. \qquad (6)$$

The adjustment speed is $ba_2 + ba_3$ with this formulation. Regressions using the form of Eq. (6) with the appropriate variables are estimated for each system.[21] The statistical results were poorer except for the Great Northern and Texas and Pacific. The best regression in the general form of (6) for the Great Northern is

$$1.1179 + 0.2107(\log Y_t - \log K_{t-1}) - 0.2188 \log C_{t-3} - 0.0201T,$$
$$(4.96) \qquad\qquad\qquad (-3.68) \qquad\qquad (-4.61)$$

$$R^2 = 0.8275, \qquad DW = 1.84, \qquad df = 11,$$

where the dependent variable is $\log K_t - \log K_{t-1}$. This regression is at least as good as that reported in Table XX, although the adjustment speed in this case is about one-third higher. The results for capacity and utilization are similar with both equations, and capacity utilization is reported below for both.

The best regression in the general form of Eq. (6) for the Texas and Pacific is

$$1.1137 + 0.5335(\log Y_t - \log K_{t-1}) - 0.0856 \log C_{t-2} - 0.0086T,$$
$$(5.51) \quad (4.42) \qquad\qquad\qquad (-2.33) \qquad\qquad (-3.29)$$

$$R^2 = .7037, \qquad DW = 1.69, \qquad df = 17.$$

This equation again is at least as good as that of Table XX. The adjustment speed is reduced to a more moderate level. The results for capacity and utilization are similar with both equations, and are reported below for both.

The elasticity of capital with respect to capital price is surprisingly high for the Great Northern and relatively low for the Texas and Pacific and Canadian Pacific, but lies in a more moderate range for the Union Pacific, Santa Fe, and Northern Pacific. Capital is quite inelastic in relation to relative profitability for the Central Pacific.

The regression results reported substantiate the hypothesis that an acceleration principle is the major determinant of investment for railroads in the early building period. These findings indicate that the accelerator mechanism dominates even in the case of these major railroad systems receiving considerable governmental subsidy and being built and operated

---

[21] The technique used here follows that suggested by Bert Hickman, *op. cit.*, pp. 47–49.

6. Building Ahead of Demand

initially in relatively undeveloped areas.[22] Availability of retained profits and subsidy revenue are found to have no significant effect on the investment decision. In six out of seven cases, capital cost acts as an important determinant of investment behavior for these pioneer railroads. Relative profitability plays a significant role in the one instance in which capital cost does not, while a trend variable representing technological change enters significantly for four systems.

Capacity Utilization

Estimates of normal capacity utilization are presented in Table XXVI for the seven systems; the alternative series for the Great Northern and Texas and Pacific are shown in Table XXVII. Normal utilization rate estimates depend on corresponding estimates of capacity, which is defined here as the output associated with minimum average total cost.[23] Capacity, at any point in time, depends on the size of the capital stock, the state of technology, and resource prices. These variables are included in the specification of desired capital stock.[24] If actual stock is substituted for desired stock in Eq. (2.1) and the desired stock relation is solved for output, the result is

$$\log CAPY_t = \frac{1}{a_2} (\log K_{t-1} - \log a_1 - a_3 \log C'_t - a_4 T), \qquad (7)$$

where $CAPY_t$ is capacity output in t. To estimate capacity in year t for each railroad system, Eq. (7) is derived from the corresponding investment regression and the optimum output associated with the actual capital stock is calculated. Capacity utilization is the ratio of expected output to capacity output, i.e., in each year $Y'_t/CAPY_t$.

The actual capital stocks used in the calculations underlying Table XXVI are midyear capital stocks, with the exception that current-year stocks are used in those years during which significant mergers occurred and for the Central Pacific and Santa Fe during their initial construction periods.[25] Current-year stock is used in merger years because this more nearly approximates the average stock in place during those years than does the midyear stock. For the Central Pacific, Great Northern, and Canadian Pacific the magnitude of the utilization rates in Table XXVI

---

[22] It should be noted again that the Great Northern's land grant subsidy was virtually a happenstance, i.e., in a policy sense the Great Northern was not a land grant railroad.
[23] For the development of the technique used to estimate capacity see Bert G. Hickman, *op. cit.*, pp. 94–97.
[24] Because of the lack of data, capital price rather than relative price is used in this study.
[25] This includes 1868–1870 for the Central Pacific and 1870–1871 for the Santa Fe.

TABLE XXVI

Normal Rates of Capacity Utilization (percent of capacity)

Year	Central Pacific	Union Pacific	Texas and Pacific	Santa Fe	Great Northern	Northern Pacific	Canadian Pacific
1868	450	—	—	—	—	—	—
1869	250	—	—	—	—	—	—
1870	157	—	—	100	—	—	—
1871	139	79	—	173	—	—	—
1872	132	98	—	147	—	—	—
1873	95	86	—	110	—	—	—
1874	106	92	102	90	—	—	—
1875	161	96	152	97	—	—	—
1876	87	101	121	143	—	—	—
1877	95	115	127	168	—	131	—
1878	110	99	128	176	—	131	—
1879	96	130	125	151	—	152	—
1880	88	152	122	110	—	216	—
1881	98	190	111	115	—	250	—
1882	100	176	103	103	—	536	—
1883	95	118	107	91	285	576	—
1884	104	104	90	106	204	154	244
1885	100	106	89	99	144	114	271
1886	105	108	98	91	119	92	152
1887	92	117	92	74	122	131	132
1888	120	112	100	62	112	149	119
1889	131	98	110	96	93	157	127
1890	—	—	102	98	99	165	150
1891	—	—	98	104	142	135	134
1892	—	—	95	107	172	121	125
1893	—	—	104	110	133	123	108
1894	—	—	104	119	92	90	107
1895	—	—	97	117	95	91	102
1896	—	—	94	117	112	73	151
1897	—	—	102	115	108	60	138
1898	—	—	101	110	108	86	122
1899	—	—	96	97	96	108	110
1900	—	—	111	96	101	150	109

suggests that the estimates of capacity are understated in the first two years included. Some unusually high utilization rates also appear in later years. The rates for 1880–1883 for the Northern Pacific appear particularly suspect. One reason for high estimated utilization rates in the very early years is that the technique used to estimate capacity understates the level of capacity when capital stock is low relative to its mean and log a_1 is positive. The magnitude of log a_1 is largely dependent here on the mean of

TABLE XXVII

Normal Capacity Utilization with
Capital–Output Elasticity of 1

Year	Texas and Pacific	Great Northern
1874	114	—
1875	188	—
1876	135	—
1877	136	—
1878	140	—
1879	136	—
1880	131	—
1881	117	—
1882	103	—
1883	100	393
1884	84	250
1885	84	157
1886	99	128
1887	90	132
1888	105	110
1889	119	91
1890	100	100
1891	95	165
1892	93	204
1893	103	139
1894	105	88
1895	96	93
1896	95	110
1897	103	112
1898	104	111
1899	96	95
1900	112	103

capital stock. When a negative-trend term representing technological change is present, this bias is accentuated, because the mean capital stock is much more productive per measured unit than that of the very early years. The explanation offered for high early-year utilization rates does not apply to the Great Northern. While there is no constant in the Great Northern regression, the utilization rates of 1883 and 1884 appear too high. In this instance the explanation is that output in 1883 is high relative to its mean for the period (about 60% of the mean), while capital stock is low relative to its mean, or about 25%. Output then varies between 51 and 65% of the mean for the period during 1884–1890, while capital stock rises to its mean value. At the same time, capacity is substantially augmented by technological change (the trend term). Although the bias in estimating capacity clouds the issue, there is no consistent indication of substantial continuing long-term excess capacity for these pioneer railroads during their early years, although such a situation has been widely implied in the historical literature.[26]

Some of the unusually high utilization rates appearing later in the series for various railroads are explainable in terms of movements of the variables underlying the rates. This is the case in 1881–1882 for the Union Pacific and 1876–1879 for the Santa Fe. In the case of the Santa Fe, the bulge in utilization rates during the 1876–1879 period is the result of a five-fold growth of output between 1875 and 1879, while capital stock only doubled. Capacity output for the Union Pacific actually declined by about one-quarter between 1878 and 1880 and then only doubled between 1880 and 1882, while output grew by 15% in the first period and 120% in the second. The movement in capacity was the result of a 75% decline and continuing relatively low level of capital cost as estimated for the Union Pacific over 1879–1882. This implies a rise in the price of labor relative to the price of capital and a lower optimum level of output given the capital stock.

The Overbuilding Hypothesis

The utilization estimates of Table XXVI provide a basis for evaluation of the hypothesis that the land grant railroads built excess capacity in their early years, and that overbuilding was a primary factor in the financial failure of land grant systems. The three systems that failed during the period covered by this study are the Texas and Pacific, the Santa Fe, and the Northern Pacific. On the basis of the *ex post* unaided private rate of return estimated in this study all three railroads were privately unprofitable without subsidy.

The Texas and Pacific went into receivership in 1885 and was sold at foreclosure in 1887.[27] The company reported a decline in business in 1884, "chiefly owing to the heavy floods in Louisiana . . . and the failure of the cotton crop in Texas."[28] This is reflected in the utilization figures, with a significant decline appearing in 1884, followed by relatively low levels of utilization in two of the three succeeding years. Since the major expansion of the railroad in 1881 was followed by declining utilization, it is not clear

---

[26] The exception here is the Union Pacific, which experienced continuing financial difficulty and near-bankruptcy in its early years (see Robert G. Athearn, *Union Pacific Country*, p. 123).

[27] *Poor's Manual*, 1900, p. lxxxiii.

[28] *Ibid.*, 1885, p. 833.

6. Building Ahead of Demand

whether the Texas and Pacific failure was primarily the result of a decline in demand or of overbuilding.

The Santa Fe System entered receivership in 1893 and was sold at foreclosure in 1895.[29] This failure is clearly related to the substantial expansion of the system by construction and merger in 1886–1889, with the low utilization levels of 1887–1890 reflecting the extent of the overexpansion. The utilization figures presented support the argument that the Santa Fe did overbuild during 1886–1889. This considerable expansion relative to demand was undoubtedly a major contributing factor in the financial failure of the Santa Fe.

The Northern Pacific System also went into receivership in 1893, and was sold at foreclosure in 1896.[30] The reported utilization rates reflect a sharp decline in utilization in 1894 and very low capacity utilization for the period 1895–1898. Overbuilding is not supported as a cause of the 1893 financial failure. The decline and low levels of utilization for 1894–1898 occur subsequent to the 1893 completion of the Great Northern System to the West Coast. Because the latter was a substantial direct competitor of the Northern Pacific, the Northern Pacific's sales were reduced. For the Great Northern itself, the utilization figures show a sharp decline in 1894, which continued in 1895. The continuing financial difficulties of the Northern Pacific do appear most likely to have been the result of the reduction in its market with the completion of the Great Northern. There is no immediate evidence that overexpansion of the Northern Pacific itself was a contributing factor.

For purposes of comparison, capacity utilization estimates based on the regressions for both the Great Northern and the Texas and Pacific, with long-run capital output elasticity constrained to 1, are presented in Table XXVII. The series for each of the roads is very similar in level and movement to the railroad's series in Table XXVI, in which the capital output elasticity was not constrained to 1.

It is interesting that three of the four systems that did not experience financial failure in the years covered also have periods of less than capacity utilization. The Canadian Pacific is the exception, with no indication of less than capacity utilization. Three of the four U.S. roads for which utilization figures are calculated in the 1890s show periods of less than capacity utilization in the mid-1890s. However, only one of these, the Northern Pacific, failed at that time.[31] The financial failure or success of

---

[29] *Ibid.*, 1900, p. lxxix.

[30] *Ibid.*, 1900, p. lxxi.

[31] The Texas and Pacific had failed earlier and presumably had been reorganized on a sounder financial basis. It should be noted that the Union Pacific also was put in the hands of receivers in 1893.

the subsidized systems studied does not appear to have been primarily related to the construction or existence of excess capacity.

Building ahead of Demand

If these railroads were built ahead of demand, the capacity utilization corollary of Fishlow's rate of return test is that capacity utilization would increase over time. This is tested here by a simple OLS regression, with the capacity utilization rate as the dependent variable and time as the independent variable. The results of these regressions are presented in Table XXVIII. With the exception of the Union Pacific, the coefficients on time are uniformly negative and significant at least at the .975 level of the t test. The coefficient on time for the Union Pacific is not significantly different from zero. The results of Tables XXI and XXVIII are inconsistent and suggest that the Fishlow test for building ahead of demand is not so clear-cut as it first seems.

The difficulty with the tests suggested by Fishlow is in determining what they really mean. It would seem reasonable to expect that Fishlow's implications would usually (if not always) be met for investment projects of relatively large size and long gestation periods. If this is the case,

TABLE XXVIII

Regression Results by System [a]

System	α	β	R^2	df
Central Pacific	207.7	−6.5539	.2848	20
	(6.81)	(−2.82)		
Union Pacific	94.5	1.5456	.0892	17
	(5.59)	(1.29)		
Texas and Pacific	127.7	−1.0494	.3355	25
	(20.14)	(−3.55)		
Santa Fe	133.0	−1.1294	.1453	29
	(13.00)	(−2.22)		
Great Northern	266.8	−5.5924	.3750	16
	(5.90)	(−3.10)		
Northern Pacific	331.2	−7.6709	.1813	22
	(4.22)	(−2.21)		
Canadian Pacific	289.3	−5.9216	.4088	15
	(6.18)	(−3.22)		

[a] Regressions of the form $u = \alpha + \beta\ Time$, where u = annual normal capacity utilization rate and *Time* represents the age of the project. The t value for each coefficient is shown in parentheses below the coefficient.

TABLE XXIX

Unaided Rate of Return and Opportunity Cost of Capital by System

	Rate of return (percent)	Opportunity cost of capital (percent)
Central Pacific	10.6	9.0
Union Pacific	11.6	9.0
Texas and Pacific	2.2	7.7
Santa Fe	6.1	7.9
Northern Pacific	6.3	7.9
Great Northern	8.7	6.3
Canadian Pacific	3.9	6.8

Fishlow's tests are not definitive, because they cannot distinguish building ahead of demand (whatever that means) from anything else. The point of interest, and what earlier writers perhaps really meant by the concept of building ahead of demand, is whether the project was profitable or unprofitable.[32] Building ahead of demand must imply that the project was unprofitable. That the accounting rate of return was less than alternatives in the project's early years, and that the rate of return rises over time, do not tell us about the profitability of the project over its lifetime.

The unaided private rate of return (internal rate of return) calculated here for each system is listed in Table XXIX, along with the estimated opportunity cost of capital relevant for each system. The real test of building ahead of demand is whether or not the unaided rate of return equals or exceeds the opportunity cost of capital. If it does not, the railroad was built ahead of demand. If the unaided rate of return equals or exceeds the opportunity cost of capital, the railroad was not built ahead of demand in any meaningful economic sense.

The test suggested here indicates that the Central Pacific, Union Pacific, and Great Northern systems were not built ahead of demand, while the other four systems were built ahead of demand. This of course conflicts with the Fishlow tests, which indicate that all seven systems were built ahead of demand. The conclusion here is that the only meaningful concept

---

[32] A related interpretation is that a railroad was built ahead of demand if the market (*ex ante*) thought that the road would fail, so that its bonds fell to a discount. Still another interpretation is that railroads built ahead of demand were (*ex post*) privately unprofitable but socially profitable (see Lloyd J. Mercer, "Building Ahead of Demand: Some Evidence for the Land Grant Railroads," *Journal of Economic History*, XXXIV, 2 (June 1974), pp. 492–500.

of building ahead of demand is one of profitability of the project in terms of the economic rate of return on the project. Unprofitable projects are built ahead of demand; profitable projects are not. Even by this test, some land grant railroads were, as Fishlow suspected, built ahead of demand.

Building ahead of demand suggests a developmental role for such pioneer railroads, but is also frequently viewed as a situation requiring governmental subsidy. The estimates presented here indicate that while the land grant systems considered were all built ahead of demand according to Fishlow's specification of the concept, they did not all (*ex post*) require subsidy for private profitability. Full evaluation of building ahead of demand requires both the Fishlow tests and the private profitability tests in order to define the extent to which the railroads were built ahead of demand.

Still a further point of interest is the social rate of return for railroads built ahead of demand. If the *ex post* social rate of return is less than the marginal opportunity cost of capital for a railroad built ahead of demand, the developmental significance of the railroad is limited even though it was "built ahead of demand." Of the systems studied here, only the Texas and Pacific falls into this category.

Chapter 7

Summary

The primary focus of this study is a quantitative appraisal of the central issue underlying government intervention in the form of land grant subsidy to pioneer railroads. This issue is the economic rationality of the subsidy measured in terms of its impact on efficiency. Our major emphasis here is on the railroad land grants. The empirical analysis of this study includes the six railroad systems that received the overwhelming bulk of the land grant aid in the United States and the heavily subsidized Canadian Pacific System in Canada. The economic rationality of the gift of land from common holding (the public domain) to a favored few (the owners of the land grant railroads) rested on the four hypotheses (A1, A2, B1, and B2) concerning the relationship of the social and private rates of return on investment in the land grant railroads to the opportunity cost of capital. These hypotheses allow us to draw a conclusion regarding the rationality of railroad land grant policy with regard to the seven systems studied.

A second major objective of this study is evaluation of the less operational and specific hypothesis regarding the building of pioneer railroads ahead of demand. The concept of building ahead of demand is especially important in historians' discussion of land grant policy. However, as we saw earlier, building ahead of demand does not by itself provide a rational basis for the land grant subsidy. Examination of building ahead of demand also provides a basis for evaluating the hypothesis that land grant railroads built excess capacity, perhaps as a result of the subsidies provided to encourage construction.

Some conclusions with regard to whether land grant policy was beneficial for society are suggested by the estimates of this study. However, as noted in Chapters 1 and 2, the study does not address a number of land grant policy issues. As a result, one must be careful about proceeding from the conclusions of this study to a macro (overall) evaluation of land grant policy.[1]

Economic Rationality of Land Grant Policy

Advocates of land grant subsidy for the pioneer railroads argued that subsidization was necessary to get the railroads built.[2] Their *ex ante* expectation was that the private rate of return on the pioneer railroads without aid would be less than the market rate of return (hypothesis A1), but at least equal to the market rate of return with the land grant subsidy (hypothesis A2). These hypotheses are tested here on an *ex post* basis.[3] The hypothesis tests also provide an evaluation of the optimality of the land grant subsidy on an *ex post* basis, i.e., an answer to the question whether too much, too little, or just enough aid was provided.[4]

Table XXX lists the estimates required for the test of hypotheses A1 and A2 for each railroad system included in this study. Hypotheses A1 and A2 are both accepted for only two of the seven systems: the Northern Pacific and the Canadian Pacific. For these systems, the estimated unaided private rate of return is less than the estimated opportunity cost of capital, but the estimated private rate of return with aid exceeds the opportunity cost of capital. For three systems, the Central Pacific, Union Pacific, and Great Northern, hypothesis A1 is rejected because the estimated unaided private rate of return is greater than the opportunity cost of capital. Hypothesis A1 is accepted for the other two systems, the Texas and Pacific and the Santa Fe, because the unaided private rate of return

---

[1] As was also noted earlier, many of these other issues have received careful and detailed study (at least on a micro basis, i.e., for specific railroads or railroad systems) by historians. The issues examined here provide a major input required for a macro evaluation of land grant policy.

[2] The argument could be taken in either an absolute or relative sense. Land grant supporters may have meant that they expected the railroads never to be built without subsidization, or they expected construction to be greatly delayed without aid to private investors.

[3] There appears to be little doubt that hypothesis A1 was correct on an *ex ante* basis. The question of interest here is, Did it turn out to be correct *ex post?*

[4] We would, of course, regard with great scepticism any finding that hypotheses A1 and A2 are correct on an *ex post* basis and that the subsidy provided was optimal, i.e., just enough to cover the actual shortfall between the opportunity cost of capital and the unaided private rate of return. Thus, the real question with regard to optimality is whether too much or too little aid was provided.

Table XXX

Estimates for the Test of Hypotheses A1 and A2

System	Private rates[a] (%) Unaided	Aided	Opportunity cost of capital (%)
Central Pacific	10.6	11.6	9.0
Union Pacific	11.6	13.1	9.0
Texas and Pacific	2.2	4.3	7.7
Santa Fe	6.1	7.1	7.9
Northern Pacific	6.3	9.2	7.9
Great Northern	8.7	10.0	6.3
Canadian Pacific	3.9	8.4	6.8

[a] Estimated rates with terminal adjustment C.

for their investment is less than the opportunity cost of capital. For these two systems, the aided private rate of return also falls below the market rate, so hypothesis A2 is rejected. Here the land grant proponents' argument with respect to the rate of return without aid was correct, *ex post,* but the aid provided was insufficient to make the project privately profitable.

Land grant aid (government intervention) was nonoptimal in the case of all seven systems studied. In the case of the Texas and Pacific and the Santa Fe the aid was nonoptimal because it was too small.[5] For the other five systems the aid provided was nonoptimal because too much was given. In three cases, the Central Pacific, Union Pacific, and Great Northern, no aid was required (*ex post*). The Northern Pacific and Canadian Pacific needed aid, but too much was provided.

The estimates developed to test hypotheses A1 and A2 allow examination of another proposition in the historical literature, namely, that the aid provided paid for the railroads. This proposition has been advanced because the comparison of the value of aid and cost of construction has typically been done incorrectly in the literature. Nominal dollar amounts of aid and cost have been compared without reference to the timing of the stream of aid and cost. The correct comparison uses the present values of the aid and cost streams at a point in time. When the comparison is made

[5] An optimal level of aid is just sufficient to raise the rate of return on an investment to the market rate (opportunity cost of capital), where it fell below the latter on an unaided basis. Notice that this implicitly implies acceptance of hypotheses B1 and B2 for the railroad concerned. Aid to a system for which either hypothesis B1 or hypothesis B2, or both, is rejected would be nonoptimal (on efficiency grounds) from society's point of view.

on this basis, we find that the subsidies did not fully pay for the investment in any system or its aided railroads (see Tables IV and V). At the same time it is shown that the aid was a significant fraction of costs in all cases (and very significant indeed in some instances), rather than being of little moment, as suggested by some writers.

This examination also reveals that government intervention in the form of the loan subsidy involved in the federal government loans to railroads in the Central Pacific and Union Pacific systems was much greater (and more significant) than previously thought. In fact, the loan subsidy was almost twice as large relative to investment costs as the land grant aid.

Rationality in terms of economic efficiency requires the land grant advocates to have had two other hypotheses in mind in conjunction with hypotheses A1 and A2. Those who supported the land grant policy believed that the object of their support—the proposed land grant railroads—would be beneficial to society, but for rationality with regard to economic efficiency their argument required more than this. In particular, it necessitated a specific belief about the relationship between the social rate of return on the land grant railroads and the market rate of return, as well as other potential social rates of return on investment in the economy. What was necessary was the expectation that the *ex post* social rate of return on the land grant railroads would exceed both the average opportunity cost of capital (hypothesis B1) and the marginal opportunity cost of capital, i.e., the social rate of return on projects curtailed or abandoned as a result of the diversion of capital resulting from the land grant policy (hypothesis B2).[6]

Table XXXI lists the estimates necessary for the hypotheses B1 and B2. On the basis of the preferred estimate (the uniform distribution for intraregional benefits and terminal adjustment C), hypothesis B1 is accepted for all seven systems, while hypothesis B2 is accepted for six systems and rejected for the Texas and Pacific.[7] The preferred social rate estimate for the Texas and Pacific is only 7.8% greater than the estimated opportunity cost of capital. It seems most probable that there were other projects in the economy with higher social rates of return that could have used the capital directed to the Texas and Pacific by land grant policy. It should also be noted that the Texas and Pacific is the only system for which the

[6] This would include all the many potential projects in the economy for which hypotheses A1 and A2 would hold.

[7] Thus, while it was concluded above that land grant aid to the Texas and Pacific was nonoptimal because it failed to raise the private rate of return to the market rate, the aid was actually nonoptimal for a different reason. On efficiency grounds, no aid should have been given to the Texas and Pacific. As a result, the previous conclusion that too little aid was given is reversed and the final conclusion must be that too much aid was provided to the Texas and Pacific.

7. Summary

TABLE XXXI

Estimates for the Test of Hypotheses B1 and B2

	Social Rates[a] (%)		
System	Uniform distribution	No intraregional benefits	Opportunity cost of capital
Central Pacific	23.2	14.0	9.0
Union Pacific	19.8	14.6	9.0
Texas and Pacific	8.3	5.7	7.7
Santa Fe	19.0	12.1	7.9
Northern Pacific	12.5	9.4	7.9
Great Northern	26.8	15.3	6.3
Canadian Pacific	13.1	7.0	6.8

[a] Estimated rates with terminal adjustment C.

estimated social rate of return without intraregional benefits (with terminal adjustment C) actually falls below the market rate of return.

Both social rates listed in Table XXXI lie sufficiently above the opportunity cost of capital that hypotheses B1 and B2 can be accepted with a high degree of confidence for the Central Pacific, Union Pacific, Santa Fe, and Great Northern systems.[8] Hypotheses B1 and B2 are accepted, with a lower degree of confidence, for the Northern Pacific and the Canadian Pacific. In the case of the Northern Pacific, the estimated social rates exceed the market rate by 58% (uniform distribution) and 19% (no intraregional benefits). While this is not so striking as for the four systems with the highest social rates, it is sufficiently high to permit acceptance of hypothesis B2. The estimated social rates exceed the market rate by 93% (uniform distribution) and 3% (no intraregional benefits) for the Canadian Pacific. Given the undeniable military and political unification benefits in the case of the Canadian Pacific, these estimates warrant acceptance of hypothesis B2.

The estimates of this study directly support the conclusion that railroad land grant policy (government intervention) was rational in terms of economic efficiency for three of the seven systems studied: the Santa Fe, Northern Pacific, and Canadian Pacific. Government intervention (land grant policy) definitely fails to meet the test of economic rationality only in the case of the Texas and Pacific. The conclusion that land grant policy was economically rational holds on a qualified basis for the other three

[8] The previous conclusion that aid provided to the Santa Fe was nonoptimal because too little was provided still holds, given evaluation of hypotheses B1 and B2.

systems—the Central Pacific, Union Pacific, and Great Northern—because their estimated *ex post* unaided private rates of return exceeded the opportunity cost of capital. However, there seems little doubt that on an *ex ante* basis the private rate of return was less than the opportunity cost of capital for the Central Pacific and the Union Pacific. On this basis the conclusion regarding the economic rationality of land grant policy holds for these two systems. Because hypothesis A1 is less likely to hold on an *ex ante* basis for the Great Northern System, the economic rationality conclusion remains qualified for that system.[9] In terms of evaluating land grant policy, it is worth noting again that the Great Northern System was not explicitly a land grant railroad as a matter of policy.

Building Ahead of Demand

A major conclusion of this study is that the widely accepted notion that American railroads were typically built ahead of demand can be best evaluated in terms of the hypothesis test regarding the economic rationality of subsidy to the railroads. This is illustrated by application of the Fishlow building-ahead-of-demand tests to each of the seven systems. With what appears to be the appropriate time periods for evaluation of Fishlow's two propositions, one would conclude that all seven systems were built ahead of demand. This result does not sit well, because on reflection it appears that Fishlow's propositions should always be true for any investment project of relatively large size and relatively long gestation period.[10] Thus, it is concluded that the Fishlow tests are inadequate because they really cannot distinguish building ahead of demand (whatever that may be taken to mean) from anything else.

The test proposed here for the concept of building ahead of demand (on an *ex post* basis) is whether the railroad investment over its lifetime was privately profitable without aid. Based on this test, we find that of the seven systems considered, the Central Pacific, the Union Pacific, and Great Northern Systems were not built ahead of demand. However, on the same basis the other four systems—the Texas and Pacific, the Santa Fe, the Northern Pacific and the Canadian Pacific—were all built ahead of

[9] Subsidy was required on an *ex ante* basis (in the 1850s) for the predecessors of the railroads forming the Great Northern System. The *ex ante* rates of return of these pioneer railroads were certainly less than the opportunity cost of capital. When the St. Paul, Minneapolis and Manitoba was formed in 1879 (by the purchase of its bankrupt predecessors) such subsidy does not so clearly appear to have been necessary. Naturally, the promoters of the new railroad sought to obtain the subsidy since it improved their wealth position and reduced their risk in the undertaking.

[10] This would seem to be a reasonable description of all railroad projects of any significant size in mileage or investment costs.

demand. This test (and definition) of building ahead of demand has the advantage of being operational and of relating to the four hypotheses regarding economic rationality of subsidization.

Because the idea of building ahead of demand suggests a developmental role for the railroads involved, evaluation of hypotheses B1 and B2 is useful in assessing the significance of building ahead of demand. Hypotheses B1 and B2 are accepted for the Santa Fe, Northern Pacific, and Canadian Pacific systems. Thus, it can be argued that they were built ahead of demand and played a developmental role. As defined here, the Texas and Pacific was built ahead of demand. However, since hypothesis B2 is rejected for the Texas and Pacific, its developmental significance is limited. This illustrates that the notion of building ahead of demand does not automatically have the developmental significance seemingly attributed to it in the literature.

As a further evaluation of both the issue of building ahead of demand and the possibility that land grant and other aid may have encouraged overbuilding of the subsidized systems, estimates of investment demand, capacity, and capacity utilization are developed here for the seven systems. The estimated investment demand functions confirm the importance of the accelerator mechanism and capital cost variables suggested by earlier studies of the entire railroad system. No evidence could be found that governmental aid led to overexpansion and excess capacity for the systems studied. The estimates of capacity utilization do reveal periods of overexpansion for specific systems, as well as the expected relationship between these episodes and financial difficulty (bankruptcy) for these systems. An evaluation of the capacity utilization corollary of Fishlow's second rate of return test is made using the capacity utilization estimates developed. The results of this test (see Table XXIX) are inconsistent with the earlier tests (see Table XXII) of the Fishlow rate of return hypothesis regarding building ahead of demand. These results further demonstrate that the Fishlow tests for building ahead of demand are not so clear-cut as has been thought.

Evaluation of the Railroad Land Grants

The railroad land grants and related subsidies have been much discussed and much maligned. There is no doubt that they were an imperfect and inefficient means to accomplish the desired ends. As we saw in Chapter 2, land grants are not the most efficient subsidy on theoretical grounds. In addition, on an *ex post* basis (as estimated here) subsidization was not even required for three of the seven systems studied. However, this conclusion must be qualified by the evidence in the historical record indicating that subsidy was required *ex ante* for at least six of the seven systems (the Great Northern is the possible exception). A very important consideration here is that the policy of land grant aid was politically feasible whatever its other shortcomings. Given the vast amount of land in the public domain, the land grant policy was one that, as a purely practical matter, could be undertaken. With the constitutional and other scruples about the alternative forms of aid, it is not clear that those policies that are theoretically more efficient could have been undertaken on the scale of the land grant policy. As a practical matter it appears that the choice for society was something resembling the land grant (and associated) policies used in the nineteenth century, or no policy at all.

Without subsidy, the land grant railroads would probably have been built, but at a later date. Thus, the land grants did aid in the acceleration of the construction and operation of these pioneer railroads.[11] The movement from the brink of one financial disaster to another during their construction periods, as illustrated by the discussion of their corporate histories in Chapter 3, indicates that the land grant railroads required all the help they could get in that early period.[12] Without subsidy (and the land grants were the principal subsidy that was both available and feasible), construction and operation of the land grant railroads would surely have been delayed for some years. With the exception of the Texas and Pacific, the systems studied here had sufficiently high social rates of return that hypotheses B1 and B2 are accepted. Thus, the acceleration of their construction and operation through subsidization made a positive contribution to nineteenth-century economic growth in the United States. On efficiency grounds government intervention in the timing of the railroad building decision was rational. Society's well-being was improved by government intervention.

This conclusion clearly applies to five of the seven systems studied, and on a qualified basis to a sixth: the Great Northern. It does not apply to the Texas and Pacific because hypothesis B2 was rejected for that system. On efficiency grounds there is no basis for subsidy to the Texas and Pacific. The conclusion is qualified for the Great Northern, because while hypotheses B1 and B2 are accepted for the Great Northern, hypothesis A1 is not only rejected on the basis of the *ex post* rate of return estimates, but in addition is less likely than in the case of the other six systems to hold on an *ex ante* basis. Thus, the economic growth conclusion must be qualified for

---

[11] An important qualification indicated by the estimates of this study is that the governmental loan played a role as important as (or more important than) that of the land grants for the Central Pacific and Union Pacific systems.

[12] Again, the Great Northern appears to be the notable exception.

7. Summary

the Great Northern in the same manner as the economic rationality conclusion above.

Because the evidence reported here offers strong support for the argument that the land grant policy for five of the seven systems made a positive contribution to growth, we may conclude that the policy in general did so. This means only that the vast bulk of the land grant acreage went to railroads that required subsidy (at least on an *ex ante* basis) and that were sufficiently beneficial to society to make a positive contribution to growth. On balance, the land grant policy was good for society in terms of economic efficiency. It is this conclusion, indicated by the micro evidence developed here, that should play a predominant role in a macro evaluation of the land grant policy, rather than the obvious imperfections of the policy in theory and practice. Such consideration will qualify the land grant legend in the historical literature and bring the story closer to describing reality.

Appendix A

Investment Expenditure

An explanation of the estimation techniques and data sources for the estimated annual expenditure on construction and equipment of the seven systems is presented here. The goal in developing these capital expenditure estimates is to arrive at the best possible estimate of the real resource cost of the investment in the railroads. Unfortunately, nineteenth-century business and accounting practices present some serious barriers to achievement of this goal.

The primary difficulty in estimating the real resource cost of the railroads' investment is created by the vast amount of "water" typically present in book values of road and equipment for nineteenth-century railroads. This water is the product of financing and accounting techniques and the discounts at which securities were sold. The best authorities are not in agreement concerning the relative magnitude of water in the book values, but the existence of any water means that the goal of estimating capital costs in terms of real resource cost cannot be achieved by simply relying on book values of construction and equipment. Perhaps the most authoritative source asserts that some 40% of the railroad capital stock outstanding in 1900 was fictitious.[1] Book values are clearly an upper

---

[1] *Poor's Manual*, 1900, pp. liv ff. The Interstate Commerce Commission estimate of original cost for the nation's railroads in 1915, when its series began, is only 8.8% less than the corresponding book value. However, if all bonds were originally sold at par, total cost would be overstated by about 20% and correspondingly more depending on the actual discount on bonds, according to Albert Fishlow, in "Productivity and Technological Change

A. Investment Expenditure

bound to the real resource cost of railroad investment, and the capital cost estimates must be developed as independently of the book values as possible.

A second major problem involves the treatment of expenditures for repair and replacement of track (rails and ties) and equipment. Most railroads charged routine expenditures on these items to operating expenses at the time expenditures were made, and as a result no appropriate entry appears in the capital account.[2] Published information on the components of annual operating expenses for the various railroads is not sufficient to allow the researcher to correct this deficiency using the railroads' accounts. Fortunately, for the rate of return computations of this study the problem introduced by this treatment of repair and replacement costs is not a severe one, because these costs enter into the annual net receipts stream in an appropriate way, even if they are included in operating expenses. However, a bias is introduced in the rate of return estimates with terminal adjustment C (value of the final year capital stock). Rates of return computed using terminal adjustment C will be slightly understated, because repair and replacement of track and equipment are excluded from the capital expenditure stream and the terminal year capital stock is a little smaller than it would otherwise be. The reader can verify that the bias introduced is relatively small by comparing the difference between the rates of return calculated using terminal adjustments A and B, whose magnitudes differ by 50%.

We turn now to explanation of the capital cost estimates with the discussion and data presented below by system.

The Central Pacific System

For the Central Pacific and Union Pacific systems, a unique data source exists for the larger part of the period covered by this study. This source is the several-volume detailed report of the United States Pacific Railway Commission (*PRC*), appointed by the U.S. Senate to investigate those railroads that had received federal government loans to aid in their construction.[3] The substantial accounting data provided by the *PRC* report

---

in the Railroad Sector, 1840–1910", in *Output, Employment, and Productivity in the United States After 1880*, Studies in Income and Wealth, Vol. 20 (New York: National Bureau of Economic Research, 1966), p. 592.

[2] Fishlow, *op. cit.*, p. 591, points out that neglect of this factor resulted in Ulmer's estimates of railroad capital in the nineteenth century being understated.

[3] U.S. Congress, Senate, *Majority and Minority Reports and Testimony Taken by the United States Pacific Railway Commission*, 50th Congress, 1st Session, Executive Document No. 51, 8 vols. (2505–2509). Hereafter cited as: U.S. Congress, Senate, *PRC*.

make possible more detailed estimates of the capital cost for individual components of the Central Pacific and Union Pacific systems than are possible for the other systems. A detailed explanation of the investment cost estimates is presented here for the Central Pacific System as a case study of the techniques and data sources used. For the other six systems, a general, rather than detailed, outline of the estimation of investment expenditure is provided.

Table A-1 lists the separate railroad companies included in the Central Pacific System as defined for this study, the year in which construction began on each railroad, the date the railroad joined the system, the legal relationship between the railroad and the system, and the current dollar value of total construction and equipment expenditures for each firm during the period of study. The construction and equipment costs shown for those railroads that joined after being partially or completely built represent the depreciated value of capital costs incurred earlier and actual costs while the railroads were in the system.[4] Table A-2 lists the annual investment expenditure for the Central Pacific System.

Even with the *PRC* reports, rather roundabout means must be used at times to estimate the construction and equipment costs for the Central Pacific System, especially with respect to placing those costs in specific years. The reason for this is the disappearance of the books of the major construction company (the Contract and Finance Company) before the *PRC* investigation.[5] A detailed explanation of the estimate of capital cost for the original Central Pacific Railroad will illustrate the problems encountered and some of the solutions used.

From Sacramento to the California state line, the annual estimate of capital cost is based on the record of payments to Charles Crocker and Company and to minor contractors who worked on this portion of the

[4] Since track replacement was charged as an operating expense, the track component of the capital stock was not depreciated after initial investment, i.e., it is assumed that the track part of real capital stock was continuously maintained. The other two components of capital stock are structures and equipment with apparent lives of 50 and 20 years, respectively, in the nineteenth century. Thus, a 5% depreciation charge was used for equipment and 2% for structures. Iron track apparently had a life of about 10 years, making 10% the appropriate straight-line charge. The estimated proportion of total capital stock represented by these major components for the original Central Pacific Railroad are: structures (65.911%); track (23.562%); and equipment (10.527%). For development of these estimates, see Lloyd J. Mercer, "The Central Pacific System: An Estimate of Social and Private Rates of Return for a Land Grant Aided Railroad System" (unpublished Ph.D. dissertation, University of Washington, 1967), Appendix IIIB. The straight-line depreciation rate resulting from the factors discussed is 1.845%, calculated as: $(0.02)(0.65911) + (0.05)(0.10527) + (0)(0.23562) = 0.01854$.

[5] U.S. Congress, Senate, *PRC*, p. 73.

TABLE A-1

Total Current Dollar Value of Construction and Equipment Cost of Individual Railroads in the Central Pacific System (1863–1889) and Information on Their Entrance into the System

Railroad	Total construction and equipment cost (thousand current $)	Year of first construction	Year railroad entered system	Legal relationship to the system at entrance
Amador Branch	379	1876	1877	Leased to C.P.[a]
Calif. & Oregon	10,452	1867	1870	Consolidated with C.P.
Calif. Pacific	3,633	1868	1876	Leased to C.P.
Central Pacific	54,393	1863	N.A.	N.A.
L.A. & Independence	473	1875	1879	Sold to S.P.
L.A. & San Diego	1,091	1874	1876	Leased to C.P.
L.A. & San Pedro	498	1868	1874	Consolidated with S.P.
Monterey	468	1875	1879	Leased to S.P.
Northern Railway	3,596	1875	1876	Leased to C.P.
San Francisco Bay	860	1869	1870	Consolidated with C.P.
S.F., Oakland & Alameda	482	1866	1870	Consolidated with C.P.
San Joaquin Valley	4,560	1870	1870	Consolidated with C.P.
San Pablo & Tulare	1,132	1876	1878	Leased to Northern
S.F. & San Jose	1,460	1863	1870	Consolidated with S.P.
Santa Cruz	779	1876	1883	Leased to S.P.
Southern Pacific (Ariz.)	8,295	1878	N.A.	N.A.
Southern Pacific (Calif.)[b]	28,971	1869	N.A.	N.A.
Southern Pacific (N.M.)	3,885	1880	N.A.	N.A.
Stockton & Copperopolis and Stockton & Visalia	1,405	1870	1874	Leased to C.P.
Western Pacific	3,573	1866	1870	Consolidated with C.P.

[a] Abbreviations: C.P. for Central Pacific; S.P. for Southern Pacific; N.A. for not applicable.
[b] Includes the Northern and Southern Divisions and the Southern Pacific Branch Railroad.

TABLE A-2

Annual Investment Expenditures by the Central Pacific System

	Investment expenditures	
Year	(thousand current $)	(thousand 1869 $)
1863	598	691
1864	575	495
1865	1,894	1,655
1866	3,537	3,192
1867	3,655	3,468
1868	14,575	14,191
1869	19,688	19,688
1870	10,983	11,952
1871	1,593	1,786
1872	7,901	8,599
1873	1,472	1,634
1874	4,502	5,206
1875	1,678	2,025
1876	16,305	20,803
1877	3,588	4,741
1878	2,842	4,044
1879	4,399	6,341
1880	4,678	6,333
1881	2,123	2,773
1882	5,008	6,391
1883	4,970	6,568
1884	1,182	1,661
1885	1,312	1,891
1886	4,992	7,291
1887	2,519	3,632
1888	1,341	1,908
1889	2,471	3,562

road.[6] Cash and note payments to these contractors are taken to be the real resource cost of construction, except for a few dollars worth of materials or equipment furnished them and $100,000 in convertible bonds paid to Charles Crocker and Company in 1863. The bonds were valued at 56 per 100.[7] One large payment of $2,502,600 to Charles Crocker and Company for track-laying, equipment, buildings, etc. on this section is divided between years by assuming that the cost in each year was proportional to

[6] *Ibid.*, pp. 3508–3510, 3038, and 3556.
[7] Stuart Daggett, *Chapters in the History of the Southern Pacific*, p. 25.

A. Investment Expenditure

the mileage of the section completed in that year.[8] The portion of this assigned to 1868 ($595,618.80) is assumed to be included in the cost given for iron, buildings, etc., in the construction account of the Central Pacific for 1868.[9]

From the California border to Promontory Point, Utah, the Central Pacific Railroad was constructed by the Contract and Finance Company. This company was owned by the four promoters of the Central Pacific Railroad (Huntington, Stanford, Hopkins, and Crocker). Construction accounts of the Central Pacific for the years 1868, 1869, and 1870 and the abstracts of the transactions between the Central Pacific and the Contract and Finance Company taken from the books of the Central Pacific furnish the data for the estimated capital costs for the line from the California border to Promontory Point.[10] After completion of the main line, additional improvements were carried out by the Contract and Finance Company in 1870 and paid for by the Central Pacific.[11]

In 1869 the Central Pacific purchased 47.5 miles of railroad between Promontory Point and Ogden, Utah from the Union Pacific for $100,000 cash, 1,338 U.S. government bonds, and 1,562 Central Pacific first mortgage bonds. To estimate the cost of this transaction, the U.S. government bonds (currency sixes) are taken at face value in currency and converted to a gold basis.[12] This last is necessary because gold was at a premium from 1862 through 1878. Dollar quotations were apparently in gold terms in the West, so in this case the currency value must be translated into gold terms to be comparable with the other values used. The Central Pacific first mortgage bonds were valued at 74.5 per 100, which is the ratio of the amount received to face value for all Central Pacific first mortgage bonds sold during the construction period of the main line.[13] This may be an underestimate since Central Pacific first mortgage bonds sold for a low of 90.5 and a high of 93 in November 1869.[14] However, since this is the only quotation on Central Pacific bonds for 1869, and the date the bonds were transferred (or the precise date the agreement was reached for the purchase of the mileage from the Union Pacific) could not be determined, the bonds are valued at 74.5.

---

[8] The source for mileage completed was U.S. Congress, *PRC*, p. 4748 and Daggett, *op. cit.*, p. 83.

[9] U.S. Congress, *PRC*, p. 3518.

[10] *Ibid.*, pp. 3512–3518.

[11] *Ibid.*, pp. 81, 3519, and 3531.

[12] The gold premium used is that from James K. Kindahl, "Economic Factors in Specie Resumption: The United States, 1865–79", *Journal of Political Economy*, LXIX, 1 (February 1961), 36.

[13] *Public Aids*, II, p. 19.

[14] *Commercial and Financial Chronicle*, November 18, 1871, p. 668.

Considerable investment in equipment by the Central Pacific occurred following completion of the main line. Comparison of the volume of equipment in 1869, valued by reported equipment prices with the value of the equipment account on the balance sheet of the Central Pacific for 1869, indicates that the book value of the equipment account was approximately equal to the original cost of the equipment held.[15] Changes in the value of this account are taken to represent investment in equipment by the railroad for the years 1871 through 1884. From 1885 on, the equipment account was not shown separately on the Central Pacific's balance sheet. Given the apparent 20-year life of equipment, it is assumed that the equipment investment of 1863–1869 was replaced by an equal current dollar volume of investment during 1883–1889 for the Central Pacific Railroad.

Early construction cost data for the Southern Pacific of California are not available primarily because of the disappearance of the Contract and Finance Company's books. The cost estimate for 1869 is for 31 miles on the Northern Division. Estimated cost per mile for construction in 1872 and 1873 was used to arrive at this number. The Contract and Finance Company handled construction in the latter years for $40,000 per mile in Southern Pacific first mortgage bonds.[16] No market value can be assigned to these bonds at the time of construction because none were sold until 1880 or 1881.[17] An assumed value of 75, which is approximately the average proportion of face value for Central Pacific first mortgage bonds during the construction period, is used to value these bonds. Hence, the estimated construction and equipment cost per mile for the Southern Pacific through 1873 was $30,000. Information in *Poor's Manual* and Kneiss is used to determine the timing of expenditure through 1873.[18] Apparently the contract cited between the Southern Pacific and the Contract and Finance Company was continued for the 90.4 miles built by the construction company in 1874.

In 1874 the four promoters formed the Western Development Company to continue construction and equipment of the Southern Pacific. The costs of various construction contracts during 1874–1877 were estimated from the books of the new construction company by the accountants for the

---

[15] *Poor's Manual*, 1871, p. 424. While there was always considerable overstatement in the balance sheet value of construction, equipment seems to have been carried on the books at something near the actual cost for the systems studied. This often proved helpful when equipment was shown separately on balance sheets.
[16] *Commercial and Financial Chronicle*, June 20, 1874, p. 621.
[17] U.S. Congress, Senate, *PRC*, p. 3416.
[18] Gilbert H. Kneiss, *Bonanza Railroads* (Stanford: Stanford University Press, 1940), p. 47, and *Poor's Manual*, 1871–1872 and 1875–1876.

A. Investment Expenditure

Pacific Railway Commission and reported in *PRC*. These costs include construction and equipment plus interest paid to the construction company for late payment. With the available data it is impossible to determine the specific mileage or years to which the various contracts apply, except for the Goshen contract, which is evidently for the 40.1 miles between Goshen and Huron, California constructed in 1876. The Goshen contract was $487,000, which, with interest at $1,162.54 per mile ($480,499.50 total interest was paid on all contracts for 413.32 miles) becomes $533,707.90.[19] Construction and equipment cost per mile for the remaining 373.22 miles was estimated by subtracting the Goshen contract estimate from the total of all costs for all contracts ($11,890,726.61) and dividing the result by mileage. Total estimated cost per mile by this procedure was $30,429.83, composed of construction and equipment cost (the Western Development Company supplying everything necessary for the original railroad) of $29,267.29 and interest of $1,162.54. The timing of investment during the years 1874–1877 was estimated from the completion date of various sections of the road and reports on progress of construction.[20] Original equipment costs of the railroad are assumed to be included in the contract cost, but postconstruction equipment costs are assumed to have been paid by the Southern Pacific of California.

Construction and equipment of the Southern Pacific from Mojave to Needles, California during 1882 and 1883 was carried out by the Pacific Development Company at an estimated cost per mile of $21,127.55. The cost per mile assumed is the same as that for construction and equipment of the Southern Pacific of New Mexico in 1880 and 1881, as reported in *PRC*.[21] Investment timing was estimated as above.[22] The Pacific Improvement Company was the third construction company formed by the four promoters, and it also built the Southern Pacific Railroads of Arizona and New Mexico.

Southern Pacific of California construction costs for 1885–1889 are for the construction of the Southern Pacific Branch Railroad from Soledad, California down the coast to a point north of Santa Barbara. The assumed cost is $20,000 per mile.

Between 1878 and 1880 the Pacific Improvement Company built and equipped the Southern Pacific of Arizona at an average cost per mile of $18,231.15, based on the estimate of total cost reported in *PRC*.[23] Average

---

[19] U.S. Congress, Senate, *PRC*, p. 4749.
[20] *Ibid.*, and *Commercial and Financial Chronicle*, September 9, 1876, p. 76.
[21] U.S. Congress, Senate, *PRC*, pp. 3526 and 4749.
[22] *Commercial and Financial Chronicle*, January 13, 1883, p. 48, and *Poor's Manual*, 1884, p. 899.
[23] U.S. Congress, Senate, *PRC*, p. 3526.

cost per mile for the Southern Pacific of New Mexico, built and equipped by the same company, was $21,127.55, again based on the *PRC* estimates of the total cost.[24] Postconstruction equipment costs are assumed to have been paid by the railroads, and information on the opening of sections of the roads provides a basis for assigning investment costs to specific years.

The Central Pacific paid the Contract and Finance Company $30,500 in cash and $6,080,000 in first mortgage bonds of the railroad for construction of the San Joaquin Valley Railroad. Evaluating the bonds at 74.5 makes the total cost $4,560,100, which is placed in years on the basis of the opening of various sections of the line.[25] Equipment cost per mile was assumed to be equal to that on the Central Pacific itself through 1869, i.e., $4,588,972/737.5 = $6,223.33 per mile.

Total construction cost of the Western Pacific is calculated from the record of bond transactions between the Central Pacific and the Contract and Finance Company involving the Western Pacific's government and first mortgage bonds.[26] These are valued by the average amount realized on all Central Pacific and Western Pacific bonds of these types.[27] Some city and county bonds were involved and are valued on the basis of the amount received for them. The cost per mile of construction is assumed to be constant, and the total placed in each year depends on the mileage built.[28]

The Contract and Finance Company also built the California and Oregon Railroad through 1872, under a contract calling for payment of $20,000 per mile in coin plus bonds of the California and Oregon.[29] Since no market existed for the bonds, it is assumed that $20,000 per mile was the actual cost. The timing of investment is estimated as above. The Central Pacific furnished the equipment on the California and Oregon. It is assumed, however, that $3,000 per mile of equipment investment occurred in 1886 since the equipment account of the Central Pacific is not reported after 1885. The Central Pacific itself constructed additional mileage on the California and Oregon in 1882, 1883, and 1884. Cost per mile is assumed to be constant, with total cost being that reported by *PRC*.[30] Mileage built per year was taken to be the increase in mileage shown in the annual volumes of *Poor's Manual* for 1879–1885. The Pacific Improvement Company, the fourth construction firm formed by the rail-

---

[24] *Ibid.*
[25] *Ibid.*, pp. 3531, 4749.
[26] *Ibid.*, pp. 3515, 1516, and 1519.
[27] *Public Aids*, II, p. 20.
[28] U.S. Congress, Senate, *PRC*, p. 4749, and Kneiss, *Bonanza Railroads*, pp. 45–46.
[29] U.S. Congress, Senate, *PRC*, pp. 77, 81, 3521, and 3531.
[30] *Ibid.*, pp. 81 and 3531.

A. Investment Expenditure

road owners, built 104 miles in 1886, with the total cost shown being the estimate found in *PRC*.[31]

The contractor who built the California Pacific Railroad could not be determined, nor could any record of the actual payments on construction be found. It is assumed that cost of construction and equipment was $20,000 per mile plus a fraction of the floating debt ($1.2 million) equal to the proportion of the total mileage built each year.[32]

The Western Development Company built the Northern Railway, with all equipment being furnished by the Central Pacific. With the exception of 1882, the annual costs shown are the amounts of the various contracts for construction as reported in *PRC*.[33] Construction on the Northern Railway in 1882 was an extension of the section of line built in 1878 through an area of similar geographic features, so construction cost per mile is assumed equal to that of 1878. The timing of construction was estimated from information in *Poor's Manual*.[34]

Phineas Banning, a stagecoach line owner who had no connection with the Central Pacific System, built most of the Los Angeles and San Pedro Railroad in 1868 and 1869.[35] The Pacific Improvement Company carried out the construction in 1882 on this railroad.

The Contract and Finance Company constructed 6.07 miles of the Los Angeles and San Diego Railroad in 1875, and the Western Development Company added 14 miles in that year and 7.53 miles in 1877.[36] A cost report of only $95,162.28 could be found by *PRC* for the more than 20 miles built by the Western Development Company.[37] This is clearly an understatement, and in the opinion of the accountants for the Pacific Railway Commission was due to clerical error. Construction cost is estimated here by taking the book value of construction as reported by the railroad to be total cost, with per mile cost constant.[38] By this procedure, estimated cost per mile was $40,343.85 for this railroad, with equipment being furnished by the Southern Pacific.

Construction of the 10 remaining railroads in the Central Pacific System as defined here was apparently completed in 1 year rather than a series of

---

[31] *Ibid*.

[32] *Poor's Manual*, 1886–1870, p. 482, and 1870–1871, p. 435, and Daggett, *Chapters in the History of the Southern Pacific*, p. 109.

[33] U.S. Congress, Senate, *PRC*, p. 3521.

[34] *Poor's Manual*, annual volumes of 1878, 1879, and 1883.

[35] Franklyn Hoyt, "The Los Angeles and San Pedro: First Railroad South of the Tehachapis", pp. 329–332. This article provided the information from which the timing of investment and estimated cost were taken.

[36] U.S. Congress, Senate, *PRC*, p. 3529.

[37] *Ibid*.

[38] *Poor's Manual*, 1885, p. 879.

years. The *PRC* estimate of cost is used for the Amador Branch Railroad.[39] All equipment for this railroad was furnished by the Central Pacific. Book value of construction and equipment provides the estimate of these costs for the Los Angeles and Independence Railroad and the Monterey Railroad.[40] While the San Francisco Bay Railroad paid the Contract and Finance Company $3,265,000 for its construction, $2,395,000 was paid in the capital stock of the company.[41] Cost of construction is taken to be the difference between the two sums cited. The *PRC* estimate of the cost of construction of the Oakland and Alameda local lines is used for the San Francisco, Oakland and Alameda Railroad, which was a consolidation of these lines.[42] Kneiss gives the cost of construction and equipment of the San Francisco and San José as $2,250,000, which is assumed to be a currency price, so the cost in gold is $1,641,138.[43] This railroad became the Northern Division of the Southern Pacific of California in 1870. The *PRC* estimate of construction cost for the San Pablo and Tulare is accepted.[44] Equipment was furnished by the Central Pacific, and the timing of investment was estimated as before.[45] Book values of construction and equipment are used as the estimate of these costs for the Santa Cruz Railroad, the Stockton and Copperopolis, and the Stockton and Visalia.[46]

The Union Pacific System

Because its major components received construction loans from the federal government, the Union Pacific System, like the Central Pacific System, came under scrutiny of the Pacific Railway Commission. The results of this investigation make it possible to estimate construction and equipment cost by individual railroad within the Union Pacific System. A list of the railroads included in the system, along with related information, is provided in Table A-3. Annual estimates of investment expenditures for the Union Pacific System are presented in Table A-4.

Construction and equipment cost estimates for the Union Pacific Railroad during that line's original construction period are based on appropriate division of the amounts paid on the Hoxie, Ames, and Davis contracts

---

[39] U.S. Congress, Senate, *PRC*, p. 3526.
[40] *Poor's Manual*, 1885, p. 879.
[41] U.S. Congress, Senate, *PRC*, p. 76.
[42] *Ibid.*, p. 81.
[43] Kneiss, *Bonanza Railroads*, p. 47.
[44] U.S. Congress, Senate, *PRC*, p. 3523.
[45] Daggett, *op. cit.*, p. 141, and *Poor's Manual*, 1878, pp. 917 and 925.
[46] *Poor's Manual*, 1887, p. 896, and 1878, pp. 917–918.

A. Investment Expenditure

during the years 1864–1869 and, for 1867, 1868, and 1869, the expenditures made directly by the railroad company.[47] The amount paid by the Central Pacific for the 47.5 miles it purchased from the Union Pacific in 1869 was deducted from the latter firm's expenditures in 1869. Annual investment expenditures for the years 1870–1886 are those reported by the accountants of *PRC* and based on their examination of the company's books.[48] Since the *PRC* investigation was primarily conducted in 1887, other sources of information are necessary to establish the investment cost of 1887–1889. Fortunately, the requisite information is available in the Union Pacific's accounts as reported in *Poor's Manual* for those years.[49]

Investment expenditure estimates for the numerous feeder lines and subsystems of the Union Pacific System are derived in three ways. First, from investment expenditure data through 1887, available in *PRC*. Second, from data provided in the company accounts in *Poor's Manual*. Finally, where no other information is available, the 75–10 rule is applied. The 75–10 rule is that in the absence of any information other than the book value of construction and equipment, the estimate of the real cost used in this study is an amount equal to 75% of the face value of the firm's mortgage bonds and 10% of its capital stock. This is based, first, on the observation that the average amount realized on all Central Pacific and Western Pacific bonds during their initial construction period was 75% of face value, and second, on the apparent practice of requiring no more than 10% of the face value of stock to be paid in for many speculative railroads.[50]

The Texas and Pacific System

Investment expenditure estimates for this system and the remaining systems are developed on a system basis, rather than by component railroads as in the case of the Central Pacific and Union Pacific Systems. The primary reason for this is that we do not have the voluminous information made available as a result of the Pacific Railway Commission investigation of those lines that received government loans. Fortunately, *Poor's Manual*

---

[47] U.S. Congress, Senate, *PRC*, pp. 4992–5005 and 5297, and Edwin L. Sabin, *Building the Pacific Railway* (Philadelphia: Lippincott, 1919), pp. 81, 94, 146, and 160, U.S. Congress, House, *Affairs of the Union Pacific Company*, 42nd Congress, 3rd Session, Report No. 78 (1577), pp. xiv and 373.

[48] U.S. Congress, Senate, *PRC*, pp. 5046–5048, 5068, and 5297.

[49] *Poor's Manual*, 1887, p. 840; 1888, p. 884; 1889, p. 868; and 1890, p. 932.

[50] U.S. Congress, Senate, *PRC*, p. 1350, for testimony supporting the 10% payment on face value of stock.

TABLE A-3

Total Current Dollar Value of Construction and Equipment Cost of Individual Railroads in the Union Pacific System (1864–1889) and Information on Their Entrance into the System

Railroad	Total construction and equipment cost (thousand current $)	Year of first construction	Year railroad entered system	Legal relationship to the system at entrance
Atchison, Colorado & Pacific	5,112	1876	1880	Consolidated with U.P.[a]
Atchison, Jewel County & Western	700	1879	1880	Consolidated with U.P.
Central Branch U.P.	556	1866	1880	Consolidated with U.P.
Cheyenne & Northern	2,731	1886	1886	Owned by U.P.
Colorado Central	6,165	1870	1876	Controlling interest by U.P.
Colorado Central of Wyoming	130	1877	1877	Leased to Colorado Central
Denver & Boulder Valley	191	1870	1880	Consolidated with U.P.
Denver & Middle Park	33	1884	1884	Owned by U.P.
Denver, Marshall & Boulder Valley	501	1881	1881	Controlling interest by U.P.
Denver Pacific	957	1868	1880	Consolidated with U.P.
Denver, South Park & Pacific	6,630	1873	1880	Controlling interest by U.P.
Echo & Park City	601	1873	1877	Owned by U.P.
Georgetown, Breckenridge & Leadville	431	1881	1881	Owned by U.P.
Golden, Boulder & Caribou	88	1877	1880	Consolidated with U.P.
Greeley, Salt Lake & Pacific	1,486	1881	1881	Owned by U.P.
Hastings & Grand Island	236	1879	1879	Owned by U.P.
Junction City & Fort Kearney	1,835	1871[b]	1880	Consolidated with U.P.
Kansas Central	622	1871[b]	1879	Owned by U.P.
Kansas City & Omaha	2,187	1886	1886	Controlling interest by U.P.
Kansas Pacific	6,503	1865	1880	Consolidated with U.P.
Laramie, North Park & Pacific	58	1880	1885	Controlling interest by U.P.
Lawrence & Emporia	66	1879	1880	Owned by U.P.
Leavenworth, Topeka & Southwestern	504	1879[b]	1883	Jointly owned with A.T. & S.F.
Lincoln & Colorado[c]	1,305	1886	1886	Controlling interest by U.P.

Manhattan, Alma & Burlingame	314	1872[b]	Jointly owned with A.T. & S.F.
Manhattan & Blue Valley	716	1881	Controlling interest by U.P.
Marysville & Blue Valley	373	1879	Controlling interest by U.P.
Montana	251	1883	Owned by U.P.
Nevada Central	413	1879	Controlling interest by U.P.
Oakley & Colby[c]	300	1886	Controlling interest by U.P.
Omaha & Republican Valley	2,761	N.A.	N.A.[d]
Omaha & Republican Valley	3,429	1876	Controlling interest by U.P.
Omaha, Niobrara & Black Hills	1,279	1879	Controlling interest by U.P.
Oregon Short Line	14,343	1881	Owned by U.P.
St. Joseph & Western	2,343	1867	Consolidated with U.P.
Salina & Southwestern	741	1879	Owned by U.P.
Salina, Lincoln & Western	1,473	1885	Owned by U.P.
Salt Lake & Western	920	1881	Owned by U.P.
Solomon Railroad	505	1877	Consolidated with U.P.
South Park & Leadville Short Line	95	1882	Owned by U.P.
Union Pacific	71,716	1864	N.A.
Utah & Nevada	372	1875	Owned by U.P.
Utah & Northern	5,444	1872	Owned by U.P.
Utah Central	710	1869	Controlling interest by U.P.
Utah Eastern	386	1880	Controlling interest by Echo & Park City
Utah Southern	1,537	1871	Controlling interest by U.P.
Utah Southern Extension	1,544	1879	Controlling interest by U.P.

[a] Abbreviations: U.P. for Union Pacific; A.T. & S.F. for Atchison, Topeka & Santa Fe; N.A. for not applicable.
[b] Year of charter or incorporation; first year of construction not available.
[c] Data are only speculation; insufficient information.
[d] A consolidation of four roads: Omaha & Republican Valley; Omaha, Niobrara & Black Hills; Manhattan and Blue Valley; Marysville & Blue Valley.

TABLE A-4

Annual Investment Expenditures by the Union Pacific System

Year	Investment expenditures	
	(thousand current $)	(thousand 1869 $)
1864	180	155
1865	1,584	1,384
1866	9,656	8,714
1867	10,320	9,791
1868	24,418	23,775
1869	9,892	9,892
1870	3,121	3,396
1871	178	200
1872	1,135	1,235
1873	123	136
1874	640	740
1875	500	603
1876	4,326	5,519
1877	2,382	3,148
1878	854	1,215
1879	2,986	5,745
1880	28,604	38,720
1881	10,133	13,232
1882	9,776	12,476
1883	8,741	11,551
1884	2,438	3,426
1885	1,469	2,118
1886	6,761	9,875
1887	7,206	10,388
1888	4,016	5,715
1889	154	222

and other sources fill the data gap adequately when we operate on a system basis. The backbone of the remaining investment expenditure estimates (where direct information is not available) is the estimate of funds available for investment and appropriate variations of the 75–10 rule.[51] Table A-5 lists the component railroads of the Texas and Pacific System and related information. Annual investment expenditure estimates for the Texas and Pacific System are presented in Table A-6.

[51] Available information allows variation of the proportion of face value received for bonds and stock from the 75–10 used for the Union Pacific.

A. Investment Expenditure

TABLE A-5

Railroads in the Texas and Pacific System and Information on Their Entrance into the System

Railroad	Year of first construction	Year railroad entered system	Legal relationship to the system at entrance
Avoyelles	1898	1900	Owned by T. & P.[a]
Denison & Pacific Suburban	1895	1895	Owned by T. & P.
Memphis, El Paso & Pacific	1869	1873	Owned by T. & P.
New Orleans Pacific	1871	1881	Consolidated with T. & P.
Southern Pacific	1868	1872	Owned by T. & P.
Texas and Pacific	1873	N.A.	N.A.

[a] Abbreviations: T. & P. for Texas and Pacific; N.A. for not applicable.

The Atchison, Topeka and Santa Fe System

Development of estimates for the Santa Fe system have been greatly aided by the large amount of information available in the books written by James Marshall and L. L. Waters.[52] Table A-7 presents the railroads included in the system and related information. Annual investment expenditure estimates for the system are presented in Table A-8. Variations of the 75–10 rule, book value when all else fails, and reports of investment expenditure in company accounts in *Poor's Manual* provide the basis for the investment expenditure estimates.

The Northern Pacific System

In the case of the Northern Pacific System, we have for the first time a situation for which *Poor's Manual* is the only substantial source of information. It is fortunate, therefore, that the Northern Pacific's reports are quite complete in matters related to investment cost, especially in the early construction years. The available data are quite adequate for application of variations of the 75–10 rule where specific information on investment expenditures is insufficient. Table A-9 lists the component roads of the system and related information, while Table A-10 presents the annual investment expenditure estimates for the Northern Pacific System. The Northern Pacific data are for a fiscal year ending June 30.

[52] James Marshall, *Santa Fe: The Railroad That Built an Empire*, and L. L. Waters, *Steel Rails to Santa Fe*.

TABLE A-6

Annual Investment Expenditures by the Texas and Pacific System

	Investment expenditures	
Year	(thousand current $)	(thousand 1869 $)
1872	950	1,034
1873	4,272	4,742
1874	160	185
1875	2,473	2,984
1876	3,677	4,691
1877	—	—
1878	417	593
1879	174	251
1880	5,220	7,066
1881	27,195	35,513
1882	—	—
1883	2,732	3,610
1884	249	350
1885	—	—
1886	—	—
1887	3,216	4,636
1888	1,057	1,504
1889	247	356
1890	117	166
1891	81	117
1892	370	540
1893	129	191
1894	32	50
1895	314	484
1896	213	333
1897	257	396
1898	162	246
1899	819	1,181
1900	639	898

The Great Northern System

The component railroads of the Great Northern System are listed in Table A-11 along with year of initial construction, year the railroad entered the system, and legal relationship to the system at entrance. The major component and forerunner of the Great Northern Railway was the St. Paul, Minneapolis and Manitoba Railroad. The latter road got its start by purchasing the St. Paul and Pacific Railroad at a judicial sale in 1879.

A. Investment Expenditure

TABLE A-7

Railroads in the Atchison, Topeka and Santa Fe System and Information on Their Entrance into the System

Railroad	Year of first construction	Year railroad entered system	Legal relationship to the system at entrance
Atchison, Topeka & Santa Fe	1869	N.A.	N.A.[a]
Atchison, Topeka & Santa Fe in Chicago	1888	1888	Controlling interest by A.T. & S.F.
Atlantic & Pacific	1880	1880	Controlling interest by A.T. & S.F.
California Central	1887	1887	Controlling interest by A.T. & S.F.
Chicago, Kansas & Western	1886	1887	Controlling interest by A.T. & S.F.
Chicago, Santa Fe & California	1886	1887	Controlling interest by A.T. & S.F.
Cowley, Sumner & Fort Smith	1879	1879	Operated under lease
Denver & Santa Fe	1887	1887	Operated under lease
Elk & Chatauqua	1879	1879	Operated under lease
Florence, El Dorado & Walnut Valley	1877	1877	Operated under lease
Gulf, Colorado & Santa Fe	1873[b]	1886	Controlling interest by A.T. & S.F.
Kansas City, Emporia & Southern	1879	1879	Operated under lease
Kansas City, Lawrence & So. Kansas	1879[b]	1880	Owned by A.T. & S.F.
Kansas City, Topeka & Western	1875	1875	Operated under lease
Kansas Southern	1883	1884	Controlling interest by A.T. & S.F.
Leavenworth, Northern & Southern	1886	1887	Operated under lease
Manhattan, Alma & Burlingame	1872[b]	1880	Jointly owned with U.P.
Marion & McPherson	1879	1879	Operated under lease
New Mexican	1882	1882	Operated under lease
New Mexico & Southern Pacific	1878	1879	Operated under lease
Pleasant Hill & DeSoto	1871[b]	1877	Operated under lease
Pueblo & Arkansas Valley	1875	1875	Operated under lease
Rio Grande & El Paso	1881	1881	Operated under lease
Rio Grande, Mexico & Pacific	1880	1881	Operated under lease
St. Joseph & Sante Fe	1887	1888	Controlling interest by A.T. & S.F.
St. Louis, Kansas City & Colorado	1884[b]	1887	Controlling interest by A.T. & S.F.
Southern Kansas & Panhandle	1887	1887	Controlling interest by A.T. & S.F.
Southern Kansas	1871	1880	Controlling interest by A.T. & S.F.
Southern Kansas of Texas	1887	1887	Controlling interest by A.T. & S.F.
Wichita & Western	1883	1884	Jointly owned

[a] Abbreviations: A.T. & S.F. for Atchison, Topeka & Santa Fe; U.P. for Union Pacific; N.A. for not applicable.

[b] Year of charter or incorporation; first year of construction not available.

Included in the sale were the 30-mile Red River and Manitoba and the 11-mile Red River Valley Railroad. At the time of the sale the length of the St. Paul and Pacific was 520 miles, with a large part of that mileage having recently been constructed.

TABLE A-8

Annual Investment Expenditures by the Atchison, Topeka and Santa Fe System

	Investment expenditures	
Year	(thousand current $)	(thousand 1869 $)
1869	431	431
1870	1,664	1,811
1871	755	846
1872	7,457	8,115
1873	174	193
1874	1,972	3,387
1875	957	1,030
1876	215	274
1877	1,578	2,085
1878	1,149	1,635
1879	14,121	20,356
1880	16,587	22,453
1881	11,763	15,361
1882	6,883	8,782
1883	2,748	3,631
1884	6,563	9,221
1885	3,929	5,664
1886	16,118	23,541
1887	51,781	74,646
1888	14,856	21,141
1889	930	1,341
1890	3,637	5,176
1891	1,270	1,831
1892	5,342	7,802
1893	1,542	2,282
1894	1,008	1,576
1895	870	1,341
1896	1,894	2,961
1897	19,232	29,649
1898	4,800	7,299
1899	8,187	11,802
1900	7,434	10,445

The price paid for the St. Paul and Pacific and the two subsidiary lines is not reported. It is assumed to be the value of the outstanding first mortgage of the St. Paul, Minneapolis and Manitoba in 1879, plus the outstanding bonds of the St. Paul and Pacific held by the former company

A. Investment Expenditure

TABLE A-9

Railroads in the Northern Pacific System and Information on Their Entrance into the System

Railroad	Year of first construction[a]	Year railroad entered system[a]	Legal relationship to the system at entrance
Central Washington	1888	1889	Operated under lease
Clealum	1886	1886	Controlling interest by N.P.[b]
Clearwater Shortline	1899	1900	Owned by N.P.
Coeur d'Alene & Navigation	1887	1888	Operated under lease
Duluth & Manitoba	1886	1887	Operated under lease
Duluth, Crookston & Northern	1890	1890	Owned by N.P.
Fargo & Southwestern	1882	1883	Operated under lease
Green River & Northern	1891	1891	Owned by N.P.
Helena & Jefferson County	1883	1884	Operated under lease
Helena & Red Mountain	1886	1887	Operated under lease
James River Valley	1885	1886	Operated under lease
Jamestown & Northern	1882	1883	Operated under lease
Jamestown & Northern Extension	1889	1890	Owned by N.P.
Little Falls & Dakota	1882	1882	Operated under lease
Montana	1884	1899	Owned by N.P.
Montana Union	1886[c]	1899	Jointly owned with U.P.
Northern Pacific	1870	N.A.	N.A.
Northern Pacific & Cascade	1885	1886	Operated under lease
Northern Pacific & Manitoba	1888	1889	Controlling interest by N.P.
Northern Pacific & Montana	1888	1888	Operated under lease
Northern Pacific & Puget Sound Shore	1883	1890	Operated under lease
Northern Pacific, Fergus & Black Hills	1882	1882	Operated under lease
Northern Pacific, LaMoure & Missouri River	1887	1887	Operated under lease
Portage & Northwestern	1899	1900	Owned by N.P.
Rocky Fork & Cooke City	1890	1890	Owned by N.P.
Rocky Mountain R.R. of Montana	1883	1883	Operated under lease
St. Paul & Northern Pacific	1874[c]	1878	Operated under lease
Seattle & Northern	1890	1890	Trackage rights
Seattle Lake Shore & Eastern	N.A.	1891	Controlling interest by N.P.
Southeastern Dakota	1887	1888	Operated under lease
Sanborn, Cooperstown & Turtle Mtn.	1882	1883	Operated under lease
Spokane & Palouse	1886	1887	Operated under lease
Spokane Falls & Idaho	1886	1887	Operated under lease
Tacoma, Orting & Southeastern	1889	1889	Operated under lease
United R.R. of Washington	n.a.	1891	Owned by N.P.
Washington & Columbia River	1892[c]	1898	Controlling interest by N.P.

[a] Fiscal years
[b] Abbreviations: N.P. for Northern Pacific; U.P. for Union Pacific; N.A. for not applicable; n.a. for not available.
[c] Year of charter or incorporation; first year of construction not available.

TABLE A-10

Annual Investment Expenditures by the Northern Pacific System

Year	Investment expenditures (thousand current $)	(thousand 1869 $)
1870	3,358	3,654
1871	5,978	6,703
1872	4,945	5,381
1873	5,277	5,857
1874	—	—
1875	—	—
1876	—	—
1877	1,144	1,512
1878	689	981
1879	1,133	1,633
1880	3,408	4,613
1881	7,024	9,172
1882	12,525	15,980
1883	24,758	32,716
1884	7,855	11,037
1885	2,276	3,281
1886	4,675	6,828
1887	6,382	9,200
1888	6,056	8,618
1889	10,433	15,040
1890	4,455	6,311
1891	8,274	11,928
1892	4,781	6,983
1893	1,676	2,480
1894	—	—
1895	—	—
1896	—	—
1897	1,051	1,620
1898	1,344	2,044
1899	3,622	5,221
1900	4,091	5,748

after purchase. These amounts are, respectively, $7,839,000 and $486,000, for a total of $8,325,000 or only $14,000 per mile. While the St. Paul, Minneapolis and Manitoba had an authorized second mortgage of $8 million dollars and capital stock of $15 million in 1879, there is no indication that any funds were received from these securities at the time. Instead, it appears that these securities were used to finance later invest-

A. Investment Expenditure

TABLE A-11

Railroads in the Great Northern System and Information on Their Entrance into the System

Railroad	Year of first construction[a]	Year railroad entered system[a]	Legal relationship to the system at entrance
Duluth, Mississippi River & Northern	1892	1899	Owned by E.R.M.[b]
Duluth, Superior & Western	1896	1898	Owned by E.R.M.
Duluth Terminal	1888	1888	Operated under lease by E.R.M.
Duluth, Watertown & Pacific	1888	1888	Owned by S.P., M. & M.
Eastern Ry. of Minnesota	1888	1888	Operated under lease
Minneapolis Union	1883	1883	Owned by S.P., M. & M.
Minneapolis Western	1894	1896	Owned by G.N.
Montana Central	1888	1888	Operated under lease
Park Rapids & Leech Lake	1898	1899	Operated under lease
Red River & Manitoba	1877	1879	Owned by S.P., M. & M.
Red River Valley	1879	1879	Owned by S.P., M. & M.
St. Paul, Minneapolis & Manitoba	1858	N.A.	N.A.
Seattle & Montana	1898	1898	Operated under lease
Superior Belt Line	n.a.	1900	Owned by E.R.M.
Willmar & Sioux Falls	1886	1888	Owned by S.P., M. & M.

[a] Fiscal years.
[b] Abbreviations: E.R.M. for Eastern Railway of Minnesota; S.P., M. & M. for St. Paul, Minneapolis & Manitoba; G.N. for Great Northern; N.A. for not applicable; n.a. for not available.

ment. The sum of $23 million is approximately equal to the difference between the increment in cost of road and equipment and the increment in value of bonds and stocks outstanding for the St. Paul, Minneapolis and Manitoba over the period 1880–1900.

Table A-12 presents the estimate of annual investment cost for the Great Northern System. Data for the Great Northern are on a fiscal year basis, with the year end being June 30.

The estimate of investment expenditure for the Great Northern System is composed of two basic parts, the major portion being the estimated cost for the St. Paul, Minneapolis and Manitoba and the smaller part made up of the cost of several branch roads built between 1887 and 1900. For the St. Paul, Minneapolis and Manitoba the investment cost estimate was derived in a relatively simple and straightforward manner. The sum of the increment to the construction and equipment account for the years 1880 through 1900, plus reported cost of construction of new lines, new equipment purchases, and expenditures on additions and improvements by the Great Northern for the St. Paul, Minneapolis and Manitoba, is taken as the estimate of construction and eqiipment cost for the latter road in those

TABLE A-12

Annual Investment Expenditures by
the Great Northern System

Year	Investment expenditures	
	(thousand current $)	(thousand 1869 $)
1879	8,325	12,001
1880	194	263
1881	3,440	4,492
1882	4,216	5,379
1883	8,618	11,388
1884	5,199	7,305
1885	1,268	1,828
1886	1,501	2,192
1887	16,898	24,360
1888	21,792	31,012
1889	6,517	9,395
1890	746	1,062
1891	12,298	17,728
1892	7,930	11,582
1893	20,935	30,984
1894	1,238	1,935
1895	508	783
1896	631	986
1897	1,353	2,086
1898	7,513	11,424
1899	4,040	5,824
1900	3,025	4,250

years.[53] This is crosschecked with the increments in the firm's various mortgages and outstanding capital stock. The sum of new bond and stock issues during 1880–1900 is $23.6 million less than estimated investments. However, another $23 million in bonds and stocks was initially on the books in 1879, so the total value of bonds and stocks issued was approximately equal to total investment. This procedure may somewhat overstate the investment expenditure, but the average estimated cost per mile for the 3,876 miles of the St. Paul, Minneapolis and Manitoba is a moderate $27,100 over the entire period. This average included equipment replacement as well as original construction and equipment.

Investment cost was estimated for most of the subsidiary railroads in the Great Northern System on the basis of the face value of their first

[53] *Poor's Manual*, annual volumes 1881–1901.

A. *Investment Expenditure* 173

mortgages. While this may somewhat overstate the cost, it should be noted that the value of outstanding capital stock for these firms was completely discounted by this procedure.[54]

The Canadian Pacific System

The Dominion government built 707 miles of railroad and gave it to the Canadian Pacific Company. The reported average cost per mile of this section of the road is $53,351.[55] Adopting the adjustments made by Peter J. George for government expenditures during 1871–1880, the average cost per mile is $49,157.[56] Writers on the history of the Canadian Pacific (and apparently many contemporaries) have suggested that the government's construction of the railroad was inefficient and much more expensive than necessary.[57] *Poor's Manual* reports that as of June 30, 1879 a total of 273 miles of the government-built road was in operation with an additional 433 miles under construction. The Dominion government at that time had spent $11,538,867 and contracted for $9,626,739 more.[58] With George's adjustments, accumulated real government expenditures through 1880 total $14.128 million, which is entered into the system investment stream in 1880. Fiscal year government expenditures are converted to a calendar year basis on the assumption of an equal monthly flow. The reported annual government expenditures over the period 1881–1886 are entered in the investment stream for those years. While the government expenditures were undoubtedly excessive (see footnote 57), they do not represent the resource cost of the railroad as actually built.

A list of railroads in the Canadian Pacific System and information on their entrance into the system is provided by Table A-13. Annual estimated cost of construction and equipment expenditures for the Canadian Pacific are shown in Table A-14.

[54] This, of course, is simply a variation of the 75–10 rule with the proportion being 100–0.

[55] For the annual government expenditures during 1871–1896, see Government of Canada, *Sessional Papers*, XXXI (1897), 10, II, 39.

[56] Peter J. George, "Rates of Return for Railway Investment and Implications for Government Subsidization of the Canadian Pacific Railway: Some Preliminary Results", pp. 745–746.

[57] Cf. John Murray Gibbon, *The Romantic History of the Canadian Pacific*, p. 207, where total investment by the government is put at $37,785,000—although actual construction is supposed to have been only $28 million. The other $9.8 million was spent on surveys, administration, etc. A considerable expense for surveys was apparently wasted (see Gibbon, p. 207). William Van Horne, President and driving force behind the construction of the Canadian Pacific, testified to the Senate Committee on Interstate Commerce, May 9, 1889, to the effect that the location of the road was bad and that it could have been built for $12–15 million. The high figure is about two-thirds of the cost per mile of the railroad built by Van Horne, so it seems very likely that his values are considerably understated.

[58] *Poor's Manual*, 1880, p. 1011.

TABLE A-13

Railroads in the Canadian Pacific System and Information on Their Entrance into the System

Railroad	Year of first construction	Year railroad entered system	Legal relationship to the system at entrance
Alberta Ry. & Coal Co.	1890	1893	Operated under lease
Atlantic & Northwest	1884	1884	Operated under lease
British Columbia Southern	1897	1897	Operated under lease
Canadian Pacific	1876	N.A.	N.A.[a]
Cap de la Magdaleine	1896	1896	Operated under lease
Columbia & Kootenay	1890	1890	Operated under lease
Columbia & Western	1896	1898	Operated under lease
Great Northwest Central	1886[b]	1900	Operated under lease
Guelph Junction	1887	1888	Operated under lease
Lake Temiscaminque Colonization	1886	1891	Operated under lease
Manitoba & Northwestern	1883	1900	Operated under lease
Manitoba & Southwestern Colonization	1882	1883	Operated under lease
Montreal & Lake Maskinonge	1888	1892	Operated under lease
Montreal & Ottawa	1890	1892	Operated under lease
Montreal & Western	1892	1892	Operated under lease
Nakusp & Slocan	1894	1893	Operated under lease
New Brunswick	1870[b]	1890	Operated under lease
North Shore	n.a.	1885	Operated under lease
Ontario & Quebec	1883	1884	Operated under lease
St. Lawrence & Ottawa	1850	1882	Operated under lease
St. Stephen & Milltown	1895	1895	Operated under lease
Shuswap & Okanagon	1886[b]	1893	Operated under lease
Tobique Valley	1893	1894	Operated under lease
Toronto, Hamilton & Buffalo	1896	1896	Operated under lease

[a] Abbreviations: N.A. for not applicable; n.a. for not available.

[b] Year of charter or incorporation; first year of construction not available.

Investment expenditures by the Canadian Pacific Railroad during the years 1881–1886 are derived from the company reports to the Dominion government.[59] Following George, the cost of acquisition of the Canada Central Railway and the Quebec, Montreal, Ottawa and Occidental Rail-

[59] These were published in the *Sessional Papers* annually from 1883 to 1887. My attention was directed to these reports by Peter J. George, in "Rates of Return for Railway Investment and Implications for Government Subsidization of the Canadian Pacific Railway: Some Preliminary Results". The expenditures reported corresponded very closely with my previous estimates on the basis of cash available derived from balance sheet information in *Poor's Manual* and other sources.

TABLE A-14

Annual Investment Expenditures in the Canadian Pacific System

	Investment expenditures			
	(thousand current $)		(thousand 1900 $)	
Year	Private[a]	Total[b]	Private[a]	Total[b]
1881	10,167	29,849[c]	8,833	26,153[d]
1882	21,971	25,516	18,264	21,211
1883	21,964	26,289	19,199	22,979
1884	38,844	42,332	35,153	38,310
1885	24,707	26,617	24,462	26,353
1886	12,734	13,349	13,083	13,719
1887	8,501	8,755	8,294	8,541
1888	8,120	8,189	7,675	7,741
1889	8,366	8,430	7,990	8,051
1890	14,110	14,149	13,646	13,684
1891	6,672	6,724	6,372	6,421
1892	7,513	7,753	7,785	8,034
1893	6,086	6,366	6,135	6,417
1894	2,321	2,419	2,520	2,626
1895	955	1,012	1,082	1,147
1896	1,901	1,934	2,288	2,327
1897	5,686	5,686	6,641	6,641
1898	14,980	14,980	16,443	16,443
1899	7,086	7,086	7,711	7,711
1900	11,184	11,184	11,184	11,184

[a] Canadian Pacific Company expenditures.
[b] Includes Dominion government and Canadian Pacific Company expenditures.
[c] Includes expenditures by the Dominion government of 16.008 million prior to 1881.
[d] Includes expenditures by the Dominion government of 14.128 million prior to 1881.

way during fiscal year 1881–1882 is estimated to have been $10,913,904.[60] Investment cost of the several leased roads included in the Canadian Pacific System was estimated in two ways. First, on the basis of funded debt, government subsidies, and book value of cost of road; and second, by capitalizing lease rentals at 5%.[61] The two methods produce quite similar results, with the estimates of the second being adopted here. The annual estimates of Canadian Pacific Company investment expenditures during the period 1887–1900 are the expenditures reported in the firm's accounts for construction, improvements, rolling stock, telegraph, lake

[60] George, *op. cit.*, p. 748.
[61] The latter is the technique used by Peter George.

TABLE A-15

Estimated and Book Value Cost per Mile by System and Mileage

System	Mileage	Estimated cost per mile (thousand $)	Book value cost per mile[a] (thousand $)
Canadian Pacific	7,733	$34.8	$43.0[b]
Great Northern	5,278	26.3	41.0
Northern Pacific	4,862	26.9	63.4
Santa Fe	7,426	28.9	54.8
Texas and Pacific	1,480	36.9	55.2
Union Pacific	6,382	25.8	47.6
Central Pacific	4,284	30.4	96.2

[a] Based on terminal year book value of railroad and equipment.
[b] Includes adjusted government expenditures.

and ferry steamers, etc.[62] To these must be added the expenditures in 1890–1893 on the China and Japan steamships, whose revenues cannot be separated from the railroad revenues of the firm.[63]

Summary

Table A-15 presents the average estimated cost and book value cost per mile for the seven systems. In terms of estimated cost there is a considerable spread between the lowest and highest system in terms of cost per mile. However, four of the systems lie within little more than a 10% per mile cost differential and, based on the private rate of return, these include one of the most successful systems (the Union Pacific) and one of the least successful (the Santa Fe). The very substantial terrain difficulties encountered on parts of the Canadian Pacific and Central Pacific Systems probably account for their relatively higher per mile cost. At the same time, the 10% of the line (approximately) built by the government seems to have done at least as much to raise the Canadian Pacific figure. It is noteworthy that on the basis of the unaided private rate of return, the Central Pacific is the second most successful system and the Canadian Pacific the second least successful. The Texas and Pacific's high figure is due largely to the necessity of rebuilding considerable mileage after the Louisiana floods in 1884 and to the large terminal facilities for the relatively short railroad. If

---

[62] *Poor's Manual*, annual volumes 1888–1901.
[63] George does not recognize this and excludes the steamship expenditures from the investment stream.

A. Investment Expenditure

only costs directly assignable to mileage are included, the Texas and Pacific average per mile cost is $30,200.

The relationship between book value cost per mile and estimated cost per mile in Table A-15 illustrates the very considerable extent of water in the book values. Even for the Canadian Pacific, whose operations and financing were closely controlled by the Dominion government, book value is 22% higher than estimated cost. Book value is more than 100% higher than the estimated real resource cost for the Northern Pacific System, and more than 200% greater for the Central Pacific System. The other roads show smaller but still very substantial excesses of book value over estimated cost. Since these railroads were heavily financed by bond sales, it is easy to see why they often encountered financial difficulties.

Appendix B

Capital Earnings

An estimate of capital earnings for each of the systems studied is discussed and presented in this appendix. Capital earnings are computed by subtraction of the sum of all noncapital costs from the firm's gross revenues. Subsidies such as earnings from land grants and cash receipts from governments are not included in capital earnings. The primary problem in preparing the estimates of capital earnings is to ensure that the earnings of all capital formed as a result of the investment expenditures discussed in Appendix A are properly included in each railroad's net receipts stream. The source of data for calculating capital earnings is the published income statements of the systems.

The Central Pacific System

Annual estimated capital earnings for the Central Pacific System are shown in Table B-1. The basic data sources for these estimates are the firm's income statements in the annual volumes of *Poor's Manual* and the accountants' reports in *PRC*. The latter source covers the years 1864–1886, but was primarily used for the years 1864–1884, when all railroads in the system, except the Northern Division of the Southern Pacific of California, were leased to the Central Pacific Railroad or its lessors. This resulted in their combined operations being reported in the income statement of the Central Pacific. Data for 1885–1889 are from the income statements for the Pacific System of the Southern Pacific Company. Rail-

B. Capital Earnings

TABLE B-1

Annual Capital Earnings of the Central Pacific System

Year	Gross revenue (thousand current $)	Noncapital expenses (thousand current $)	Capital earnings[a] (thousand current $)	(thousand 1869 $)
1864	113	68	45	39
1865	396	144	252	220
1866	860	235	625	564
1867	1,422	399	1,023	971
1868	1,962	803	1,159	1,128
1869	5,968	3,292	2,675	2,675
1870	7,487	5,092	2,395	2,606
1871	9,074	5,526	3,548	3,986
1872	12,292	6,504	5,787	6,298
1873	13,067	5,938	7,130	7,914
1874	14,034	6,578	7,456	8,621
1875	16,104	7,938	8,166	9,852
1876	17,232	9,621	7,611	9,711
1877	17,622	9,689	7,932	10,482
1878	18,523	10,046	8,477	12,063
1879	18,081	9,808	8,273	11,926
1880	21,506	11,058	10,449	14,144
1881	25,226	11,357	13,870	18,112
1882	26,916	13,728	13,188	16,826
1883	26,004	13,514	12,489	16,503
1884	23,583	14,720	8,863	12,453
1885	20,692	10,066	10,627	15,520
1886	23,635	12,897	10,739[b]	15,685
1887	26,951	16,991	9,960[c]	14,358
1888	32,978	21,662	11,315[d]	16,102
1889	31,372	21,216	10,157	14,642

[a] Gross revenue minus noncapital costs may not equal capital earnings because of rounding.

[b] Taxes and other expenses assumed equal to 1885.

[c] Operating expenses for the Pacific System assumed to be the same proportion of the total for the Southern Pacific Company as in 1888.

[d] Taxes for the Pacific System assumed to be the same proportion of the total for the Southern Pacific Company as in 1887.

roads acquired from 1885 on are excluded, although the rental of the Colorado Division (Mojave to Needles, California) of the Southern Pacific of California to the Atlantic and Pacific Railroad is included.

A major problem in computing the Central Pacific System's capital earnings is the estimation of the capital earnings for the Northern Division of the Southern Pacific in order not to double-count the capital earnings of the Southern Division, which are already included in the Central Pacific figures. While the Northern Division was operated independently from 1870 to 1884, its revenues and operating expenses are only shown separately from 1879 to 1884.[1] Since the Southern Pacific's earnings are reported on a June 30 fiscal basis through 1877 (while the Central Pacific is on a calendar year), it is also necessary to convert these earnings to a calendar year basis. This is done throughout this study on the assumption of an equal monthly flow.

Construction began on the Southern Division of the Southern Pacific in 1872. Earnings and operating expenses reported for the Southern Pacific in 1870–1871 are assumed to be those of the Northern Division. To calculate earnings and operating expenses of the Northern Division for the years 1872–1873, 1873–1874, 1874–1875, 1875–1876, 1876–1877, and the last half of 1877, it is necessary to remove the Southern Division rental earnings and operating expenses (which are included in the earnings and operating expenses of the Central Pacific for the same period) from the earnings and operating expenses of the Southern Pacific. Rental receipts and operating expenses attributable to the Southern Division during the year in question are estimated on the basis of the rental agreement between the Central Pacific and the Southern Pacific for the Southern Division, and the average number of miles operated by the latter. Under the lease, the Central Pacific paid the Southern Pacific rental of $500 per mile per month and charged $250 per mile per month for operating expenses.[2] Subtraction of the estimated rental and operating expenses of the Southern Division from the gross revenues and operating expenses of the Southern Pacific yields the estimate of revenue and operating expenses of the Northern Division.

With the exception of mail earnings for 1864–1869, all data through 1869 in *Poor's Manual* are in terms of currency, while data for 1871–1878 are partly in gold and partly in currency. Since construction and equipment costs for the years 1863–1878 are assumed to be in gold (while gold was at a premium), all revenue and expense figures must also be in terms of gold. Kindahl's series on the currency price of a gold dollar are used for this adjustment, which is included in the data shown in Table B-1.[3]

One additional adjustment was necessary to arrive at the system figure in Table B-1. From 1877 through 1884, the rental of leased lines was included in the operating expenses contained in the income statements of

---

[1] *Poor's Manual*, 1885, p. 879.

[2] Daggett, *Chapters in the History of the Southern Pacific*, p. 144. Operated mileage for the Southern Division was obtained from information in annual volumes of *Poor's Manual*.

[3] Kindahl, "Economic Factors in Specie Resumption", p. 36.

B. Capital Earnings

the Central Pacific. Since these rentals were a part of the capital earnings of the system rather than an expense, it was necessary to deduct them from the Central Pacific's operating expenses during 1877–1884. Rentals for 1877 and 1878 were shown separately in the Central Pacific's income statements, while those paid to the various leased lines for the years 1879–1884 are obtained from the lessors' income statements.[4]

The Union Pacific System

The Union Pacific System's estimated capital earnings by year for the period 1866–1889 are listed in Table B-2. Data for the Union Pacific are on a calendar year basis.

Estimation of the Union Pacific System's capital earnings is primarily a matter of straightforward data collection from *PRC* and *Poor's Manual*. The worst problem is that while part of the railroad was operated in 1866, no revenue and expense figures are available for that year. Capital earnings for 1866 are estimated as the product of capital earnings per average operated mile in 1867 and average operated mileage in 1866.

Two branch lines were owned jointly with the Santa Fe. These were the Leavenworth, Topeka and South Western and the Manhattan, Alma and Burlingame. One-half of the capital earnings of these branch railroads for the appropriate years is included in the Union Pacific totals.

One railroad, the South Park and Leadville Short Line, was not operated during the period considered. No earnings for this railroad are included in the system totals.

The Texas and Pacific System

The major difficulty in preparing the capital earnings estimates for the Texas and Pacific is the necessity to convert fiscal year data to a calendar year basis. For 1871–1881 the raw data are reported by fiscal years, while the remaining 19 years of the period included are reported by calendar years. Since the basic data for the longer and, in value terms, more important period are already on a calendar year basis, the calendar year basis is used for this system. Annual capital earnings are given in Table B-3 for the Texas and Pacific System.

Revenue and expenses for the Texas and Pacific are first reported for a fiscal year ending April 3, 1873. The second report that is used here is for the fiscal year to April 30, 1873. The next report is for the fiscal year

---

[4] *Poor's Manual*, annual volumes 1878–1885.

TABLE B-2

Annual Capital Earnings of the Union Pacific System

Year	Gross revenue[b] (thousand current $)	Noncapital expenses[c] (thousand current $)	Capital earnings[a] (thousand current $)	(thousand 1869 $)
1866	1,144	459	685	618
1867	3,499	1,404	2,095	1,918
1868	6,109	4,169	1,940	1,889
1869	8,182	6,161	2,021	2,021
1870	7,625	4,677	2,948	3,208
1871	7,522	3,601	3,921	4,396
1872	8,893	4,801	4,092	4,453
1873	10,266	4,975	5,291	5,873
1874	10,560	4,652	5,908	6,831
1875	11,994	4,982	7,012	8,460
1876	12,887	5,268	7,619	9,721
1877	12,473	5,273	7,200	9,514
1888	13,121	5,377	7,745	11,022
1889	13,201	5,476	7,726	11,138
1890	26,135	12,780	13,335	18,078
1891	32,134	17,133	15,000	19,588
1892	32,865	16,709	16,156	20,613
1893	32,398	17,351	15,047	19,883
1894	28,324	16,808	11,515	16,179
1895	28,149	17,448	10,701	15,426
1896	29,094	18,650	10,444	15,254
1897	30,897	18,957	11,941	17,214
1888	32,881	21,726	11,156	15,876
1889	32,959	21,355	11,604	16,728

[a] Gross revenue minus noncapital costs may not equal gross capital earnings because of rounding.

[b] Includes gross revenues of subsidiary companies not reported in the Union Pacific total 1880–1889 plus net earnings of the Central Branch Union Pacific Railroad 1880–1889.

[c] Includes operating expenses of subsidiary lines not reported in the Union Pacific total 1880–1889.

ending June 30, 1874, and succeeding reports through the 1881 fiscal year are for fiscal years ending May 31.[5] Since no further information is available, the first two fiscal years (those ending April 30, 1873 and June 30, 1874) are treated as May 31 fiscal years, and the fiscal year data are

[5] *Ibid.*, annual volumes 1873–1874 through 1882.

B. Capital Earnings

TABLE B-3

Annual Capital Earnings of the Texas and Pacific System

Year	Gross revenue (thousand current $)	Noncapital expenses (thousand current $)	Capital earnings[a] (thousand current $)	(thousand 1869 $)
1872	301	193	108	118
1873	635	496	139	154
1874	1,054	769	284	329
1875	1,406	943	463	558
1876	1,844	1,289	544	708
1877	2,211	1,546	666	880
1878	2,217	1,419	798	1,136
1879	2,410	2,740	−331	−477
1880	2,947	3,061	−114	−154
1881	4,990	3,478	1,512	1,975
1882	6,266	4,657	1,609	2,053
1883	7,046	5,587	1,459	1,928
1884	5,919	5,420	499	700
1885	5,826	4,731	1,096	1,579
1886	6,042	5,516	526	769
1887	6,182	5,801	381	549
1888	6,505	5,072	1,434	2,040
1889	7,097	5,246	1,851	2,668
1890	7,479	6,256	1,223	1,740
1891	7,323	5,716	1,607	2,317
1892	7,104	5,678	1,425	2,082
1893	7,452	5,422	2,031	3,005
1894	7,425	5,735	1,690	2,642
1895	7,102	5,401	1,701	2,622
1896	6,935	5,368	1,567	2,450
1897	7,697	5,637	2,060	3,176
1898	8,105	6,004	2,101	3,196
1899	8,300	6,098	2,201	3,175
1900	9,811	6,858	2,953	4,150

[a] Gross revenue minus noncapital expenses may not equal gross capital earnings because of rounding.

transformed to an estimate for the appropriate calendar years using the procedure discussed above.

Calendar year revenue and expense data for the years 1882–1900 are reported in the Texas and Pacific's accounts in *Poor's Manual*, with no other adjustments or estimation required.[6]

[6] *Ibid.*, annual volumes 1883–1901.

The Atchison, Topeka and Santa Fe System

Table B-4 presents the capital earnings for the Santa Fe System. Through 1888 the system's accounting was on a calendar year basis, with operations for the remaining years reported in terms of June 30 fiscal years. Because most of the raw data were already on a calendar year basis, the data for the fiscal years 1889 through 1901 are converted to a calendar year basis for the period 1889–1900.

Only a few minor problems required solution in preparing the estimates of Table B-4. Capital earnings for some companies not included in the revenue and expense reports for the consolidated system are not available in all years. Kansas Southern System data are available in 1881 and 1883 but not for 1882. Moreover, the Kansas and Southern group of railroads is not the same in 1882 as in 1881, so one cannot simply assume that the 1882 figure is equal to that of 1883. The 1882 capital earnings for the Kansas Southern are estimated by assuming that the proportional change in its capital earnings between 1881 and 1882 is the same as that for the rest of the Santa Fe System between these years. Capital earnings for the Atlantic and Pacific are available for 1896 but not for 1897. It is assumed that 1897 capital earnings were equal to those for 1896. For the Manhattan, Alma and Burlingame and the Wichita and Western, capital earnings for the 1895 and 1896 fiscal years are not available, but are assumed equal to 1897 ($28,045).

Taxes for the system are reported separately and quite well from 1876 on, with a few exceptions. No taxes are reported for 1889 and the 1890 report is for only 9 months. It is assumed that taxes for the 9 months were three-quarters of the 1890 total and that taxes in 1889 were equal to the estimated level for 1890. Taxes for 1901 are estimated by interpolation between the figures for 1900 and 1902. All data for the Santa Fe System are from *Poor's Manual*.[7]

The Northern Pacific System

Revenue and expense data for the Northern Pacific System did not require conversion from one base to another because the data for all included years are reported on a June 30 fiscal year basis. Table B-5 gives the annual gross capital earnings data for the Northern Pacific System. All raw data are from the accounts of the included firms recorded in *Poor's Manual*.[8]

Although the Northern Pacific operated during 1872, no earnings and

[7] *Ibid.*, annual volumes 1871–1872 through 1903.
[8] *Ibid.*, annual volumes 1872–1873 through 1901.

B. *Capital Earnings* 185

TABLE B-4

Annual Capital Earnings of the Atchison, Topeka and Santa Fe System

Year	Gross revenue (thousand current $)	Noncapital expenses (thousand current $)	Capital earnings[a] (thousand current $)	Capital earnings[a] (thousand 1869 $)
1870	183	104	79	86
1871	447	295	152	170
1872	1,172	715	457	497
1873	1,217	786	431	479
1874	1,251	558	693	801
1875	1,520	699	822	991
1876	2,487	1,350	1,137	1,450
1877	2,679	1,799	880	1,163
1878	3,951	1,989	1,962	2,792
1879	6,381	2,926	3,455	4,981
1880	8,557	4,386	4,171	5,646
1881	13,011	8,087	4,924	6,430
1882	15,351	8,637	6,713	8,565
1883	14,891	6,748	8,143	10,760
1884	16,363	8,976	7,387	10,380
1885	15,814	8,315	7,499	10,810
1886	15,733	8,614	7,119	10,398
1887	18,215	10,408	7,806	11,253
1888	16,759	11,027	5,732	8,156
1889	29,289	22,114	7,175	10,343
1890	32,334	23,729[b]	8,606	12,246
1891	35,051	25,799[c]	9,252	13,338
1892	37,807	27,146	10,662	15,572
1893	35,756	26,826	8,931	13,217
1894	30,533	24,714	5,819	9,097
1895	28,911	23,595	5,316	8,195
1896	29,902	23,833[d]	6,069	9,488
1897	34,949	27,079	7,870	12,133
1898	39,849	29,497	10,352	15,741
1899	43,373	29,066	14,307	20,624
1900	50,353	31,486	18,868	26,510

[a] Gross revenue minus noncapital costs may not equal gross capital earnings because of rounding.

[b] Taxes for 1980 are estimated by division of 9-month report by 0.75.

[c] Taxes in 1891 assumed equal to 1890.

[d] Taxes for 6 months ending June 30, 1896 are doubled to estimate 1896 taxes.

TABLE B-5

Annual Capital Earnings of the Northern Pacific System

Year	Gross revenue (thousand current $)	Noncapital expenses (thousand current $)	Capital earnings[a] (thousand current $)	Capital earnings[a] (thousand 1869 $)
1872	296	126[b]	169	184
1873	355	152	203	225
1874	364	319	45	52
1875	407	323	83	101
1876	466	323	143	183
1877	604	334	270	356
1878	680	330	350	498
1879	977	464	514	741
1880	2,230	1,904	326	441
1881	2,995	1,873	1,122	1,465
1882	5,478	3,686	1,791	2,286
1883	7,855	5,126	2,729	3,607
1884	12,643	7,357	5,286	7,428
1885	11,259	6,227	5,031	7,252
1886	11,750	6,196	5,554	8,112
1887	12,802	7,179	5,623	8,106
1888	15,846	9,285	6,562	9,338
1889	19,956	12,277	7,679	11,069
1890	23,684	13,717	9,967	14,184
1891	26,208	15,643	10,564	15,229
1892	27,652	14,652	12,999	18,986
1893	27,157	15,095	12,063	17,852
1894	17,148	12,365	4,783	7,478
1895	17,721	12,179	5,541	8,543
1896	20,126	12,635	7,491	11,711
1897	17,931[c]	11,502[c]	6,429	9,911
1898	24,108	11,778	12,330	18,748
1899	26,286	13,100	13,187	19,010
1900	30,253	15,245	15,008	21,087

[a] Gross revenue minus noncapital costs may not equal gross capital earnings because of rounding.

[b] Estimated by assuming expenses per mile operated in 1872 equal to those per operated mile in 1873.

[c] Ten-month total reported is divided by 0.8333 to estimate 1897 amount.

B. Capital Earnings

expense data could be found. The revenue data in Table B-5 are estimated on the basis of 1872 operated mileage and revenue per mile operated in 1873. Operating expenses for 1872 and 1874 are estimated as the product of operated mileage in those years and operating expenses per mile operated in 1873.

Because of financial difficulties in 1897, the Northern Pacific reported revenue and expenses only for the first 10 months of that year. The annual figure in Table B-5 for 1897 is computed on the assumption that the reported figures are five-sixths of the year's total.

Capital earnings for some subsidiary lines whose accounts were not included in those of the consolidated system are included in the system's miscellaneous revenue figures for 1898–1900.

TABLE B-6

Annual Capital Earnings of the Great Northern System

Year	Gross revenue (thousand current $)	Noncapital expenses (thousand current $)	Capital earnings[a] (thousand current $)	(thousand 1869 $)
1880	2,885	1,387	1,498	2,028
1881	3,701	1,856	1,845	2,410
1882	6,630	3,516	3,114	3,973
1883	9,091	4,596	4,496	5,941
1884	8,257	3,930	4,327	6,080
1885	7,776	3,510	4,266	6,150
1886	7,322	3,839	3,483	5,087
1887	8,028	4,315	3,714	5,353
1888	9,562	5,420	4,142	5,894
1889	8,587	5,000	3,586	5,170
1890	9,583	4,973	4,610	6,560
1891	11,847	5,464	6,383	9,202
1892	14,885	7,501	7,384	10,784
1893	15,706	7,711	7,995	11,832
1894	13,545	6,901	6,645	10,388
1895	15,140	7,606	7,534	11,615
1896	19,613	10,864	8,749	13,678
1897	19,436	11,310	8,126	12,528
1898	22,578	11,556	11,022	16,759
1899	25,018	13,091	11,927	17,193
1900	28,911	15,868	13,042	18,325

[a] Gross revenue minus noncapital costs may not equal gross capital earnings because of rounding.

TABLE B-7

Annual Capital Earnings of the Canadian Pacific System

Year	Gross revenue (thousand current $)	Noncapital expenses (thousand current $)	Capital earnings[a] (thousand current $)	Capital earnings[a] (thousand 1900 $)	Cash subsidy (thousand 1900 $)
1881	968	748	220	191	823
1882	3,018	2,550	468	389	5,086
1883	4,491[c]	3,954[c]	538	470	5,737
1884	5,745	4,559	1,186	1,073	6,194
1885	8,368	5,143	3,225	3,193	4,257
1886	10,082	6,378	3,703	3,806	473
1887	11,606	8,102	3,504	3,419	73
1888	13,196	9,325	3,871	3,659	4
1889	15,031	9,025	6,006	5,736	35
1890	16,553	10,253	6,300	6,092	—
1891	20,241	12,231	8,010	7,650	—
1892	21,409	12,989	8,420	8,726	180
1893	20,962	13,221	7,741	7,804	125
1894	18,752	12,329	6,423	6,974	554
1895	18,941	11,460	7,481	8,472	18
1896	20,682	12,574	8,108	9,756	95
1897	24,050	13,746	10,304	12,037	661
1898	26,139	15,705	10,434	11,453	2,535
1899	29,230	17,000	12,230	13,308	462
1900	29,595[b]	18,263[b]	11,333	11,373	254

[a] Gross revenue minus noncapital costs may not equal gross capital earnings because of rounding.

[b] Amount for January 1 to June 30, 1900 plus one-half fiscal year total for period ending June 30, 1901.

[c] Data for full year 1883 not available. It is assumed that the calendar year total for 1883 is equal to that of the fiscal year ending June 30, 1883.

The Great Northern System

Accounts for the St. Paul, Minnesota and Manitoba, and later the Great Northern System, were always on a June 30 fiscal basis, so that conversion of the raw data from one base to another was not required. Table B-6 presents the annual gross capital earnings for the Great Northern System, with all basic data collected from *Poor's Manual*.[9]

[9] *Ibid.*, annual volumes 1881–1901.

B. *Capital Earnings* 189

The Canadian Pacific System

Capital earnings for the Canadian Pacific System are shown in Table B-7. Data for 1881–1883 are converted from a fiscal year to a calendar year basis. Revenue and expense data for 1884 through 1899 were reported on a calendar year basis. The firm switched from a calendar year to June 30 fiscal year in 1900. Revenue and expense data for calendar year 1900 are the sum of the amounts reported for January 1 to June 30, 1900 and one-half of the amounts for fiscal year 1901. Again, all raw data are from the annual reports of *Poor's Manual*.[10]

---

[10] *Ibid.*, annual volumes 1882–1902.

Appendix C

Net Land Grant Revenue

This appendix is devoted to explanation and presentation of the estimates of net land grant revenue for each system included in this study. The aim is to develop the best possible estimate of the contribution of the land subsidy to the aided private net receipts stream (and rate of return) of the subsidized railroads.

Several problems arise in estimating net land grant revenue. One major difficulty is that it is not possible to develop estimates that are exactly alike for all systems because of the firms' differences in reporting land grant transactions. Moreover, individual firms did not follow a consistent method of reporting over the entire period. Ideally, one would like to know all the income derived from the land grant. The best measure would be cash receipts, including not only cash receipts from sales but also interest received on time sales, payments on time contracts, rents, stumpage, etc. If cash receipts are not used for gross land grant revenue, value of sales is the other alternative. Since some sales contracts were subsequently canceled, it would be best to have an accurate accounting of the net sales in each year rather than gross sales when the value of sales is used for gross land grant revenue. The gross sales measure is the poorest estimate of total land grant revenue available.

By the later years of this study, reporting of land transactions was becoming reasonably complete for most of the systems. However, if reporting for a particular system allowed only the use of gross sales value for the early years, this study could not switch to cash receipts even if that information became available for later years. To make a switch from gross

C. Net Land Grant Revenue

sales value to cash receipts would involve double-counting of some part of land revenues. The net effect of relying on the gross sales value for the revenue estimate is most likely an overstatement of the land grant revenue's impact on the private rate of return. The best method of consistently estimating land grant revenue was selected individually for each system, rather than using the same method for all systems, on the grounds that it is better to have a consistent method for each system than one for all, given that the only consistent method across all systems would be the gross sales technique.

Another significant problem involves the costs associated with the land grants, in particular the matter of taxes on lands included in the land grant. It is not clear that land taxes are always included in the land office costs reported by the railroads. Land taxes in some instances do not appear to have been separated from all other taxes reported in income statements elsewhere. Where taxes on land in the land grant are lumped with total taxes, capital earnings are understated. If they are not included in land grant costs, net land grant revenue is overstated. The end result of this situation is that unaided private rates of return are understated and aided private rates of return are overstated. Neither of these biases appears to be of great magnitude. No effort is made to correct for them.

The Central Pacific System

Railroads in the Central Pacific system that received a land grant include the Central Pacific, the California and Oregon, the Southern Pacific of California, and the Western Pacific. The land grant of the Western Pacific was retained by one of the original contractors and did not pass to the Central Pacific at the merger of the two roads.[1] For the Central Pacific System, value of total land sales is used as the gross land grant revenue of the system. Where possible, this is corrected to net sales to reduce the inherent overstatement involved. Taxes on the land grant were not shown separately during the early years, and it is not known whether they are included in land office expenses. Because gross sales are used for the land revenue figure, it is likely that the aided rate of return for the Central Pacific is overstated.

Table C-1 presents the estimated annual net land grant revenue for the Central Pacific System during the period 1869–1927.[2] It is necessary to

---

[1] Daggett, *Chapters in the History of the Southern Pacific*, p. 84.
[2] Land grant data for the Central Pacific System are primarily from *Poor's Manual*, annual volumes 1870–1871 through 1927. The distribution of acres sold from July 1, 1877 to the end of 1884 is from Leslie E. Decker, *Railroads, Land and Politics: The Taxation of Railroad Land Grants, 1864–1897*.

TABLE C-1

Annual Net Land Grant Revenue of the Central Pacific System (Thousand Current $)[a]

Year	Southern Pacific			Central Pacific[b]			System net land revenue
	Land sales	Land expenses	Net land revenue	Land sales	Land expenses	Net land revenue	
1869	—	—	—	168.6	16.4	152.3	152
1870	—	—	—	180.3	17.5	162.8	163
1871	—	—	—	215.2	20.9	194.3	194
1872	—	—	—	215.2	20.9	194.3	194
1873	—	—	—	410.3	39.8	370.5	370
1874	—	—	—	388.8	37.7	351.1	351
1875	362.7	34.8	327.9	163.7	15.9	147.8	476
1876	285.4	27.4	258.0	275.4	26.7	248.7	507
1877	200.4	19.2	181.1	1,203.9	116.8	1,087.1	1,268
1878	115.3	11.1	104.3	643.8	47.3	596.5	701
1879	115.3	11.1	104.3	201.7	66.1	135.6	240
1880	115.3	11.1	104.3	344.4	59.5	284.9	389
1881	612.2	58.8	533.4	382.2	30.8	351.4	905
1882	341.7	32.8	308.9	504.5	23.7	480.8	790
1883	275.8	26.5	249.3	967.6	32.5	935.1	1,184
1884	1,170.0	112.3	1,057.7	712.5	66.3	646.2	1,704
1885	1,198.7	59.9	1,138.8	501.9	61.5	440.4	1,579
1886	884.4	84.9	799.5	292.6	28.4	263.2	1,063
1887	2,369.8	74.7	2,295.1	405.3	64.3	341.1	2,636
1888	440.5	83.4	357.0	205.4	19.9	185.5	543
1889	194.5	78.5	116.0	583.8	52.7	491.0	607
1890	594.1	73.2[c]	520.9	295.8	93.5[f]	202.3	723
1891	204.9	67.9[e]	137.0	532.9	107.5	425.4	562
1892	157.4	62.6[e]	94.8	140.7	101.0[a]	39.7	134
1893	1,406.1	57.4	1,348.7	141.1	115.9	25.2	1,374
1894	19.4	57.9	−38.5	1181.	133.4[a]	−15.3	−54
1895	24.7	53.5	−28.8	224.8	378.2[a]	−153.4	−182
1896	123.0	68.5	54.5	105.5	211.9[a]	−106.4	−52

Year							
1897	132.2	—	120.7	11.5	43.8	173.4^e	−129.6	−118
1898	131.3	—	20.5	110.8	170.3	189.3^e	−19.0	92
1899	119.3	—	120.0^a	−0.7	368.2	205.2^e	163.0	162
1900	626.9	—	120.0^a	506.9	288.9	221.1^e	67.8	575
1901	168.1	—	120.0^a	48.1	1,239.1	237.0^e	1,002.1	1,050
1902	1,478.0	—	120.0^a	1,358.0	2,013.1	252.4^f	1,760.7	3,119
1903	77.4	—	32.1	45.3	242.8	281.5^c	−38.7	7
1904	65.2	—	107.8	−42.6	29.4	309.7^f	−280.3	−323
1905	7.6	—	120.3	−112.7	6.2	328.3^c	−322.1	−435
1906	2.5	—	146.3^c	−143.8	32.2	346.9^c	−314.7	−458
1907	13.8	—	172.3^c	−158.5	484.2	365.5	118.7	−40
1908	5.6	—	198.3^c	−192.7	4.2	383.9^g	−379.7	−572
1909	4.1	—	224.3^c	−220.2	15.8	397.8^g	−382.0	−602
1910	636.6	—	250.3^c	386.3	425.7	419.9^g	5.8	392
1911	398.9	—	276.6	122.3	645.3	263.3^f	382.0	504
1912	4,465.9	—	293.4	4,172.5	969.5	279.2^f	690.3	4,863
1913	—	—	—	—	—	295.1^f	−295.1	−295
1914	—	—	—	—	510.2	311.0^f	199.2	199
1915	—	—	—	—	655.2	326.9^f	328.3	328
1916	—	—	—	—	569.6	342.8^f	226.8	227
1917	—	—	—	—	321.6	358.7^f	−37.1	−37
1918	—	—	—	—	1,371.4	375.4	996.0	996
1919	—	—	—	—	1,310.5	360.8	949.7	950
1920	—	—	—	—	1,683.6	538.3	1,145.3	1,145
1921	—	—	—	—	175.7	368.1^h	−192.4	−192
1922	—	—	—	—	485.4	368.1^h	117.3	117
1923	—	—	—	—	1,012.4	368.1^h	644.3	644
1924	—	—	—	—	—	368.1^h	−368.1	368
1925	—	—	—	—	—	368.1^h	−368.1	368
1926	—	—	—	—	—	368.1^h	−368.1	368
1927	—	—	—	—	26,980.9^e	368.1^h	26,612.8	26,613

^{a} Columns may not add because of rounding.
^{b} Includes California and Oregon.
^{c} Estimated by interpolation.
^{d} Based on observations for 1897, 1904, and 1905.
^{e} Total reported as of December 12, 1927 minus total reported 1869–1923.
^{f} Central Pacific expenses estimated by interpolation.
^{g} California and Oregon expenses estimated by interpolation.
^{h} Estimated as the average of the observations for 1918 and 1919.

include the years 1890–1927, because the estimated market value of the firm's bonds and stocks is used in terminal adjustments A and B to the net receipts stream. Market value of the bonds and stocks includes the market value of future net land grant revenues. For the unaided private rate the correct terminal adjustment, using the market value of bonds and stocks outstanding, is the bond and stock market value, excluding the contribution of future net land grant revenues. Hence, net land grant revenues after the terminal year (1889 in this case) must be subtracted in calculation of the net receipts stream.

With the exception of the Union Pacific, which recorded a value for unsold land in its balance sheet in 1889, and the Texas and Pacific, which made a paper transfer of all its remaining lands in 1887, the United States railroads included in this study did not carry a value of unsold land on their books that makes the preceding calculation necessary. Fortunately, there is a record of total land grant receipts and costs for the land grant railroads through 1927.[3] These figures provide a useful benchmark for estimation of net land grant revenues after the terminal year and a convenient stopping point for that portion of the net receipts stream.

The Union Pacific System

The Union Pacific, Denver Pacific, Kansas Pacific, and Central Branch of the Union Pacific System all received land grants. However, the Union Pacific System apparently did not receive any revenue from the Central Branch's grant. Net sales plus other receipts, when available, are used to value land grant revenue for the Union Pacific System. Other receipts from the land grant are available for the Union Pacific Railway during 1879–1889, and for the Kansas and Denver Pacific during 1880–1885 and 1887. Table C-2 presents the net land grant revenue of the Union Pacific System.

Gross sales for the Union Pacific were obtained from *PRC* for 1869–1886 and *Poor's Manual* for 1887–1889.[4] The annual values of cancelled contracts for 1880–1889 are from *Poor's Manual*. Total cancelled contracts through 1886 are reported in *PRC*. The difference between this total and the total of the annual reports for 1880–1886 is assumed to be the total for 1869–1879, which is divided equally among these years. Estimated net sales are the value of gross sales minus the value of cancelled contracts. Annual land taxes for the Union Pacific during 1865–1886 are from *PRC*.[5]

---

[3] *Public Aids*, II, pp. 107–117.
[4] U.S. Congress, Senate, *PRC*, p. 524, and *Poor's Manual*, annual volumes, 1888–1890.
[5] U.S. Congress, Senate, *PRC*, p. 4283.

C. Net Land Grant Revenue

Land grant data for the Kansas and Denver Pacific Railroads for the period 1880–1889 are taken from the annual reports in *Poor's Manual*. Net sales are reported for 1880–1887 and other receipts as noted earlier. Land taxes are given separately in 1880–1881 and are included in general land grant expenses for 1882–1887. Only net proceeds from the land grants are reported in 1888–1889.

The book value of land unsold is reported on the Union Pacific Railway's balance sheet in 1890.[6] This value of $12,567,500 for 6,283,000 unsold acres is used to adjust the estimated market value of the firm's bonds and stocks for terminal adjustments A and B in calculating the unaided private rates of return.

The Texas and Pacific System

Net land grant revenues for the Texas and Pacific System are shown in Table C-3. The Texas and Pacific did not fare very well with its land grant. It was originally entitled to receive 12,723,200 acres from the State of Texas. Because it did not build its line in time it received only 5,173,120, of which 5,167,360 were located and 256,046 later reclaimed by the state. Thus, the Texas and Pacific in the end received only 4,911,314 acres from the state.[7] A total of 1,001,783 acres was received from a federal grant, making the total acreage received 5,913,097.

In 1887 the Texas and Pacific was reorganized and the balance of the land grant was taken over by a committee of creditors, to be disposed of and the proceeds applied to liquidation of the bonds issued with these lands as security. The Texas and Pacific Land Trust Company was organized to handle this land.[8] The revenue to the company from this transaction is valued as the difference between total gross proceeds of sales reported in *Public Aids* and the total otherwise reported up to 1887. Because of this transaction, no adjustment for land grants sold after 1900 is required for this system.

The Atchison, Topeka and Santa Fe System

In the Santa Fe System, the Santa Fe itself and the Atlantic and Pacific were land grant recipients. Tables C-4 contains the annual net land grant revenue for the Santa Fe System on a cash receipts basis.

[6] *Poor's Manual*, 1890, p. 939.
[7] Reed, *A History of the Texas Railroads*, p. 371.
[8] *Poor's Manual*, 1888, p. 824.

TABLE C-2

Annual Net Land Grant Revenue of the Union Pacific System (Thousand Current $) [a]

Year	Union Pacific			Kansas Pacific and Denver Pacific			System net land revenue
	Land re-ceipts	Land ex-penses	Net land revenue	Land re-ceipts [c]	Land ex-penses	Net land revenue	
1865	—	−0.3	−0.3	—	—	—	−0.3
1866	—	−0.5	−0.5	—	—	—	−0.5
1867	—	—	—	—	—	—	N.A.
1868	—	−1.0	−1.0	—	—	—	−1
1869	430.2	74.3	355.9	—	—	—	356
1870	563.1	127.0	436.1	—	—	—	436
1871	638.9	190.2	448.7	—	—	—	449
1872	598.8	180.3	418.4	—	—	—	418
1873	826.4	125.2	701.2	—	—	—	701
1874	942.8	139.8	803.1	—	—	—	803
1875	253.3	219.7	33.6	—	—	—	34

Year							
1876	233.1	123.3	109.8	—	—	—	110
1877	236.8	178.8	58.0	—	—	—	58
1878	1,450.1	305.8	1,144.3	—	—	—	1,144
1879	970.8	223.8	747.1	—	—	—	747
1880	723.3	180.8	542.5	336.1	125.8	210.3	753
1881	388.7	128.5	260.2	359.7	121.2	238.4	499
1882	937.2	157.9	779.3	392.3	137.5	254.8	1,034
1883	2,517.4	226.1	2,291.2	1,038.1	185.4	852.7	3,144
1884	6,669.4	246.4	6,423.0	1,961.9	245.0	1,716.8	8,140
1885	1,327.6	49.9	1,277.7	2,839.7	458.6	2,381.1	3,659
1886	324.6	17.2	307.4	1,341.3[e]	83.7[e]	1,257.6	1,565
1887	251.8	2.2	249.5	2,531.4	126.6	2,404.9	2,654
1888	206.6	1.2	205.4	—	—	777.5[d]	983
1889	273.8	89.4	184.4	—	—	317.8[d]	13,070[b]

[a] Columns may not add because of rounding.
[b] Includes estimated book value of unsold land, which is $12,567,500.
[c] Interest received on land contracts is excluded because these railroads did not join the system until 1880. Premiums on land grant bonds are excluded from expenses.
[d] No data other than net revenue available.
[e] No breakdown available on land receipts or expenses.

TABLE C-3

Annual Net Land Grant Revenue of the Texas and Pacific System (Thousand Current $)[a]

Year	Land sales	Land expenses	Net land revenue
1876	—	137.1	−137
1877	15.1	111.4	−96
1878	27.5	27.0	0
1879	97.5	77.2	20
1880	101.5	77.4	24
1881	29.0	22.0	7
1882	—	—	—
1883	624.8	—	625
1884	1,676.2	206.9	1,469
1885	—	—	—
1886	—	—	—
1887	13,800.6[b]	91.4	13,709

[a] Columns may not add because of rounding.

[b] This is the difference between sales reported through 1927 and sales reported through 1886. The firm's land grant was transferred to land trust in the reorganization of 1887.

The Northern Pacific System

Table C-5 presents the annual net land grant revenues of the Northern Pacific System. While some minor land grants were received by subsidiaries of the Northern Pacific, almost all the approximately 40 million acres received by the system went to the Northern Pacific Railroad. Land grant revenue for the Northern Pacific is in terms of gross sales.

The Great Northern System

Annual estimates of net land grant revenue for the Great Northern System are listed in Table C-6. The Great Northern was not a land grant railroad, but its predecessor—the St. Paul, Minneapolis and Manitoba—received the lands remaining in the land grants of the various divisions of the St. Paul and Pacific when it purchased the latter road at a judicial sale in 1879. In addition, the new railroad in 1880–1881 acquired the charter of the Minneapolis and St. Cloud Railway Company, to which was attached a land grant of 10 sections per mile.[9] Unless otherwise noted, the revenue

[9] *Ibid.*, 1884, p. 748.

TABLE C-4

Annual Net Land Grant Revenue of the Atchison, Topeka and Santa Fe System
(Thousand Current $) [a]

Year	Land receipts	Land expenses	Net land revenue	Year	Land receipts	Land expenses	Net land revenue
1871	148.0[b]	58.2[e]	90	1900	7.0	—	7
1872	148.0[b]	37.0[e]	111	1901	−3.4[f]	—	−3
1873	269.2	103.2[e]	166	1902	66.6[f]	—	67
1874	147.3	123.8[e]	23	1903	1.6[f]	—	2
1875	364.2	57.1[e]	307	1904	681.3[f]	—	681
1876	245.2[c]	91.5[e]	153	1905	—	—	318[g]
1877	245.2[c]	58.2[e]	187	1906	—	—	318[g]
1878	763.3[d]	112.3	651	1907	—	—	318[g]
1879	592.3	116.1	476	1908	—	—	318[g]
1880	600.0	80.6	519	1909	—	—	318[g]
1881	558.6	54.0	505	1910	—	—	318[g]
1882	889.8	233.7	676	1911	—	—	318[g]
1883	1,390.9	240.4	1,151	1912	—	—	318[g]
1884	1,209.7	149.9	1,060	1913	—	—	318[g]
1885	1,813.7	209.4	1,605	1914	—	—	318[g]
1886	1,422.5	99.2	1,323	1915	—	—	318[g]
1887	509.6	10.2	500	1916	—	—	318[g]
1888	256.0	13.4	243	1917	—	—	318[g]
1889	1,724.0	124.0	1,600	1918	700.0[f]	—	700
1890	1,770.0	133.0	1,644	1919	750.0[f]	—	750
1891	96.0	51.0	45	1920	400.0[f]	—	400
1892	110.0	60.0	50	1921	—	—	318[g]
1893	76.0	58.0	18	1922	400.0[f]	—	400
1894	13.0	35.0	−22	1923	—	—	318[g]
1895	10.0	11.0	−1	1924	—	—	318[g]
1896	6.0	9.0	−3	1925	—	—	318[g]
1897	10.0	3.0	7	1926	—	—	318[g]
1898	16.0	—	16	1927	—	—	318[g]
1899	14.0	—	14				

[a] Columns may not add because of rounding.

[b] Reported cumulative total through 1895 (*Poor's Manual*, 1896, p. 360) for Atchison, Topeka and Santa Fe is $296,000 more than the sum of individual year reports. This is divided equally between 1871 and 1872.

[c] The increment to cumulative receipts from the end of 1875 to the end of 1877 is divided equally between 1876 and 1877.

[d] This is the increment in cumulative receipts.

[e] Total expenses through December 31, 1877 are reported. These are divided among the years 1871–1877 in proportion to sales for which most expenses were incurred.

[f] Reported as addition to net earnings from the land department.

[g] Reported total net receipts as of December 31, 1927 are $22,588,000, while the sum of individually reported net receipts through that date is $16,860,000, leaving $5,728,000 unaccounted for. Since it appears that the firm did not report land earnings after 1904 until the government ran the railroads in 1918–1920, the missing total of $5,728,000 is divided among the 18 years in which there was no report.

TABLE C-5

Annual Net Land Grant Revenue of the Northern Pacific System
(Thousand Current $)

Year	Land sales	Land expenses	Net land revenue	Year	Land sales	Land expenses	Net land revenue
1874	1,842[a]	341[c]	1,501	1901	6,838[b]	2,702[c]	4,136
1875	1,842[a]	341[c]	1,501	1902	5,917[b]	2,338[c]	3,579
1876	887	222[c]	665	1903	5,863[b]	2,317[c]	3,546
1877	1,217	266[c]	951	1904	1,056[b]	417[c]	639
1878	3,379	735[c]	2,644	1905	795	182	613
1879	918[b]	363[c]	555	1906	1,110	271	839
1880	813	74	739	1907	1,703	218	1,485
1881	2,231	828[c]	1,403	1908	1,217	340	877
1882	1,556	485[c]	1,071	1909	1,808	397	1,411
1883	3,393	746[c]	2,647	1910	3,978	532	3,446
1884	2,282	482	1,800	1911	1,496	625	871
1885	1,698	425	1,273	1912	1,525	540	984
1886	1,394	300	1,094	1913	3,040	704	2,336
1887	1,072	402	670	1914	3,458	818	2,640
1888	1,495	375	1,120	1915	4,125	997	3,128
1889	1,982	458	1,524	1916	6,433	884	5,549
1890	1,805	536	1,269	1917	7,776	742	7,034
1891	1,450	556	894	1918	1,989	1,045	944
1892	2,340	879	1,461	1919	1,672	127[c]	1,545
1893	331	577	−246	1920	2,114	124[c]	1,990
1894	174	387	−213	1921	1,404	71[c]	1,333
1895	475	121[c]	354	1922	1,817	155[c]	1,662
1896	411[b]	162[c]	249	1923	1,990	87[c]	1,903
1897	418	130[c]	288	1924	2,162	125[c]	2,037
1898	15,962[b]	6,308[c]	9,654	1925	2,253	112[c]	2,141
1899	2,347[b]	928[c]	1,419	1926	1,862	131[c]	1,731
1900	6,893[b]	2,724[c]	4,169	1927	1,613	131[c]	1,482

[a] Total sales reported as of September 29, 1875 divided between fiscal years 1874 and 1875.

[b] Estimated as the product of acreage sold and average proceeds per acre ($2.48) through 1927.

[c] Estimated as the product of acreage sold and average expenses per acre ($0.98) through 1927.

from the relatively small grant of the Minneapolis and St. Cloud is in terms of gross sales, while that of the St. Paul, Minneapolis and Manitoba (the grant made originally to the St. Paul and Pacific) is in terms of cash receipts.

TABLE C-6

Annual Net Land Grant Revenue of the Great Northern System (Thousand Current $)[a]

Year	Minneapolis and St. Cloud			St. Paul, Minneapolis and Manitoba			System net land revenue
	Land sales	Land expenses	Net land revenue	Land receipts	Land expenses	Net land revenue	
1880	—	—	—	—	—	—	598[b]
1881	—	—	—	—	—	—	224[b]
1882	—	—	—	—	—	—	861[b]
1883	—	—	—	901.3	87.3	813.9	814
1884	—	—	—	581.3	163.0	418.3	418
1885	—	—	—	408.9	277.6	131.3	131
1886	—	—	—	505.4	155.2	350.1	350
1887	—	—	—	569.4	153.6	415.8	416
1888	—	—	—	366.9	94.9	271.9	272
1889	—	—	—	253.2	91.4	161.9	162
1890	—	—	—	276.7	73.4	203.3	203
1891	12.6	3.4	9.2	370.8	64.0	306.8	316
1892	16.1	25.4	−9.3	948.1	73.8	874.3	865
1893	11.5	5.0	6.5	237.3	54.1	183.2	190
1894	7.7	7.6	0.1	150.6	42.3	108.3	108
1895	12.1	2.1	10.0	239.1	40.3	198.8	209
1896	12.1	3.9	8.2	474.0	76.1	397.8	406

(Continued)

TABLE C-6 (*Continued*)

	Minneapolis and St. Cloud			St. Paul, Minneapolis and Manitoba			System net land revenue
Year	Land sales	Land expenses	Net land revenue	Land receipts	Land expenses	Net land revenue	
1897	7.6	0.4	7.2	317.9	52.5	265.4	273
1898	19.5	7.8	11.7	679.1	71.5	607.6	619
1899	38.5	12.8	25.7	584.5	57.1	527.4	553
1900	66.4	15.1	51.3	714.2	60.0	654.1	705
1901	366.2	23.7	342.5	955.5	103.4	852.1	1,195
1902	495.7	6.1	489.6	1,273.0	68.8	1,204.2	1,694
1903	19.9	4.4	15.5	925.5	40.9	884.6	900
1904	10.6	85.6	−75.0	649.9	24.4	625.5	551
1905	5.1	2.4	2.8	793.8	29.2	764.6	767
1906	1.2	4.1	−2.9	614.4	26.5	587.9	585
1907	1.9	2.4	−0.5	359.8	21.2	338.6	338
1908	3.2	2.9	0.3	189.1	18.0	171.1	171
1909	3.2	2.9	0.3	195.5	14.0	181.5	182
1910	2.1	—	2.1	51.9[a]	—	51.9	54
1911	2.6	—	2.6	74.0[a]	—	74.0	77

1912	21.7	4.0	17.8	94.8	32.1	62.7	80
1913	34.1	—	34.1	202.9[d]	—	202.9	237
1914	4.3	—	4.3	107.1	33.9	73.2	77
1915	39.6	2.4	37.2	97.0	37.3	59.7	97
1916	2.9	2.7	0.2	146.8	35.2	111.6	112
1917	—	—	—	—	—	—	—
1918	13.0	—	13.0	242.5[e]	24.9	217.6	231
1919	22.8	—	22.8	396.3	46.8	349.5	372
1920	2.8	—	2.8	484.9	47.9	437.0	440
1921	—[c]	—	—[c]	—	—	—	—
1922	-0.1	—	-0.1	427.2	56.4	370.8	333
1923	0.6	—	-5.0	656.3[f]	12.3	644.0	644
1924	—	5.7	-5.0	399.5	23.4	376.1	371
1925	—	4.2	-4.2	113.2	25.1	88.1	84
1926	—	4.7	-4.7	167.8	31.5	136.3	132
1927	—	—	—	—	—	—	—

[a] Columns may not add because of rounding.
[b] Reported as net cash receipts for the system.
[c] Net receipts of $47 reported.
[d] Sales.
[e] Net receipts east of Red River.
[f] Net receipts west of Red River.

TABLE C-7

Annual Net Land Grant Revenue of the Canadian Pacific System
(Thousand Current $)

Year	Net land receipts	Year	Net land receipts
1882	3,372	1900	1,141
1883	2,846	1901	1,262
1884	2,777	1902	5,133
1885	−423	1903	9,632
1886	9,643 [a]	1904	4,301
1887	−50	1905	2,757
1888	325	1906	6,892
1889	335	1907	5,887
1890	159	1908	1,569
1891	124	1909	5,086
1892	280	1910	14,469
1893	155	1911	9,558
1894	−36	1912	10,710
1895	−165	1913	7,487
1896	−628	1914	2,771
1897	280	1915	2,328
1898	626	1916	5,396
1899	888	1917	90,269 [b]

[a] In 1886 the government took back 6,792,014 acres of the original grant as an offset at $1.50 per acre ($10,188,021 total) against cash advanced the previous year. This amount is included in the net land receipts of the company. See J. Lorne McDougall, *Canadian Pacific*, p. 126.

[b] Includes $75,938,000 book value of agricultural lands as given in December 31, 1917 inventory of assets and property shown in general balance sheet.

The Canadian Pacific System

Net land receipts (apparently net cash receipts) from the Canadian Pacific System's land grant provide the annual estimates of the system's net land grant revenues reported in Table C-7. System figures include proceeds from the land grants of the Canadian Pacific, Manitoba, Southwestern, and Great Northwest Central. Net receipts in 1882 are the amount of land grant bonds redeemed by payments from lands sold.[10] The

---

[10] *Ibid.*, 1883, p. 961.

C. Net Land Grant Revenue

1883 estimate is the difference between total cash receipts to date and the 1882 figure.[11] Annual net land revenues for 1884–1900 are the first difference of the net land receipts account on the Canadian Pacific's balance sheet. In 1886 this includes the proceeds from 6,792,014 acres of the original grant, which the government took back at $1.50 an acre as an offset against cash advanced the previous year.[12] The 1900 estimate is one-third of the difference between the December 3, 1899 and the June 30, 1901 balances.

Net land grant revenue for 1901–1917 is on a June 30 fiscal year basis. For 1901–1916 this is simply net proceeds of sales recorded in the annual statement of receipts and expenditures.[13] In 1917 the value placed (for the first time) on unsold lands in the firm's inventory of assets and property in the general balance sheet is added to the net proceeds from sales so that terminal adjustments A and B will be appropriate.

---

[11] *Ibid.*, 1884, p. 940.
[12] J. Lorne McDougall, *Canadian Pacific*, p. 126.
[13] *Poor's Manual*, appropriate annual volumes.

Appendix D

Zero Rent Perimeters

The first step in estimation of the intraregional benefits resulting from the operation of a particular railroad system is determination of the geographic area over which these benefits accrue. This necessitates an estimate of the airline distance of the zero rent perimeter (extensive margin) from the railroad, i.e., the distance from the railroad where the product of labor and capital in conjunction with land is just sufficient to pay the opportunity cost of labor and capital and the cost of transporting the product to market.

Technique for Estimation of the Zero Rent Perimeter

The algorithm outlined here for estimating the distance of the zero rent perimeter from the railroad is basically the same as that used by Robert W. Fogel.[1] Fogel estimates that the boundary of feasible agricultural pro-

---

[1] Robert W. Fogel, *Railroads and American Economic Growth: Essays in Econometric History* (Baltimore: Johns Hopkins Press, 1964), pp. 75–79. Two modifications are made. First, no account is taken of the saving in hauling from water shipping points, rather than from rail shipping points, to primary markets. Second, shipments by water to primary markets are not deducted from total shipments in estimating tonnage shipped per acre in farms. Since the extensive margin around a railroad rather than a water transportation facility is desired, the additional computations are irrelevant. In addition, the second modification produces a downward bias in the distance estimate for the extensive perimeter.

D. Zero Rent Perimeters

duction (the zero rent perimeter) fell 40 miles from a navigable waterway in 1890.[2] Four of the six zero rent perimeters estimated here fall between 34.6 and 42.8 miles from the railroad; the other two are at 60.9 and 89.2 miles.[3]

Let us begin with an outline of the technique used to estimate the distance to the zero rent perimeter within the geographic area of operation of a railroad. The first estimate required is the tonnage of agricultural products shipped to primary markets. Output minus estimated farm use in the area provides an estimate of this tonnage. This estimate allows calculation of the "acre-weight," i.e., the average tonnage shipped to primary markets per acre in farms. The third necessary piece of information is the average wagon cost per ton-mile for hauling agricultural produce to shipping points.[4] The product of the wagon cost per ton-mile and the acre weight is the acre-weight transport cost, i.e., the cost of hauling an acre-weight 1 mile by wagon. The fourth estimate required is the average value per acre of "pure" farm land, excluding that portion of the value of farms attributable to capital improvements. Average value per acre is transformed into average annual rent per acre by decapitalizing the former value by the appropriate mortgage interest rate. Division of average annual rent per acre by the acre-weight transport cost yields an estimate of potential wagon haul mileage, i.e., the incremental miles that an acre-weight would have had to travel by wagon to exhaust the average rental value of land. The Andrews study cited above contains data on actual average wagon haul mileage from farms to shipping points. The sum of potential and actual acreage wagon haul mileage from farms to shipping points is the average wagon haul miles required to exhaust the rent to land in the affected area.

The mileage estimate produced by the technique described refers to the average road miles from the railroad to the zero rent perimeter. The distance desired for our purposes is the average airline miles between the railroad and the extensive margin. Conversion of road to airline miles requires an estimate of the average ratio of road to airline miles. A sample of actual modern road and airline miles between points in the appropriate geographic area is used to derive this ratio. Division of average road miles to the extensive margin by this ratio provides an estimate of the average airline mileage from the railroad to the zero rent perimeter.

[2] *Ibid.*, p. 79.

[3] Since farm values are not reported in the Canadian Census until 1901, the zero rent perimeter is not estimated for the Canadian Pacific.

[4] The source of information on wagon haulage costs is a Department of Agriculture study for the 1905–1906 crop year. Frank Andrews, *Cost of Hauling Crops from Farms to Shipping Points*, U.S. Department of Agriculture, Bureau of Statistics, Bulletin No. 49 (Washington: Government Printing Office, 1907).

The zero rent perimeter estimated by the technique described differs from what would be expected in the simple abstract model.[5] Imagine a railroad that runs from A to D in Fig. D-1, serving the area between those two points. Let D be the only primary market within this region. Suppose wheat is the only commercial crop. Assume that every acre of land produces one ton of wheat. Let the price of wheat be P per ton and the cost of labor and capital required to produce a ton of wheat be everywhere equal to $P/2$. Assume that the cost of transporting a ton of wheat from A to D by the railroad is $P/3$, with a constant rate being charged per ton-mile. The rent per acre at A is $P/6$. Producers for some distance around A will receive rent depending on the cost of transporting wheat by wagon to a shipment point. Assume that the acre-weight transport cost is everywhere equal to $P/36$. The zero rent perimeter would be 6 miles from A.

Now assume two other shipping points B and C in addition to A. Let B be one-third of the distance from A to D and C two-thirds of the distance. The rent at B, C, and D is, respectively, $10P/36$, $14P/36$, and $18P/36$ per acre. Given the assumptions of the example, the distance to the zero rent perimeter would be 10 miles at B, 14 miles at C, and 18 miles at D. The zero rent perimeter described would lie along the lines EF and GH. Lands within the zero rent perimeter receive rent depending on their distance from the railroad.

The algorithm to be used here does not provide a zero rent perimeter like EF and GH. Instead, it provides an average perimeter, equidistant from the railroad at all points, such as that shown in Fig. D-1 by the dashed lines $E'F'$ and $G'H'$, which are parallel to AD. To the extent that the real extensive margin corresponds to EF and GH, an average distance zero rent perimeter like $E'F'$ and $G'H'$ will include relatively less of the higher-valued land and relatively more lower-valued land, so that the estimated incremental rent with the railroad is likely to be less than the true incremental rent. Insofar as this is the case, the social rate of return will be understated.

An important question concerning the estimated zero rent perimeter is whether it is in fact, given the technique, an estimate of the *zero* rent perimeter. Consider the point E in Fig. D-2, which is representative of any point on the zero rent perimeter. Point C is the closest point on the railroad from E. Is C the optimal shipping point from E, or is some point between C and D, such as F, the optimal shipping point? Such will be the case when the additional wagon haulage cost per ton incurred in going from E to some point F, rather than C, is less than the railroad transport

---

[5] Cf. Roger L. Ransom, "Social Returns from Public Transport Investment: A Case Study of the Ohio Canal", *Journal of Political Economy*, (September/October, 1970), 1043–1047.

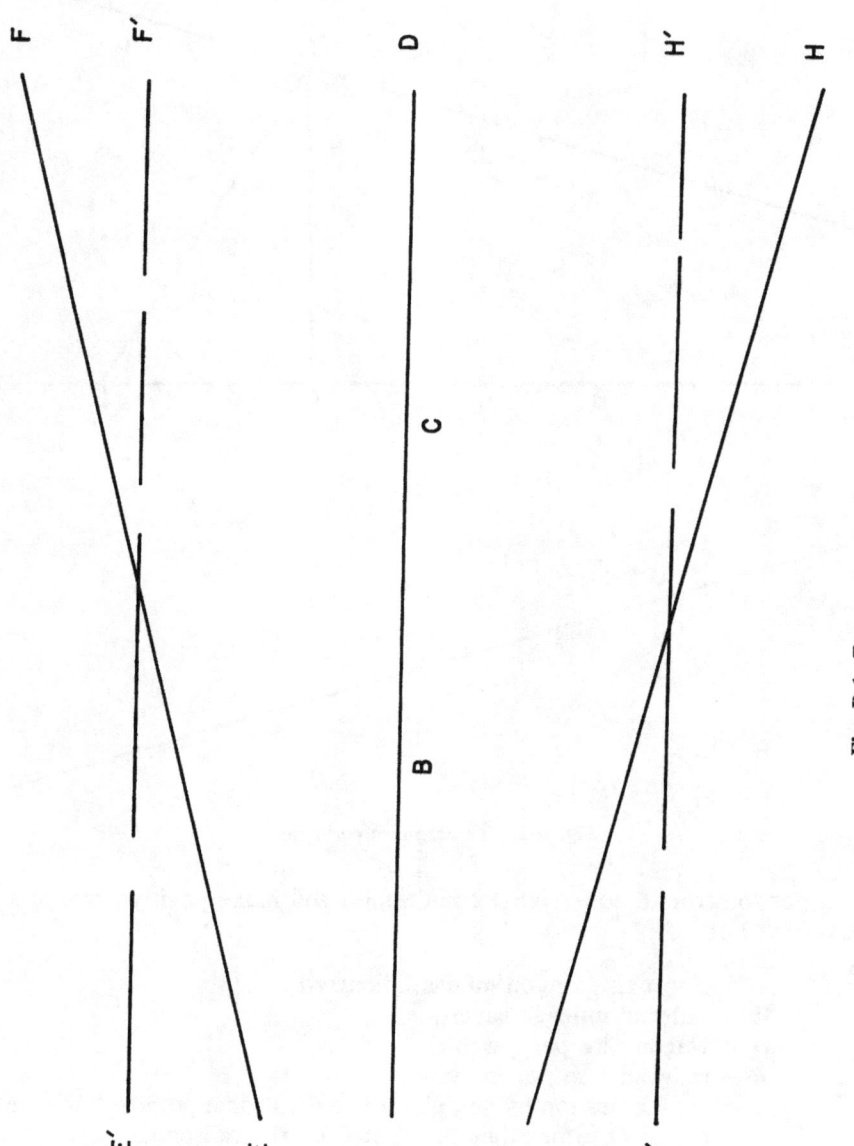

Fig. D-1. Zero rent perimeters.

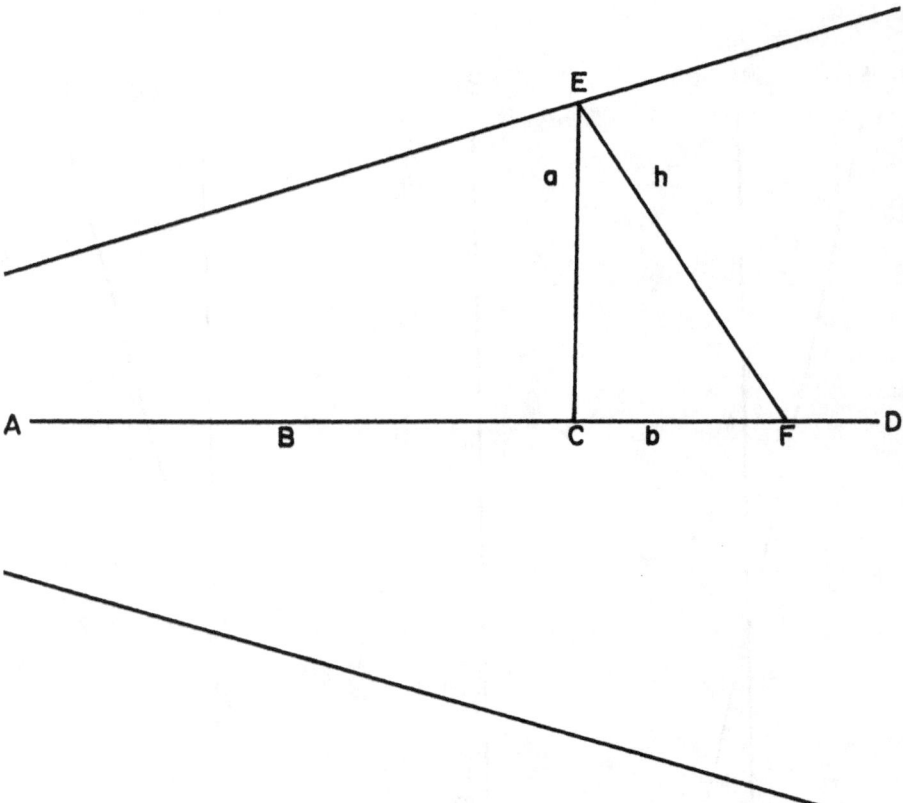

Fig. D-2. The zero rent perimeter.

cost per ton from C to F. What condition(s) will make positive rent at E possible? Let

$h - a = d =$ extra wagon mileage incurred,
$b =$ railroad mileage saved,
$W =$ wagon rate per ton-mile,
$R =$ railroad rate per ton-mile,
$s =$ saving per ton by shipping from E to some point F between C and D rather than to point C on the railroad.

$$s = bR - dW. \qquad (1)$$

D. Zero Rent Perimeters

Assume that R is some fraction of W, say $1/N$, so that $R = W/N$, i.e., W is some multiple N of R.[6]

$$\begin{aligned}
&\text{(a)} \; s = 0 &&\text{when} \quad b = Nd \\
&&&\text{for} \quad s = NdW/N - dW, \\
&\text{(b)} \; s < 0 &&\text{when} \quad b < Nd \\
&&&\text{for} \quad s = MdW/N - dW, \quad \text{where} \quad M < N, \quad\quad (2)\\
&\text{(c)} \; s > 0 &&\text{when} \quad b > Nd \\
&&&\text{for} \quad s = LdW/N - dW, \quad \text{where} \quad L > N.
\end{aligned}$$

Condition (2c) must hold in order for producers to ship to a point such as F rather than the nearest point on the railroad, such as C. The distance b must be a multiple of d greater than the multiple W is of R. Fortunately, we can go beyond this general statement and define precisely the condition required for rent at point E to be zero.

The object of the producer at E is to minimize the cost of shipping his products to the primary market at D. Let T represent transportation cost from point E to the primary market at D. Whether the route selected is from E to C to D or from E to some point F to D, or even from E to D, transportation cost can be defined as follows:

$$T = (W)(EF) + (R)(FD)$$

by definition: $\cos \theta = \dfrac{EC}{EF}$, $\tan \theta = \dfrac{CF}{EC}$, $\sin \theta = \dfrac{CF}{EF}$,

$$\sec \theta = \frac{1}{\cos \theta} = \frac{EF}{EC}; \quad\quad (3)$$

$$T = (W)(EC)(\sec \theta) + (R)(CD) - (R)(CF) = (W)(EC)(\sec \theta) \\ + (R)(CD) - (R)(EC)(\tan \theta). \quad\quad (4)$$

Minimize T with respect to θ:

$$\frac{\partial T}{\partial \theta} = 0 = (W)(EC)(\tan \theta)(\sec \theta) - (R)(EC)(\sec \theta)^2; \quad\quad (5)$$

$$0 = (W)(EC)\left(\frac{CF}{EC}\right)\left(\frac{EF}{EC}\right) - (R)(EC)\left(\frac{EF}{EC}\right)^2; \quad\quad (6)$$

$$(W)(EC)\left(\frac{CF}{EC}\right) = (R)(EC)\left(\frac{EF}{EC}\right); \quad\quad (7)$$

---

[6] Railroad ton-mile rates were a relatively small fraction of the cost of wagon haulage per ton-mile in the period under consideration. Moreover, Fogel, *op. cit.*, p. 56, reports that there is no evidence that real wagon rates decreased between 1840 and 1890. No major productivity improvements occurred in either roads or wagons, while substantial gains were achieved in railroad productivity.

$$(W)(CF) = (R)(EF); \qquad (8)$$

$$\frac{R}{W} = \frac{CF}{EF} = \sin \theta. \qquad (9)$$

When $\theta = 0$, $\sin \theta = 0$, that is, $CF = 0$. But this requires $R = 0$.[7] Since $R > 0$, the zero rent perimeter estimated is really a minimum rent perimeter. Given the relatively small fraction that R is of W, the understatement of the perimeter following the procedures used here is not substantial. However, it does tend to understate the intraregional external benefits and the social rate of return.

As the ratio R/W declined during the nineteenth century, the estimated zero rent perimeter would more closely approximate the true zero rent perimeter. The zero rent perimeters of this study are estimated for the terminal year for each system. This terminal year estimate of the zero rent perimeter tends to reduce the understatement of the perimeter, the intraregional external benefits, and the social rate of return.

Zero rent perimeters are first estimated by state, and a system average is computed as the weighted mean of the state distances. Estimated shipments to primary markets are used as weights. This produces a lower estimate of system zero rent perimeters than does calculation of the perimeter for the system without reference to state distances. Use of the system average described produces a lower estimate of intraregional external benefits than would be the case if the state distances were used for each state.

Calculation of the Zero Rent Perimeters

Estimation of the acre-weight shipped to primary markets in counties affected by the railroad is the first step in calculating the zero rent perimeters. Counties included in the zero rent perimeter computations for a specific railroad system are those containing lines of the system and all counties contiguous to this set in the year for which the zero rent perimeter estimate is made. In addition, based on Fogel's estimate cited above, when part of a county was within 40 airline miles of the railroad it is included in the computations, even though the rule just stated would have excluded it.

---

[7] I am indebted to Michael Viren for this proof. Note the limits involved. By assumption, $R < W$.

$$\lim_{R \to 0} \sin \theta = 0$$

$$\lim_{R \to W} \theta = \angle CED$$

D. Zero Rent Perimeters

For the included counties, data are obtained from the census of 1890 or 1900, as appropriate, on either the output of agricultural products in 1889 and 1899 or the stock of those items, e.g., swine and chickens on farms on June 1, 1890 or 1900, where output was not reported in the preceding year.[8] Shipments to primary markets are estimated by subtracting total farm use from total output in the counties concerned.

For most of the output items, the census provides data on output either in pounds or tons or in measures that can readily be converted to tons. Outputs reported in bushels, dozens, gallons, etc., are converted to a weight basis using standard conversion factors. However, in several cases special problems arise in estimating total output in tons. The most serious problems concern livestock.

Sheep and lambs present an especially throny problem. The 1890 census reports spring lambs sold for consumption but not other sales of sheep for consumption. Lambs dropped in 1889, slaughter for use on farms in 1889, and total sheep on farms June 1, 1890 are also reported. For 1900 the census reports only lambs younger than 1 year, ewes 1 year old and over, and rams and wethers 1 year old and over on farms and ranges as of June 1, 1900. Neither the total nor sales of any kind are reported, although the subgroups can be added by county to arrive at the total of sheep and lambs by county as of June 1, 1900.

Two major problems must be resolved. One is estimation of the total sales of sheep and lambs. The second arises because the only sales figure we have to operate on is spring lambs sold for consumption in 1889. Thus, we need an estimate of spring lambs sold for consumption in 1899 based on the available data. The solution adopted is to calculate the total sheep and lambs on farms by county on June 1, 1900, and multiply this by the ratio of spring lambs sold for consumption in 1889 to total sheep and lambs on farms June 1, 1890 for the same county. The product is an estimate of spring lambs sold for consumption in 1899.

Available data allow two alternative methods of estimating total sales of sheep and lambs for consumption. One of these is for 1899, the other for 1889. The first involves an alternative method of estimating spring lambs sold for consumption in 1899. This is the product of total sheep and lambs June 1, 1900 and the ratio of spring lambs sold for consumption in 1889 to total sheep and lambs on June 1, 1890.[9] This estimate of spring lambs sold for consumption during 1899 is 5.78 million. Total sheep and lamb slaugh-

---

[8] U.S. Bureau of the Census, *Eleventh Census of the United States: 1890. Reports on the Statistics of Agriculture in the United States,* Vol. V, and *Twelfth Census of the United States: 1900. Agriculture,* Vols. V and VI.

[9] The data are totals for the United States from the respective census reports.

ter for 1899 is estimated to be 11.82 million.[10] The estimated ratio of spring lambs sold for consumption to total sheep and lamb slaughter is 0.4898 in 1899 by this procedure.

The second method starts with an estimate of total sheep and lamb slaughter for 1889. This is calculated as the ratio of estimated total 1889 consumption in live weight equivalent to the average live weight of inventories.[11] The estimated total of sheep and lamb slaughter is 6.8 million, while the census reports total spring lambs sold for consumption as 3.37 million in 1889. By this technique the ratio of spring lambs sold for consumption to total sheep and lamb slaughter is 0.4956 for 1889. This figure is used here to adjust spring lambs sold for consumption to total sales of sheep and lambs for consumption. Average shipment weight of sheep and lambs is assumed to be 85 pounds.[12]

Problems like those concerning sheep and lambs must be solved to estimate the tonnage of cattle and calves shipped to primary markets. First, for 1889 the census report of cattle sold living and slaughtered by county includes calves.[13] The average live weight equivalent of total cattle and calves slaughtered is required to transform the number provided by the census into tons. The average live weight of slaughtered cattle and calves separately is computed for 1889 and 1899 from Strauss and Bean, and a weighted mean live weight for each year calculated with numbers of cattle and calves as the weights.[14] For 1889 the mean live weight is 759.9 pounds, with average cattle weight being 949.9 pounds and average calf weight 170.1 pounds. In 1899 the mean live weight is 744.6 pounds, with average cattle weight being 958.5 pounds and average calf weight 168.2 pounds. The 1889 average weight is used throughout.

The second problem with respect to cattle and calves is that while several classifications of the inventory are reported by county for June 1, 1900, no sales in 1899 are reported. Sales by county are estimated as the product of the total number of cattle and calves on farms and ranges June 1, 1900 and the ratio of the number sold living and slaughtered in 1889 to the total number on farms June 1, 1890 for the same counties.

Sales of swine for consumption are not reported by the census in either

---

[10] Frederick Strauss and Louis H. Bean, *Gross Farm Income and Indices of Farm Production and Prices in the United States, 1869–1937*, U.S. Department of Agriculture, Technical Bulletin, No. 703 (1940), p. 123, provide an estimate of live weight equivalent, which, when divided by the average live weight of inventories (85 pounds per head based on the 1920 census and observations made by the Department of Agriculture) reported on p. 122, yields the figure 11.82 million. This is cited hereafter as *Gross Farm Income*.

[11] *Ibid.*, p. 122.

[12] *Ibid.*

[13] *Census of Agriculture: 1890*, p. 35.

[14] Strauss and Bean, *Gross Farm Income*, pp. 111, 114.

D. Zero Rent Perimeters

1890 or 1900. The number on hand as of June 1 is reported for both years. It is assumed that production in the preceding year is equal to the June 1 stock.[15] Average live weight of swine slaughtered is taken as 222.6, which is the weight estimated for 1898 by Strauss and Bean.[16] Per capita consumption is estimated on the basis of a Department of Agriculture study (in 1913 and 1914) of consumption by farm families.[17] Pork consumption per capita by Northern and Western families adjusted for the proportion supplied by the farm provides the basic figure of 94.9 pounds dressed weight.[18] This figure then requires conversion to the live weight equivalent. Data for 1930–1939 and 1944–1948 indicate that carcass weight is about 75% of live weight.[19] Rural per capita pork consumption in live weight equivalent is estimated to be 127 pounds for this study.

Chicken production is also not given by the census, although stock on hand June 1, 1890 and June 1, 1900 is reported. Later studies indicate that the number of chickens on hand as reported by the census was high for 1889 and low for 1900. To account for this the 1890 stock is reduced by 25% and the 1900 stock increased by 12%.[20] The number of chickens produced in a census year is assumed to be 145% of the stock.[21] It is further assumed that chickens represent 90% of poultry production. The average weight of chickens produced is taken to be 4 pounds.[22]

Rural per capita consumption of chickens is calculated using the sources and methods cited for swine. Annual consumption per capita of 45.4 pounds is adjusted to a live weight equivalent basis of 60.5 pounds.[23]

For several tree crops of special importance in the state of California the 1890 census provides data on output and bearing trees in the state but only the number of bearing trees by county. Output per bearing tree (in pounds) was computed for the state and the product of this ratio and the number of bearing trees per county is the estimate of output for the items concerned. The affected crops are almonds, figs, lemons, Madeira nuts, and olives.

An important factor in estimating total farm use for several items is

---

[15] *Ibid.*, p. 116. Strauss and Bean compute slaughter for 1869–1898 as 102.2% of inventory.

[16] *Ibid.*, p. 119.

[17] W. C. Funk, *Value to Farm Families of Food, Fuel, and Use of House*, U.S. Department of Agriculture, Bulletin No. 410 (Washington: U.S. Government Printing Office, 1916).

[18] *Ibid.*, p. 26.

[19] P. Thomas Ziegler, *The Meat We Eat* (Danville, Ill.: The Interstate Printers and Publishers, 1958), pp. 68–69.

[20] Strauss and Bean, *Gross Farm Income*, p. 99.

[21] *Ibid*.

[22] *Ibid.*, p. 101.

[23] Ziegler, *The Meat We Eat*, p. 239.

the estimated rural population of the affected counties. Total population for the counties was obtained from the census. The estimate of urban population by county is the sum of the population of all towns with a population of 1,000 or more. Estimated rural population by county is total population minus estimated urban population.

On-farm use does not need to be estimated for several items because: (a) sales are reported directly; (b) partial sales, as in the case of sheep and lambs or cattle, form the basis for an estimate of total off-farm shipment; or (c) virtually none of the items would be used on farms, e.g., wool and hops. Rural per capita consumption of several items—beef, pork, milk, butter, cheese, poultry, eggs, honey, potatoes, apples, cherries, peaches, pears, oranges, lemons and plums—is estimated on the basis of data in the Department of Agriculture study cited above.[24] Per capita consumption of apricots is assumed to equal that of peaches, while prune consumption is assumed equal to that of plums. Domestic disappearance of dry edible beans averaged 6.4 pounds per capita in 1909–1918, and this value is used as the estimate of rural per capita consumption.[25] For the decade 1909–1918, per capita raisin consumption is reported to be 1.8 pounds.[26] However, because of the concentration of raisin production it is assumed that the entire crop is shipped. Olives are treated in the same manner. Nominal rural consumption per capita of 1 pound is assumed for figs and tree nuts.[27] Where rural per capita consumption is estimated, total farm use is calculated as the product of per capita consumption and rural population for the appropriate counties.

Total farm use of wheat and corn in 1889 and 1899 is based on the proportion of the crop shipped from the county where grown (by state) for the 1892 crop.[28]

The proportion of the hay crop needed for feeding animals in cities is estimated as 20.5%.[29] It is assumed that this is the proportion shipped to primary markets in 1889 and 1899.

Total farm use of barley, oats, buckwheat, and rye are estimated in the following fashion. Strauss and Bean define gross farm income as the value (at farm prices) of farm products sold by producers to the nonfarm economy or consumed in the producer's households.[30] Farm value and gross

[24] W. C. Funk, *op. cit.*, p. 26.
[25] U.S. Department of Agriculture, *Consumption of Food in the United States, 1909–1952*, Agriculture Handbook No. 62 (Washington: Government Printing Office, 1953), p. 232.
[26] *Ibid.*, p. 115.
[27] *Ibid.*, pp. 111, 125 reports much smaller amounts for these items during 1909–1918.
[28] U.S. Department of Agriculture, *Report of the Secretary of Agriculture, 1892* (Washington: Government Printing Office, 1893), pp. 446, 450.
[29] Strauss and Bean, *Gross Farm Income*, p. 62.
[30] *Ibid.*, p. 7.

D. Zero Rent Perimeters

farm income are reported for barley, oats, and rye in 1889 and 1899.[31] The ratio of gross farm income to farm value is an estimate of the proportion of the output of these crops shipped off the farm and consumed in producers' households. The product of total output of these crops and the indicated ratio is an estimate of the tonnage shipped to primary markets and consumed in producers' households. Call this net production. Total output minus net production provides an estimate of feed and seed use. It is assumed that household consumption of barley was zero. For 1890 Fogel has estimated that 75.61% of net production of oats and 91.23% of net production of rye was shipped off the farm.[32] Net production of oats and rye is divided between farm household use and shipments to primary markets in 1889 and 1899, using these factors. Total farm use of the three grains discussed is the sum of estimated feed and seed and farm household use.

Estimation of tonnage shipped to primary markets and the acreage in farms in the affected counties allows calculation of the acre-weight for each system by state. Average ton-mile wagon haul costs and average wagon haul mileage to shipping points by state are estimated using data from the Andrews study and the estimate of tonnage shipped to primary markets.[33] Average wagon haul mileage to shipping points and information allowing the calculation of average cost per ton-mile are reported by state for several products in the Andrews study. The weighted mean wagon haul ton-mile cost and wagon haul mileage to primary market by state are calculated using the estimated tonnage shipped to market as weights. The only livestock reported in the Andrews study are swine, and even this is for only the major producing states. The United States average is used for those states not reporting swine shipments. Although other livestock are excluded, the products reported represent the bulk of shipments for each state included.

Average wagon ton-mile costs and average wagon haul mileage to shipping points estimated by the procedure described are presented by state for each of the United States systems in Tables D-1 to D-6. The zero rent perimeter estimates by state and other related estimates to be discussed are also listed in these tables.

The wagon ton-mile rates estimated in the manner described are overstated for three major reasons. First, the rates reported are computed on the basis of the cost of hiring a team, wagon, and driver in the counties covered.[34] Since most farmers did their own hauling, the actual cost to the

---
[31] *Ibid.*, pp. 43, 44, 48–50.
[32] Fogel, *Railroads and American Economic Growth*, p. 76.
[33] Frank Andrews, *op. cit.*
[34] *Ibid.*, pp. 11–12.

TABLE D-1

Zero Rent Perimeter and Related Estimates by State for the Central Pacific System

Data or estimate	Arizona	California	Nevada	New Mexico	Utah
Farm acres (thousand)	177	20,179	1,587	95	685
Estimates					
Land clearing cost (thousand $)	187	34,942	1,672	56	377
Farm fence cost (thousand $)	330	27,748	988	168	834
Value irrigation (thousand $)	400	10,769	1,570	101	844
Value of buildings (thousand $)	523	73,503	1,707	272	1,663
Farm value (thousand $)	3,112	670,074	11,538	1,586	9,053
Land value (thousand $)	1,672	523,111	5,600	988	5,335
Land value/farm value	0.5375	0.7807	0.4854	0.6228	0.5893
Land value ($/acre)	9.43	25.92	3.53	10.44	7.79
Rent ($/year/acre)	1.15	2.27	0.38	0.86	0.73
Average ton-mile haul cost ($)	0.20	0.15	0.19	0.26	0.14
Average actual haul (miles)	9.6	10.2	20.8	17.3	15.7
Farm shipments (thousand tons)	79	2,547	76	5	37
Potential haul miles	12.5	116.8	41.7	57.5	96.9
Zero rent perimeter (road miles)	22.1	127.0	62.5	74.8	112.5
Zero rent perimeter (air miles)	17.9	92.7	50.4	57.5	85.3

TABLE D-2

Zero Rent Perimeter and Related Estimates by State for the Union Pacific System

Data or estimate	Colorado	Idaho	Kansas	Montana	Nebraska	Utah	Wyoming
Farm acres (thousand)	3,543	748	19,405	921	16,743	1,281	1,447
Estimates							
Land clearing cost (thousand $)	3,737	803	23,798	1,318	23,992	1,168	1,194
Farm fence cost (thousand $)	4,924	1,380	48,284	1,411	41,109	2,762	966
Value irrigation (thousand $)	4,668	888	7	990	30	2,636	610
Value of buildings (thousand $)	11,188	1,673	65,769	2,237	55,513	5,669	1,402
Farm value (thousand $)	70,345	9,815	375,014	14,029	345,958	27,578	10,648
Land value (thousand $)	45,808	5,070	237,157	8,073	225,314	15,342	6,477
Land value/farm value	0.6512	0.5166	0.6324	0.5755	0.6513	0.5563	0.6083
Rent ($/acre)	12.93	6.78	12.22	8.76	13.46	11.98	4.48
Average ton-mile wagon haul cost ($)	1.06	0.71	1.04	0.96	1.08	1.13	0.44
Average actual wagon haul miles	0.22	0.20	0.14	0.24	0.14	0.14	0.24
Farm shipments (thousand tons)	11.4	13.8	8.0	12.4	9.1	15.7	25.3
Potential haul miles	267	120	3,865	241	4,236	107	45
Zero rent perimeter (road miles)	64.9	22.2	37.8	15.5	29.5	98.4	59.5
Zero rent perimeter (airline miles)	763	36.0	45.8	27.9	38.6	114.1	84.7
	66.3	28.8	35.2	20.2	31.4	86.5	73.7

TABLE D-3

Zero Rent Perimeter and Related Estimates by State for the
Texas and Pacific System

Data or estimate	Arkansas	Louisiana	Texas
Farm acres (thousand)	183	7,091	45,897
Value of buildings (thousand $)	286	23,522	47,960
Estimates			
Land clearing cost (thousand $)	198	8,331	22,741
Farm fence cost (thousand $)	362	14,213	40,431
Value irrigation (thousand $)	0	1,553	547
Farm value (thousand $)	1,204	103,050	300,167
Land value (thousand $)	359	55,432	188,489
Land value/farm value	0.2978	0.5379	0.6279
Land value ($/acre)	1.96	7.82	4.11
Rent ($/year/acre)	0.15	0.53	0.33
Average ton-mile haul cost ($)	0.24	0.26	0.20
Average actual haul miles	12.1	9.9	14.0
Farm shipments (thousand tons)	6	1,217	1,076
Potential haul miles	20.0	12.0	72.5
Zero rent perimeter (road miles)	32.1	21.9	86.5
Zero rent perimeter (airline miles)	27.5	18.6	69.8

farmer was probably less than the for-hire rate. Also, the reported rates assume no loads carried from shipping point to farm.[35] Farmers did carry loads on the return trip at least part of the time. Thus, attributing the total cost of a trip to the tonnage going from farm to shipping point overstates the actual ton-mile cost for that tonnage. In the algorithm we use to estimate the distance to the zero rent perimeter, the effect of the overstatements suggested is to understate the distance. No correction is made in this study for this bias.

The third factor leading to overstatement of the wagon ton-mile cost is that the Andrews study is for the 1905–1906 crop year. Prices in general rose between 1889 or 1899 and 1906. An adjustment is made here for this factor by multiplying the estimated wagon ton-mile costs by the ratio of the 1889 to 1906, or 1899 to 1906 index numbers of the Snyder–Tucker price index. The wagon ton-mile rates in Tables D-1 to D-6 includes this adjustment.

To estimate "pure" land value by county it is necessary to estimate the value of buildings, land improvements, and fences for the Central Pacific and Union Pacific Systems, since none of these are reported separately in

[35] *Ibid.*, pp. 12–13.

D. Zero Rent Perimeters

1889. Buildings are reported separately in 1899. The other four United States systems require estimation only of the value of land improvements and fences. In the case of the Central Pacific and Union Pacific Systems, the value of farm buildings by county in 1889 is estimated as the product of the ratio of value of buildings to the total value of buildings, land, and improvements. This rests on the not-unreasonable assumption that the value of buildings by county was the same proportion of the total in 1900 as in 1890.

The estimate of value of fences uses the estimate prepared by Martin L. Primack of the average cost per rod for farm fences in the United States in 1890 and 1900.[36] Primack's estimates are $0.77 and $0.59 in current dollars in 1890 and 1900, respectively.[37] A separate estimate is made of the average rods of fence per farm by county. Average acres of improved land per farm are converted into average square rods of improved land per farm and the square root of the latter is multiplied by 4. The product of the average rods of fence per farm, the number of farms, and the cost per rod is the estimate of value of fences by county.

Estimated value of land improvements is composed of two parts. One is the estimated cost of improving land for cultivation. The second is an estimate of the cost of obtaining irrigation, i.e., the first cost of water rights.

The estimate of land improvement costs is understated because it omits nonlabor costs. Estimates of man-days required per acre to improve land for cultivation are taken from another study by Primack.[38] The labor requirements per acre depend upon the type of natural vegetation. Each included county is classified as to natural vegetation, i.e., forest, grassland, or semiarid, on the basis of the natural vegetation map of the United States in the *Atlas of American Agriculture*.[39] For counties classified as forest, the costs of clearing, gathering, and burning are assumed to be the cost of producing wood products and so not chargeable as costs of land improvement. The median labor per acre of stump removal with blasting powder (3.4 man-days) is taken as the labor requirement per acre of land clearing in forest counties.[40] Labor for land clearing in both grasslands

---

[36] Martin L. Primack, "Farm Fencing in the Nineteenth Century", *The Journal of Economic History*, XXIX, 2 (June 1969), 287–289.

[37] *Ibid.*, 288.

[38] Martin L. Primack, "Land Clearing under Nineteenth Century Techniques: Some Preliminary Calculations", *The Journal of Economic History*, XXII, 4 (December 1962), 484–497.

[39] H. L. Shantz and Ralph Zon, *Atlas of American Agriculture*, "Section E: Natural Vegetation", U.S. Department of Agriculture (Washington: Government Printing Office, 1924), pp. 4–6.

[40] Primack, *op. cit.*, p. 495.

TABLE D-4

Zero Rent Perimeter and Related Estimates by State for the Atchison, Topeka and Santa Fe System

Data or estimate	Arizona	California	Colorado	Illinois
Farm acres (thousand)	1,892	5,074	5,532	14,242
Value of buildings (thousand $)	2,223	17,778	7,480	131,238
Estimates				
Land clearing cost (thousand $)	643	4,070	2,377	22,535
Farm fence cost (thousand $)	870	5,326	2,817	33,146
Value irrigation (thousand $)	4,431	3,487	3,523	0
Farm value (thousand $)	13,086	183,077	52,181	965,543
Land value (thousand $)	4,919	152,417	35,984	778,626
Land value/farm value	0.3759	0.8325	0.6896	0.8064
Land value ($/acre)	2.60	30.04	6.50	54.67
Rent ($/year/acre)	0.28	2.28	0.46	3.11
Average ton-mile haul cost ($)	0.18	0.22	0.23	0.16
Average actual haul miles	11.9	10.4	11.0	5.8
Farm shipments (thousand tons)	93	764	274	3,390
Potential haul miles	30.8	70.1	41.3	80.7
Zero rent perimeter (road miles)	42.7	80.5	52.3	86.5
Zero rent perimeter (airline miles)	31.4	63.9	38.5	68.1

and semiarid counties is taken as 1.5 man-days per acre.[41] In grassland this is the midpoint of the cost using the common breaking plow, while for semiarid vegetation it is the estimate of the requirement for clearing by hand. In each case man-days are valued by the 1889 or 1899 daily wage rate for farm labor in nonharvest work, as reported by state in George K. Holmes' study.[42] Land clearing costs by county are the product of the man-day requirement per acre, the wage rate, and the number of improved acres on farms in the county in 1889 or 1899.

The second part of the value of land improvements is computed from data in the 1890 and 1900 censuses.[43] Irrigated acreage per county and the average first cost of water rights per acre by state are reported. The product of these two factors by county is the estimated cost of irrigation improvements.

For each county the sum of the estimated land clearing cost and esti-

---

[41] *Ibid.*

[42] George K. Holmes, *Wages of Farm Labor*, U.S. Department of Agriculture, Bureau of Statistics, Bulletin No. 99 (Washington: Government Printing Office, 1912), pp. 40–41.

[43] U.S. Bureau of the Census, *Eleventh Census, Agriculture*, "Report on Agriculture by Irrigation in the Western Part of the United States at the Eleventh Census: 1890", and *Twelfth Census: 1900*, Vol. VI, Part IX.

D. Zero Rent Perimeters

(Table D-4 continued)

Iowa	Kansas	Missouri	New Mexico	Oklahoma	Texas
1,641	36,044	8,390	4,644	9,442	45,202
13,494	102,774	54,479	3,253	11,794	71,485
2,568	42,185	9,554	463	7,092	33,221
3,769	54,755	20,323	1,554	14,511	53,138
0	477	0	3,713	2	170
69,572	594,451	314,917	17,816	97,910	451,843
49,741	394,261	230,562	8,833	64,511	293,833
0.7150	0.6632	0.7321	0.4958	0.6589	0.6503
30.31	10.94	27.48	1.90	6.83	6.50
1.97	0.81	1.75	0.14	0.55	0.52
0.22	0.14	0.18	0.21	0.16	0.19
6.2	8.0	9.1	23.0	11.3	14.5
233	4,341	990	95	433	1,547
63.6	48.7	84.2	31.5	77.6	81.3
69.8	56.8	93.3	54.5	89.0	95.8
57.7	45.4	74.6	44.3	70.0	83.3

mated cost of irrigation improvements is the estimate of the value of land improvements. The estimated value of "pure" farm land per county is the census value of buildings, lands, and improvements minus the estimated or reported value of buildings, fences, and land improvements.

Computation of the annual rent per acre is the next step and is done by decapitalizing the average land value per acre. State average interest rates on land mortgages for 1889 provide the basis for this step.[44] In the case of the Central Pacific and Union Pacific, these rates are used directly. Because these data were not available after the 1890 census, it is necessary to estimate the 1899 rates for use with the other United States systems. The ratio of 1899 to 1889 mean annual yield on railroad bonds is calculated from data in Frederick R. Macaulay's study.[45] The product of the 1889 land mortgage interest rate by state and this ratio is the estimate of 1889 land mortgage interest rate by state used in computation of annual rent per acre for the four United States systems involved.

Addition of the potential wagon haul miles and actual wagon haul miles

---
[44] U.S. Bureau of the Census, *Eleventh Census of the United States: 1890. Report on Real Estate Mortgages*, XII, p. 248.
[45] Frederick R. Macaulay, *Some Theoretical Problems Suggested by the Movements of Interest Rates, Bond Yields and Stock Prices in the United States since 1856*, pp. A37–60.

TABLE D-5

Zero Rent Perimeter and Related Estimates by State for the Northern Pacific System

Data or estimate	Idaho	Minnesota	Montana	North Dakota	Oregon	South Dakota	Washington	Wisconsin
Farm acres (thousand)	1,008	15,080	7,019	14,332	672	1,845	5,614	793
Value of buildings (thousand $)	1,865	56,591	7,905	24,197	3,020	2,277	11,371	2,859
Estimates								
Land clearing cost (thousand $)	2,535	49,839	6,397	22,767	856	3,033	7,114	1,216
Farm fence cost (thousand $)	1,430	27,010	3,641	17,625	945	2,331	6,221	1,162
Value irrigation (thousand $)	14	0	3,559	2	0	0	1,298	0
Farm value (thousand $)	12,186	317,430	46,307	190,810	19,021	16,835	76,745	10,507
Land value (thousand $)	6,342	183,989	24,804	126,219	14,201	9,195	50,741	5,269
Land value/farm value	0.5204	0.5796	0.5356	0.6615	0.7466	0.5462	0.6612	0.5015
Land value ($/acre)	6.29	12.20	3.53	8.81	21.14	4.98	9.04	6.65
Rent ($/year/acre)	0.57	0.79	0.34	0.71	1.73	0.39	0.69	0.39
Average ton-mile haul cost ($)	0.19	0.14	0.24	0.14	0.15	0.14	0.20	0.15
Average actual haul miles	13.4	8.7	13.1	10.8	10.4	12.0	12.8	9.4
Farm shipments (thousand tons)	57	2,242	291	2,146	94	238	621	81
Potential haul miles	53.3	36.6	34.2	32.7	83.7	21.4	31.7	25.2
Zero rent perimeter (road miles)	66.6	45.3	47.2	43.5	94.2	33.3	44.5	34.6
Zero rent perimeter (airline miles)	50.9	35.9	37.2	32.2	67.7	26.5	34.8	28.4

TABLE D-6
Zero Rent Perimeter and Related Estimates by State for the Great Northern System

Data or estimate	Idaho	Minnesota	Montana	North Dakota	South Dakota	Washington
Farm acres (thousand)	254	20,200	5,495	13,692	13,140	5,477
Value of buildings (thousand $)	366	76,511	6,756	23,437	25,506	9,286
Estimates						
Land clearing cost (thousand $)	325	71,852	5,394	22,095	22,682	7,465
Farm fence cost (thousand $)	261	36,457	3,199	17,314	17,570	5,731
Value irrigation (thousand $)	3	0	3,499	16	7	1,459
Farm value (thousand $)	1,948	457,746	40,570	188,289	185,660	68,902
Land value (thousand $)	993	272,927	21,722	125,426	119,896	44,962
Land value/farm value	0.5099	0.5962	0.5354	0.6661	0.6458	0.6526
Land value ($/acre)	3.91	13.51	3.95	9.16	9.12	8.21
Rent ($/year/acre)	0.36	0.88	0.38	0.73	0.71	0.62
Average ton-mile haul cost ($)	0.20	0.14	0.24	0.14	0.14	0.20
Average actual haul miles	13.8	8.6	13.1	10.8	11.7	12.7
Farm shipments (thousand tons)	8	3,244	257	2,096	1,690	556
Potential haul miles	57.3	37.9	33.8	33.1	39.0	31.4
Zero rent perimeter (road miles)	71.0	46.5	46.9	43.9	50.7	44.1
Zero rent perimeter (airline miles)	54.2	36.9	36.9	32.5	40.2	34.5

by state produces the estimate, by state, of road miles to the zero rent perimeter. This is converted to airline miles to the zero rent perimeter by multiplying the road mileage figure by a ratio of airline to road mileage obtained from a random sample of airline and road distance between points on modern highway maps. An average of the airline-to-road-mileage ratio is computed for each state by system.

The zero rent perimeter distance is used to determine which counties to use in the estimation of intraregional benefits.[46] Some deletions and additions with respect to the original set of counties are made at this point. The geographic area to be used in calculation of intraregional benefits for the United States systems is then determined and the next step is estimation of the intraregional benefits.

---

[46] Counties at least partially within the zero rent perimeter measured vertically from the railroad line are included, except for a few cases in which the portions of a county included are trivial relative to the overall size of the county. The procedure followed includes some "excess" area already, so it appears best to exclude extreme cases of this type. It should be noted that some counties or census districts are excluded from the zero rent perimeter and the intraregional external benefits estimate because of geographic features. For the United States these include (1) the exclusion of Toole County in Utah from the Central Pacific estimate because the Great Salt Desert lies between farming areas in that county and the Central Pacific Railroad, and (2) the exclusion of counties in Arkansas (except Miller County) when making the estimates for the Texas and Pacific. In the latter case the Texas and Pacific only crosses through Texarkana, Arkansas, which is in Miller County. The Red River is the northern and eastern boundary of Miller County. In Canada, census districts across the St. Lawrence River or a mountain range from the Canadian Pacific are excluded.

Appendix E

Intraregional Benefits

This appendix provides further details on the estimation of intraregional benefits. The general technique followed is that discussed in Chapter 5. A major input for the estimation of intraregional benefits by system is the estimated zero rent perimeter of Appendix D.

Adjustments to the Intraregional Benefits Estimates

An important consideration for the estimation of intraregional external benefits in the manner described in Chapter 5 is the likely overstatement of those benefits because the total value of farms (and land) in the area served by the railroad would have increased in time without the railroad. This increase would result from the rise in demand by importing regions as their population and income growth proceeded in the absence of the railroad in any particular exporting region. Correction for this factor requires an estimate of the change in land value for each railroad's region that would have occurred without the railroad. It is assumed here that given the increase in capital and labor that occurred in the economy over the period involved, real farm values in aggregate in the region served by each railroad would have increased without the railroad by the same proportion as total real farm values in the United States increased.[1] To establish the base for estimation of intraregional benefits the change in

[1] Robert W. Fogel, *The Union Pacific Railroad: A Case in Premature Enterprise*, p. 100.

farm values reported in the census is adjusted downward by this proportion.

Two implicit assumptions underlie this adjustment.[2] One is that the nation's population growth would have been unaffected by the absence of a specific railroad system. This is likely because the increase in income due to any one railroad was a negligible fraction of national income over the study period. It is also assumed that the rate of capital accumulation would have been unchanged in the absence of the railroads studied. If the rate of return on capital depends on factor proportions and the rate of capital accumulation depends on the rate of return to capital, the absence of any of these railroads would have resulted in little change in the rate of capital accumulation. This is because the amount of supramarginal land within the zero rent perimeter for any railroad was a very small proportion of the nation's supramarginal land.

Another source of overstatement in the estimate of intraregional external benefits for any one railroad system is that other railroads may also affect land values within the estimated zero rent perimeter for a specific system. A technique is required to attribute the appropriate proportion of estimated intraregional benefits to each system. The following method was used here. The 1890 census contains a volume on railroad transportation with detailed information by railroad and by region, with the United States divided into 10 regions.[3] The data in the census include tonnage of commodities carried by railroads in the United States for the year ending June 30, 1890 and ton-mileage by railroads in the United States for the same period.[4] Agricultural tonnage, as a percent of total tonnage carried, is computed for each system by region and for each region in total. Ton-mileage in transporting agricultural goods is estimated for each region as the product of ton-miles in the region and the percentage which agricultural tons carried are of total tons carried. In the same way, agricultural ton-mileage is estimated for each system by region. The ratio of system to region estimated agricultural ton-mileage is the fraction of estimated intraregional benefits that are attributed to a specific system by state in each region.

Computation of Intraregional Benefits

Computation of incremental land values is based on the value of farms in the counties affected by each system, as determined by application of

[2] *Ibid.*, p. 101.
[3] U.S. Bureau of the Census, *Eleventh Census, Statistics of Steam Railroad Transportation*, XIV.
[4] *Ibid.*, Tables 8 and 9.

E. Intraregional Benefits

the estimated zero rent perimeter. The year in which a county first fell within the zero rent perimeter is determined from information on the timing of construction.

The reported current dollar farm values—i.e., in 1870, 1880, and 1890 the value of buildings, land, and improvements, and in 1900 the value of land and improvements plus buildings reported separately—are obtained from the respective censuses.[5] The change in real farm values, adjusted for the change that would have occurred without the railroad, is calculated for the census pairs 1870 to 1880, 1880 to 1890, and 1890 to 1900, as appropriate by county and system. These changes in farm value are converted to changes in land value by county by multiplying the change in farm value by the estimated ratio of value of farm land to value of farms by county. Derivation of the value of farm land is discussed in Appendix D. The product of each system's proportion of estimated regional agricultural ton-miles by state and the estimated incremental land values by county is the estimate of intraregional external benefits attributed to each system by county.

The computations described are those used with the six United States systems. Estimation of intraregional benefits for the Canadian Pacific system is discussed below.

The placement of estimated intraregional benefits in the social returns stream has a significant effect on the computed internal rate of return. Various hypotheses concerning the length of lag between the time a railroad begins operating in an area and the time external benefits start to accrue to landowners (and others) in the area come to mind. Given observations on incremental value every 10 years, the maximum lag is 10 years. Social rates are computed here for all lags (by years) from 10 years to 1 year. A uniform distribution of intraregional benefits is also used. For this, the incremental land value estimated for a particular county between two censuses is entered into the social returns stream by placing one-tenth of the total in each year, from the year following the first census in a census pair through the year of the second census in the pair.[6] Table E-1 presents the estimated intraregional benefits in appropriate constant dollar terms,

---

[5] For 1870 from the U.S. Bureau of the Census, *Ninth Census of the United States: 1870, Statistics of Wealth and Industry*, III. For 1880 from *Tenth Census of the United States: 1880, Statistics of Agriculture*, III. For 1890, from *Eleventh Census of the United States: 1890, Statistics of Agriculture*, V. For 1900 from *Twelfth Census of the United States: 1900, Agriculture*, V. Intraregional benefits before 1870 for the Central Pacific and Union Pacific Systems are not estimated. The primary reason for this is that real total farm values in the United States declined between 1860 and 1870, so that adjustment for rise in value in the absence of the railroads cannot be made. The resulting understatement of social rates of return for the systems in question is relatively very small.

[6] See footnote 13, Chapter 5.

TABLE E-1

Intraregional External Benefits by System with Uniform Distribution
(Thousand Constant $)

Year	Central Pacific	Union Pacific	Texas and Pacific	Santa Fe	Northern Pacific	Great Northern	Canadian Pacific
1871	6,195	3,092	—	348	—	—	—
1872	6,195	3,092	4	888	111	—	—
1873	7,436	3,092	4	1,251	111	—	—
1874	7,436	3,092	355	1,251	457	—	—
1875	7,436	3,092	355	1,251	473	—	—
1876	8,484	3,092	355	1,343	473	—	—
1877	9,576	3,193	503	1,343	473	—	—
1878	9,753	3,193	503	1,343	473	—	—
1879	9,753	3,193	503	1,343	473	—	—
1880	9,784	4,035	503	1,399	473	—	—
1881	35,245	17,455	830	4,446	2,091	1,393	—
1882	35,245	17,756	830	4,464	3,180	2,317	3,568
1883	35,245	17,961	1,224	5,014	3,445	3,322	3,752
1884	35,278	18,696	1,224	5,014	4,434	3,465	5,078
1885	35,278	18,710	1,224	5,086	4,918	3,471	8,360
1886	35,278	18,710	1,224	5,101	5,167	3,471	10,841
1887	35,278	19,218	1,224	6,605	5,167	3,633	10,370
1888	35,278	19,218	1,224	8,302	6,385	4,104	10,580
1889	35,289	19,218	1,224	8,539	6,424	4,983	10,691
1890	35,278	19,218	1,224	8,540	6,424	5,002	10,826
1891	—	—	1,665	4,308	6,113	7,222	10,691
1892	—	—	1,665	4,308	6,185	7,222	7,721
1893	—	—	1,665	4,308	6,185	7,222	7,510
1894	—	—	1,665	4,308	6,185	7,696	8,089
1895	—	—	1,665	4,308	6,185	7,696	8,437
1896	—	—	1,665	4,308	6,185	7,696	8,965
1897	—	—	1,665	4,308	6,185	7,696	8,703
1898	—	—	1,665	4,308	6,185	7,696	8,178
1899	—	—	1,665	4,308	6,185	7,696	8,107
1900	—	—	1,665	4,308	6,185	7,696	7,450
1901	—	—	—	—	—	—	7,465

by system for the seven systems, with the uniform distribution for placement of these benefits in the social returns stream.

Rather than the method discussed for the United States systems, a much simpler technique is used to estimate intraregional benefits for the Canadian Pacific. This is necessary because the Canadian census did not collect farm values until 1901. As a result of this and other data problems, the distance to the zero rent perimeter is not estimated for the Canadian

E. Intraregional Benefits

Pacific. Intraregional benefits are estimated for the census districts through which the system ran, census districts contiguous to these, and census districts within 40 airline miles of the railroad.[7]

The information we do have from the Canadian census is the average value of land in farms by census district for 1901 and the acreage occupied by farms by census district for each census year included.[8] The intraregional benefits estimate by census district for each successive pair of census years is the product of the average land value per acre in 1901, and the increment in acreage occupied by farms between the two census years.[9] No adjustment is made for the existence of other railroads in the same area. In the greater part of the area served by the Canadian Pacific it was virtually the only railroad, so the upward bias introduced into the intraregional benefits estimate is probably small. Also, no adjustment is made for the rise in land values in the absence of the railroad, since this probably was virtually zero for the time period covered.

The method described to estimate Canadian Pacific intraregional benefits relies primarily on the extensive expansion of land in farms. However, the average price per acre is the average value of all land at or within the assumed extensive margin. This represents the effect through 1901 of expansion of both the extensive and intensive margins. As the extensive margin expands, the value of supramarginal land rises, both because more land is brought into production and because the intensive margin also rises. Because of this rise of the intensive margin as the extensive margin expands, the following relationship is likely to hold:

$$P_i^3 > P_i^2 > P_i^1, \tag{1}$$

where P_i is the value of land per acre in the ith census district and the superscripts 1, 2, and 3 refer, respectively, to the census years of 1880–1881, 1890–1891, and 1901.

The relationship between acreage in farms by census year is generally

$$A_i^3 > A_i^2 > A_i^1, \tag{2}$$

where A_i^t is the acreage in farms in the ith census district in census year t.

---

[7] Districts across the St. Lawrence River or a high mountain range from the railroad are not used, even though they fall within the limits described by the stated rule.

[8] Canada, Department of Agriculture, *Census of Canada: 1880–81*, Vol. 3; *Census of Canada: 1890–91*, 2; and Census Office, *Fourth Census of Canada: 1901*, 2.

[9] Because the area of lands occupied by farms in British Columbia in 1891 includes forest, while that for 1901 does not, it is necessary to adjust the 1891 figures for the province. The figure used for 1891 is corrected field crop acreage (*Census of 1901*, 2, ix) plus acreage of pasture, gardens, and orchards from the 1891 census. For Quebec it is necessary to adjust the 1891 acreage figures from arpents to acres. See *Fourth Census of Canada: 1901*, 2, ix–x.

Intraregional benefits are calculated by

$$IB_{in} = P_i^3(A_i^{t+1} - A_i^t), \qquad (3)$$

where IB_{in} is the estimate of intraregional benefits in the ith census district for the census year pair n. The superscripts t and $t+1$ refer to the earliest and latest years, respectively, in each census pair. In contrast to (3) is the "true" estimate of intraregional benefits (IB_{in}^*):

$$IB_{in}^* = P_i^{t+1}(A_i^{t+1}) - P_i^t(A_i^t) = P_i^t(A_i^{t+1} - A_i^t) + A_i^{t+1}(P_i^{t+1} - P_i^t). \qquad (4)$$

The relationship between IB_{in}^* and IB_{in} is a question of significance. Given the assumed extensive margin, it can be shown that IB_{in} is an underestimate of intraregional benefits for 1890–1891, while the relationship between IB_{in}^* and IB_{in} is indeterminate for 1880–1881 to 1890–1891. Let $D = IB_{in} - IB_{in}^*$. Then

$$D = [P_i^3(A_i^{t+1} - A_i^t)] - [P_i^t(A_i^{t+1} - A_i^t) + A_i^{t+1}(P_i^{t+1} - P_i^t)]. \qquad (5)$$

We want to know whether D is less than, greater than, or equal to zero. If $D > 0$ the present estimate exceeds the "true" estimate, if $D < 0$ the present estimate understates the "true" value, and for $D = 0$ the present estimate is identical with the true value.

Equation (5) can be rewritten as

$$D = (A_i^{t+1})(P_i^3 - P_i^{t+1}) - (A_i^t)(P_i^3 - P_i^t). \qquad (6)$$

Writing Eq. (6) for the census pair 1890–1891 and 1901, we have

$$D = (A_i^3)(P_i^3 - P_i^3) - (A_i^2)(P_i^3 - P_i^2), \qquad (7)$$

in which case $D < 0$, i.e., the present estimate understates the "true" value. Equation (6) for the census pair of 1880–1881 and 1890–1891 becomes

$$D = A_i^2(P_i^3 - P_i^2) - A_i^1(P_i^3 - P_i^1) = A_i^2(Y_i) - A_i^1(Z_i) = X_i - W_i \qquad (8)$$

where $Y_i = P_i^3 - P_i^2$ and $Z_i = P_i^3 - P_i^1$. From (1) we know that Z_i is likely to be greater than Y_i and from (2) that A_i^2 is generally greater than A_i^1. Unfortunately, this does not tell us which of the products, X_i or W_i, is greater. Thus the relationship of D to zero is indeterminate. If the present estimate is an overstatement of the true value for the census pair 1880–1881 and 1890–1891, it does not appear likely that the overstatement would be very substantial. Moreover, since intraregional benefits are only estimated to 1901 (the terminal year), some downward bias is automatically built into the estimated social rates of return for the Canadian Pacific, as is also the case for the other six systems.

Appendix F

Interregional Benefits

Interregional external benefits are estimated only for the Central Pacific System for two reasons. First, the Central Pacific System is the only one for which sufficient data are available on through shipments over the period covered to allow an estimate. Even for the Central Pacific only seven observations are available for 21 years; this crucial piece of information is not available in even such a limited amount from the records of the other six systems. Moreover, through freight rates are also not available in general and are available in only 3 of 21 years for the Central Pacific. Second, following the estimation technique discussed here, interregional benefits for the Central Pacific System turn out to have an effect on the social rate of return of 0.1% or less. There is little reason to expect that this result would be changed for the other systems.[1] Some slight downward bias is introduced into the social returns streams and social rates of return for the other six systems because interregional external benefits are not included.

The computation of interregional external benefits is based on the estimated saving accruing to shippers engaged in interregional trade when it becomes possible to use the lower cost services of the railroad for shipments between regions rather than alternatives. The magnitude of the estimated benefits depends on the alternative chosen. It is assumed here

---

[1] Fogel, in *Railroads and American Economic Growth*, finds interregional social savings for transport of agricultural goods to be small relative to intraregional social savings for the transport of these goods. In terms of his first approximation α estimate of intraregional social savings, interregional social savings are about 22% of intraregional (see pp. 47 and 91).

that the relevant alternative in the case of the Central Pacific System during the period of this study was water transportation between the Pacific and Atlantic coasts by way of the isthmus of Panamá and the Panamá Railroad. The Cape Horn route is evidently not the relevant route, because most of what are labeled the best intercoastal freight accounts were transferred from the Cape Horn route to the Panamá route upon completion of the Panamá Railroad in 1855.[2] This apparently refers to the trade in items of relatively high value per unit of weight. From the 1860s on, the principal trade of the Cape Horn route was the export grain trade between the Pacific coast and Europe.[3] Thus, the trade in which the railroad became the principal competitor was the one in which the Panamá route was dominant.

In the 1890 census it is reported that the trade between Pacific coast ports and Atlantic ports was confined on the Pacific side to San Francisco.[4] It is assumed that the terminal of the intercoastal water route in the region served by the Central Pacific System was San Francisco during the period studied. New York is chosen as the Atlantic coast terminal. Thus the relevant alternative to the Central Pacific System for interregional shipments is assumed to be the Panamá route between San Francisco and New York. While there was undoubtedly some trade by wagon prior to the railroad between the region served by the Central Pacific System and other regions, it appears that this must have been of small volume relative to water shipments and does not represent a relevant alternative to shipments by rail for use in computing interregional benefits.

For the purpose at hand, it is assumed that the average interregional rail shipment traveled a distance equal to the distance between Oakland, California and the city of New York. This surely overstates the distance traveled by the average interregional rail shipment; however, no data could be found to estimate the actual average distance involved in interregional shipments. The rail distance between Oakland and New York was determined from information in the annual volumes of *Poor's Manual* and a map showing present rail mileage between points in the United States.[5] Additional information affecting the estimated average distance of interregional shipments is taken from other sources.[6] For 1869 through 1879, the

[2] Raymond A. Rydell, *Cape Horn to the Pacific* (Berkeley and Los Angeles: University of California Press, 1952), pp. 141 and 144.
[3] *Ibid.*, p. 145.
[4] U.S. Department of the Interior, *Eleventh Census, Transportation by Water*, p. 167.
[5] Rand McNally and Company, *Commercial Atlas and Marketing Guide: 1966* (New York: Rand McNally and Company, 1965), p. 16.
[6] Wilson and Taylor, *Southern Pacific* (New York: McGraw-Hill, 1952), p. 196; Daggett, *Chapters in the History of the Southern Pacific*, p. 106; U.S. Congress, Senate, *PRC*, p. 4750.

F. Interregional Benefits

distance used to compute the cost of shipping a ton from Oakland to New York is 3,284 miles, while for 1880 through 1889, the distance used is 3,269.04 miles. The Central Pacific formed only part of the assumed average rail route for interregional shipments. Other railroads assumed to form a part of this line are the Union Pacific, the Chicago, Rock Island, and Pacific, and the Pennsylvania. These railroads then and now form the shortest route from Oakland to New York.[7] From the sources cited in footnotes 5 and 6, the mileage used by railroad was: Central Pacific 833.5 for 1869 and 1879 and 818.5 for 1880 to 1889; Union Pacific 1,042.34; Chicago, Rock Island, and Pacific, 499.2; and Pennsylvania 909.0.

No complete series of the tonnage of interregional shipments on the Central Pacific System could be obtained. However, in 1869, 1876, 1877, 1880, 1887, 1888, and 1889 the through tonnage shipped on the system was reported.[8] For the missing years through tonnage was estimated by linear interpolation. Column 1 of Table F-1 presents this data.

The Pacific Mail Steamship Company gained control of the San Francisco to New York route via Panamá in 1865.[9] Its rates, after completion of the Central Pacific in 1869, cannot be used as the effective alternative to the transcontinental railroad because of agreements entered into between the railroads and the Pacific Mail with respect to the maintenance of rates during the period of this study.[10] Fortunately, data are available for the computation of an estimated rate per ton on the water route between San Francisco and New York. The calculation is based on San Francisco tonnage receipts of merchandise imports via Panamá by steamer for 1865, 1866, and 1867.[11] The estimated freight costs per ton were $74.12, $62.91, and $62.94 for these years, respectively. *Poor's Manual* presents information on through and local tonnage shipped on the Panamá route of the Pacific Mail and freight earnings from these in 1868, and concludes that the freight cost between New York and San Francisco was $46 per ton in 1868.[12] Unfortunately, this is incorrect, because the $46 per ton is the ratio of all freight earnings to the total (both local and through) tonnage on the route. Costs per ton of local freight undoubtedly were less than the freight

---

[7] Rand McNally and Company, *Commercial Atlas and Marketing Guide*, p. 16.

[8] *Poor's Manual*, reports on the Central Pacific or the Pacific System in the annual volumes of 1869–1870, 1876–1877, 1878, 1888, 1889, and 1890; and U.S. Bureau of the Census, *Tenth Census of the United States: 1880*, IV, *Report on the Agencies of Transportation of the United States*, p. 243.

[9] John Haskell Kemble, *The Panama Route, 1848–1869* ("University of California Publications in History", XXIX; Berkeley and Los Angeles: University of California Press, 1943), pp. 95 and 148.

[10] Daggett, *Chapters in the History of the Southern Pacific*, pp. 229–236.

[11] *Commercial and Financial Chronicle*, May 4, 1867, p. 557.

[12] *Poor's Manual*, 1868–1869, pp. 391–392.

TABLE F-1

Estimate of External Benefits Accruing to Interregional Shipments on the Central Pacific System by Year

Year	Interregional shipments (tons) (1)	Cost per ton between		External benefits[b]	
		S.F. and N.Y. by water[a] ($) (2)	Oakland and New York by rail ($) (3)	Total (thousand 1869 $) (4)	C.P. system (thousand 1869 $) (5)
1869	5,187	59.71	49.35	54	14
1870	34,588	54.87	45.33	359	91
1871	60,284	53.26	44.05	490	124
1872	85,980	54.87	45.33	626	159
1873	111,677	53.79	44.48	756	192
1874	137,373	51.64	42.72	887	225
1875	163,069	49.49	40.93	1,052	267
1876	188,774	46.80	38.77	1,145	291
1877	187,633	45.19	37.34	1,152	292
1878	197,025	41.96	34.65	1,206	306
1879	206,417	41.42	34.22	1,251	318
1880	215,812	44.11	36.31	1,322	331
1881	271,497	45.73	37.63	1,619	405
1882	327,182	46.80	38.58	1,897	475
1883	382,868	45.19	37.15	2,218	555
1884	438,553	42.50	34.99	2,335	585
1885	494,238	41.42	34.05	2,806	703
1886	549,923	40.88	33.64	3,090	774
1887	605,628	41.42	34.05	3,397	851
1888	658,249	41.96	35.30	3,283	822
1889	594,486	41.42	35.03	2,901	726

[a] San Francisco and New York by the Panama route.
[b] Accruing to interregional rail shipments.

cost per ton for through freight, which would make the $46 figure an understatement of the actual 1868 per ton through freight cost.

The freight rate between San Francisco and New York via Panamá for the years 1869–1889 is estimated on the assumption that in the absence of the railroad the freight rate on this route would have moved with the general price level. The Snyder–Tucker price index for the period is converted to 1867 = 100 and with the 1867 per ton freight cost of $62.94 cited above is used to estimate the average annual freight cost per ton on the Panamá route for 1869–1889 in the absence of the railroad. These estimates are given in column 2 of Table F-1.

In order to estimate the cost of shipping a ton of freight from Oakland to

F. Interregional Benefits

New York by rail, it is necessary to have a series of through freight rates per ton-mile on the four railroads involved for 1869–1889. No series of through freight rates could be found. Information allowing the computation of through freight rates is available for all the railroads only for the fiscal year ending nearest June 1, 1880.[13] The only other information on through rates consists of those average rates for the Central Pacific System that can be calculated from data for 1888 and 1889.[14] Average through freight rates by years and railroads are estimated in the following way. It is assumed that the average rates computed from data for the fiscal year ending nearest June 1, 1880 are equal to the annual average of 1880. Also, it is assumed that freight rates moved in the same manner as the general price level. The Snyder–Tucker price index is converted to 1880 = 100 and used to generate a series of annual through freight rates per ton-mile by extrapolation of the 1880 through rates for each railroad for 1869–1889. Table F-2 lists these estimates.

The annual sum of the products of the estimated through freight rates for each railroad and its mileage on the Oakland to New York route is the estimated annual average railroad freight cost per ton for interregional shipments. This estimate is provided in column 3 of Table F-1.

The difference between the estimated water and rail transport costs per ton for interregional shipments is the r^* of Chapter 5. It is assumed that the estimated through tonnage of 1870 is the tonnage shipped in the absence of the railroad (Q). The annual interregional benefits (IR_t) are calculated as: $IR_t = r^*Q + r^*/2(Q'_t - Q)$ for 1871–1889, where Q'_t is the through tonnage with the railroad in year t. For 1869 and 1870, the calculation is: $IR_t = r^*Q^*$, where Q^* is the through tonnage shipped by rail. Interregional benefits are computed first in current dollars and then in 1869 dollars and are shown in column 4 of Table F-1.

The share of the total annual interregional benefits to be attributed to the Central Pacific System is estimated on the basis of the proportion of the Oakland to New York mileage in the system. For 1869–1879 this is 25.38%, and for 1880–1889 it is 25.04%. The product of the applicable percentage and the annual total benefits provides the estimate of the benefits attributable to the Central Pacific System. Column 5 of Table F-1 presents this estimate.

This estimate of the interregional external benefits produced by the Central Pacific is probably an understatement of the true interregional external benefits because it includes only the saving in direct freight costs. Several costs of water transportation are neglected. These are the costs of the extra cargo loss involved in water shipment, the extra time required

---
[13] U.S. Bureau of the Census, *Tenth Census, Transportation*, pp. 215, 235, 241, and 245.
[14] *Poor's Manual*, 1890, p. 973.

TABLE F-2

Estimated Annual Average Through Freight Rates per Ton-Mile by Railroad System

Year	Central Pacific	Union Pacific	Chicago, Rock Island, and Pacific	Pennsylvania
1869	1.62	1.91	1.30	1.04
1870	1.49	1.75	1.19	0.96
1871	1.45	1.70	1.16	0.93
1872	1.49	1.75	1.19	0.96
1873	1.46	1.72	1.17	0.94
1874	1.41	1.65	1.12	0.90
1875	1.35	1.58	1.08	0.86
1876	1.27	1.50	1.02	0.82
1877	1.23	1.44	0.98	0.79
1878	1.14	1.34	0.91	0.73
1879	1.13	1.32	0.90	0.72
1880	1.20	1.41	0.96	0.77
1881	1.24	1.46	1.00	0.80
1882	1.27	1.50	1.02	0.82
1883	1.23	1.44	0.98	0.79
1884	1.16	1.36	0.92	0.74
1885	1.13	1.32	0.90	0.72
1886	1.11	1.31	0.89	0.71
1887	1.13	1.32	0.90	0.72
1888	1.24	1.34	0.91	0.73
1889	1.25	1.32	0.90	0.72

for water shipment, capital costs involved in governmental tax financed aid to water transportation facilities which are not included in water freight rates, additional wagon haul mileage required with water transportation to secondary markets not on water transportation facilities, and transshipment costs. Transshipment costs appear to have been included in the through charge on the Panamá route, since the Pacific Mail quoted through rates between San Francisco and New York.[15] Insurance charges added to the freight charge in water shipment are a measure of the additional cargo loss by water, since this is included in rail freight rates. Data on the value of interregional shipments and marine insurance rates for the Panamá route could not be obtained. Neglected capital costs could not be obtained and are probably relatively unimportant, since they would involve only improvements to the harbors and port facilities of San Fran-

---

[15] Daggett, *Chapters in the History of the Southern Pacific*, p. 233.

F. Interregional Benefits

cisco and New York, and would be spread over a much greater tonnage than that dealt with here. The costs of extra time involved in water shipments by the Panamá route would depend on the value of additional inventories required with dependence on water shipments and the market rate of interest to find the opportunity cost of the additional capital tied up in these inventories. The additional time involved was 15 to 18 days in 1910.[16] Thus, it appears that this neglected cost is relatively small. Supplementary wagon haulage for these interregional shipments in the absence of the Central Pacific System is not estimated, since no data, e.g., origin and destination of interregional shipments, are available to allow such a computation.

The paucity of data in this area of neglected costs of water transportation for interregional shipments precludes an attempt to calculate these costs. They are neglected with the realization that this undoubtedly understates this category of external benefits. However, it appears that this understatement is likely to be of minor significance, so that the conclusion above concerning the lack of importance of interregional benefits is unchanged. In any event, the product of these problems is understatement of the social rate of return estimates.

---

[16] Frank Andrews, *Marketing Grain and Livestock in the Pacific Coast Region*, U.S. Department of Agriculture, Bureau of Statistics, Bulletin No. 89 (Washington: U.S. Government Printing Office, 1911), p. 72.

Appendix G

Passenger Benefits

As in the case of interregional freight, the amount of existing data for estimation of the external benefits accruing to passengers falls considerably short of that desired. However, available data are sufficient to allow construction of an estimate of these benefits for each system studied. This is fortunate, because passenger benefits are much more substantial than interregional benefits, and ignoring them would produce a substantial understatement of the social returns stream and the social rates of return.

The Central Pacific System

Some of the estimates developed to compute passenger benefits for the Central Pacific System are used to estimate these benefits for the other six systems. For this reason the Central Pacific passenger benefits estimates are discussed in greater detail. Because the Northern Division of the Southern Pacific of California was operated separately until 1885, it is necessary to add the appropriate data for the Northern Division to that for the Central Pacific for 1870–1885. The data on passenger numbers, passenger earnings, and passenger miles are from *Poor's Manual*.[1]

Passenger numbers for the Northern Division are reported for all years except the last 6 months of 1877 and the year 1878. For 1870–1877 all

---

[1] *Poor's Manual*, annual volumes 1873–1874 and 1886.

G. Passenger Benefits

reported data are on the basis of a fiscal year ending June 30. The passenger figure for 1870–1871 covers 9 months. One-third of the reported figure is alloted to 1870 and two-thirds to the first 6 months of 1871. The numbers reported for fiscal years 1871–1872 through 1876–1877 are divided in half on the assumption that the number of passengers within each 6-month period was the same in each fiscal year. Calendar year passenger estimates for 1871–1876 are the sum of the 6-month figures for each fiscal year in which a calendar year appeared. Annual passenger numbers are reported for the calendar years 1879–1885. Estimated passenger totals for 1877 and 1878 are a linear interpolation between 1876 and 1879 passenger numbers.

Passenger earnings for the Northern Division are reported for fiscal years 1872–1873 to 1876–1877 and calendar years 1879–1885. Using the same techniques and assumptions as for passenger numbers, the fiscal year passenger earnings for years 1872–1873 to 1876–1877 are converted to calendar year figures for 1873–1876. For calendar years 1870–1872 passenger earnings are estimated as the product of the number of passengers and the mean earnings per passenger reported for 1873–1876. Passenger earnings for 1877 and 1878 are the product of the estimated passenger numbers and a linear interpolation of earnings per passenger between 1876 and 1879. For 1885 passenger earnings are estimated as the product of reported passenger numbers and 1884 earnings per passenger.

Passenger miles for the Northern Division are reported for 1879–1884. These and reported passenger numbers allow computation of miles per passenger for 1879–1884. This rises from 32.2 in 1879 to 36.0 in 1884. Passenger miles for 1870–1878 are estimated as the product of passenger numbers and an assumed 30 miles per passenger, while passenger miles in 1885 are estimated on the assumption that miles per passenger were equal in 1884 and 1885.

Passenger numbers are reported for the Central Pacific and leased lines for the years 1869, 1875–1885, and the Pacific System for 1888 and 1889.[2] The number reported includes ferry passengers on the Oakland and Alameda to San Francisco ferries operated by the Central Pacific.[3] Rail passengers are reported separately only for 1876, 1884, 1885, 1888, and 1889. Passenger earnings are reported for every year, but include rail and ferry passenger earnings. Total passenger miles, including ferry passenger miles, are reported for 1877–1889, with rail passenger miles reported separately for 1884, 1885, 1888, and 1889.

[2] *Ibid.*, annual volumes containing Central Pacific or Pacific System reports for these years.
[3] *Ibid.*, 1877–1878, total passengers for 1876 are given as 5,772,659, with 789,702 rail and 4,982,957 ferry passengers.

For the Central Pacific and leased lines, it is assumed that the 283,972 passengers reported for 1869 are rail passengers. In 1888 and 1889 through passengers are less than 5% of total passengers.[4] Through rail passengers in 1869 are reported as 29,100 for only 7 months of through operation.[5] On this basis it appears reasonable that the reported 1869 passenger total is for rail passengers. Rail passengers for 1870–1875, 1877–1883, 1886, and 1887 are estimated by linear interpolation between reported totals.

The estimated rate per rail passenger mile in 1869 is 9.9 cents. It is assumed that the average rate for 1864–1868 is 10 cents per rail passenger mile. Dividing passenger earnings by 10 cents provides the estimated rail passenger miles for 1864–1868. Average miles per rail passenger (all local traffic) is assumed to be 20 for 1864–1867 and 30 for 1868. Passenger miles divided by the assumed miles per passenger produces the estimates of rail passengers for 1864–1868.

Ferry passengers for the Central Pacific System in 1876, 1884, 1885, 1888, and 1889 are reported by *Poor's Manual*. Wilson and Taylor report ferry passenger numbers for 1871.[6] Ferry passengers for 1872–1874 are estimated by linear interpolation between the reported or estimated totals for 1871 and 1875. The 1875, 1877–1883, 1886, and 1887 ferry passenger estimate is the difference between the total passengers reported for these years for the Central Pacific and leased lines, or the Pacific System, and their estimated rail passengers for these years. Linear extrapolation of the 1871–1875 average annual ferry passenger increase provides the 1869 and 1870 ferry passenger estimates.

With the exception of 1877, 1878, and 1885 for the Northern Division of the Southern Pacific, total passenger miles for the Central Pacific System are reported for the years 1877–1889.[7] The reported average passenger miles for all passengers (rail and ferry) on the Central Pacific and leased lines for 1877–1885 is 30.02. The product of this average and the estimated or reported total passengers for 1869–1876 produces an estimate of total passenger miles for those years. Division of reported passenger earnings by the assumed rate per passenger mile of 10 cents provides the estimate of total passenger miles for 1864–1868.

Estimated ferry passenger miles are the product of estimated ferry passengers and 9.4 miles per ferry passenger, except for 1888 and 1889, which are reported. Average miles per ferry passenger were 9.34 and 9.43 in 1888 and 1889, respectively.[8] Since the same ferry routes were used

[4] *Ibid.*, 1890, p. 973.
[5] *Ibid.*, annual volume 1870–1871.
[6] Wilson and Taylor, *Southern Pacific*, p. 193.
[7] *Poor's Manual*, annual volumes 1876–1877 to 1890.
[8] *Ibid.*, 1890, p. 973.

G. Passenger Benefits

throughout the period, the use of 9.4 miles as the average per ferry passenger appears reasonable.

Subtraction of ferry passenger miles from total passenger miles produces an estimate of rail passenger miles. Rail passenger miles for 1864–1868 are derived as discussed above.[9] Miles per rail passenger are assumed to be 20 for 1864–1867 and 30 for 1868.[10] Division of rail passenger miles by rail passenger numbers provides the miles per rail passenger estimates for 1869–1889. Estimated miles per rail passenger are shown in the column "passenger miles per trip" of Table G-2.

For 1864–1884, 1888, and 1889 total passenger earnings (rail and ferry) are reported or estimated as in the case of the Northern Division of the Southern Pacific (also for 1885) as discussed above.[11] Passenger earnings are not reported separately for 1885–1887. The average rates based on all passenger miles are calculated for 1884 and 1888, and the annual average per passenger miles for 1885–1887 is estimated by linear interpolation between 1884 and 1888 rates. The product of these rates and total passengers for 1885–1887 is the estimate of total passenger earnings in these years.

For 1888 and 1889 the average rate per ferry passenger mile is reported as 0.956 cents.[12] The rate per passenger in 1869 is assumed to be 25 cents.[13] Leland Stanford fixed the commutation rate on the ferries at $3 per month and the regular fare at 10 cents soon after the Central Pacific took over full control of the ferry route between Oakland and San Francisco with these rates remaining in effect for years.[14] For 9.4 miles this works out to 1.06 cents per passenger mile on regular fare and 0.80 cents on commutation fare. The average fare per passenger mile would lie between these figures, with the exact rate depending on the relative numbers of regular and commutation passengers. For 1870–1889 it appears reasonable to use 0.956 cents as the average rate per ferry passenger mile. The product of this rate and total ferry passenger miles provides an annual estimate of ferry passenger earnings. The difference between total passenger earnings and ferry passenger earnings becomes the estimate of rail passenger earnings. Dividing rail passenger earnings by rail

---

[9] This produces an upward bias in rail passenger miles and rail passengers for 1865–1868. The Central Pacific began operating ferries between Oakland and San Francisco in 1865 and purchased two more ferry lines on this route by 1869. Wilson and Taylor, *Southern Pacific*, pp. 192–193.

[10] Based on mileage in operation during these years and average rail passenger miles (all local) on Northern Division. U.S. Congress, Senate, *PRC*, p. 4749.

[11] *Poor's Manual*, appropriate annual volumes.

[12] *Ibid.*, 1890, p. 973.

[13] Wilson and Taylor, *Southern Pacific*, p. 192.

[14] *Ibid.*, pp. 194 and 196.

passenger miles produces the estimate of average rates per rail passenger mile.

The relative magnitude of external benefits accruing to passengers from the railroad's operation depends crucially on the alternatives used in preparing the estimate. For the Central Pacific both land (stagecoach) and water would have been alternatives for passenger travel in the absence of the railroad. Table G-1 presents the data and methods upon which an estimated combination alternative fare per passenger mile was calculated for 1855. This alternative average rate per passenger mile in 1855 is 7.36 cents in current dollars. In order to estimate the alternative rate per passenger mile over the period studied in the absence of the railroad it is assumed that this rate would have moved in the same manner as the general price level after 1855. Conversion of the Snyder–Tucker general price index to 1855 = 100 and multiplication of 7.36 cents by the resulting index numbers generates the estimated alternative rate per passenger mile. The difference between this estimated alternative rate per passenger mile and the estimated rail rate per passenger mile is the saving per passenger mile given in Table G-2. This is the p^* of Chapter 5 with respect to passengers. Total passenger miles that would have been traveled without the railroad in the region it served are assumed equal to the rail passenger miles of 1870, which is the first full year of operation of the railroad following completion of the transcontinental link. This is the Q of Chapter 5, while observations of 1871 and later are Q'_t for passengers. For 1871 and later, annual direct external benefits (DB) to passengers are estimated as: $DB_t = p^*Q + p^*/2\,(Q'_t - Q)$. For 1864–1870 DB is estimated as: $DB_t = p^*Q^*$ where Q^* in these years is passenger miles with the railroad. Direct external benefits accruing to passengers on the Central Pacific System are presented in Table G-2.

Table G-2 gives annual estimated indirect external benefits to passengers (in 1869 dollars) on the Central Pacific System and the data upon which they are based. Hours required for average rail passenger trip are based on average miles per rail passenger and assumed or reported average speeds for passenger trains. An average speed of passenger trains on the Central Pacific main line is reported as 19 miles per hour in 1879.[15] In 1887 the fastest normal passenger runs on the New York Central and Pennsylvania Railroads under favorable conditions were reported to be around 40 miles per hour.[16] Few technical changes increasing the average speed of passenger locomotives were made in 1860–1880. However, about 1880, changes to increase average passenger locomotive speeds

---

[15] Daggett, *Chapters in the History of the Southern Pacific*, p. 85.

[16] J. L. Ringwalt, *Development of Transportation Systems in the United States* (Philadelphia: Published by the Author, 1888), p. 321.

G. Passenger Benefits

TABLE G-1

Estimate of Alternative Rates per Passenger Mile by
Stagecoach and Steamship in 1855

Alternative	From	To	Miles	Fare ($)	Rate per passenger mile (¢)
Stagecoach[a]	Sacramento	Placerville	26	3	11.54
	Sacramento	Auburn	35[b]	5	14.29
	Sacramento	Shasta	175[b]	20	11.43
	Sacramento	Yankee Jim's	55[b]	11	20.00
	Sacramento	Iowa Hill	64[b]	8	12.50
	Sacramento	Coloma	33	5	15.15
	San Francisco	Redwoods[c]	20[b]	1	5.00
	San Francisco	San Jose	47[b]	4	8.51
	San Francisco	Santa Cruz	67[b]	5	7.46
	San Francisco	St. Louis	2,795	200[d]	7.89
	Mean rate/passenger mile				11.38
Steamship[e]	San Francisco	Sacramento	125	10	8.00
	San Francisco	Marysville	166	12	7.23
	San Francisco	Stockton	127	8	6.30
	Mean rate/passenger mile				7.18[f]
Combination					7.36[g]

[a] All from Oscar O. Winther, "The Express and Stagecoach Business in California, 1848–60" (Unpublished Ph.D. dissertation, Dept. of History, Stanford University, 1934), pp. 174 and 234, except for San Francisco to St. Louis, which is from Oscar O. Winther, *The Transportation Frontier: Trans-Mississippi West, 1865–1890* (New York: Holt, Rinehart, and Winston, 1964), p. 50.

[b] Modern road distance.

[c] Assumed to be Redwood City.

[d] Fare in 1860 dollars; rate/passenger mile in 1855 dollars.

[e] Jerry MacMullen, *Paddle-Wheel Days in California* (Stanford University: Stanford University Press, 1944), pp. 21 and 144.

[f] Cabin fares. Deck fares appear to have been one-third of cabin fares, i.e., 2.39 cents here, Daggett, *Chapters in the History of the Southern Pacific*, p. 244.

[g] Assumes half passenger miles stagecoach; half steamship with 80% deck passage at 2.39 cents and 20% cabin passage at 7.18 cents per passenger mile. Combination steamship fare 3.35 cents.

were initiated.[17] The Central Pacific System had 317 locomotives in 1880 and 445 in 1884.[18] The proportion of passenger miles run on flat lands or

[17] *Ibid.*, p. 320.
[18] *Poor's Manual*, 1881 and 1885.

TABLE G-2
Passenger External Benefits for the Central Pacific System by Year

Year	Rail rate per mile (current ¢)	Saving per mile (current ¢)	Direct benefits (thousand 1869 $)	Passenger miles per trip	Time saved per trip hours	Value of time saved (current $)	Indirect benefits (thousand 1869 $)	Total benefits[a] (thousand 1869 $)
1864	10.0	2.1	13	20	0.74	0.14	1	14
1865	10.0	1.9	22	20	0.74	0.14	2	24
1866	10.0	1.6	35	20	0.74	0.14	5	40
1867	10.0	1.0	33	20	0.74	0.14	6	38
1868	10.0	0.8	40	30	1.11	0.22	10	50
1869	9.9	0.6	135	87	3.22	0.69	49	184
1870	9.0	0.6	243	100	3.70	0.79	84	326
1871	5.8	3.5	1,931	89	3.29	0.70	129	2,060
1872	5.5	4.0	2,494	90	3.33	0.71	159	2,653
1873	4.9	4.5	3,176	97	3.58	0.76	193	3,369
1874	4.6	4.4	3,617	102	3.77	0.66	190	3,807
1875	4.6	4.0	3,869	101	3.73	0.65	229	4,099
1876	3.8	4.3	4,963	111	5.21	0.91	365	5,328
1877	3.7	4.2	5,098	101	4.74	0.66	314	5,412
1878	3.8	3.6	4,490	85	3.99	0.56	319	4,809
1879	3.4	3.8	4,883	79	3.71	0.59	378	5,260
1880	3.7	4.0	4,585	79	3.71	0.57	387	5,815
1881	3.6	4.4	6,461	83	3.90	0.60	436	6,898
1882	3.4	4.8	7,933	89	4.18	0.64	505	8,439
1883	3.1	4.7	9,160	93	4.37	0.66	600	9,759
1884	3.0	4.4	8,598	79	3.71	0.58	611	9,209
1885	3.0	4.2	7,910	78	4.18	0.65	654	8,564
1886	2.8	4.3	9,255	67	3.60	0.56	768	10,023
1887	2.7	4.6	11,574	66	3.54	0.54	918	12,493
1888	2.5	4.9	15,699	73	3.92	0.60	1,210	16,909
1889	2.4	4.8	15,399	73	3.92	0.58	1,171	16,570

[a] May not equal the sum of direct and indirect benefits because of rounding.

G. Passenger Benefits

reduced grades and the change in the mix of stations with respect to average distance between stations would affect average speeds without technical changes. From 1875 to 1881 the Central Pacific System expanded greatly in areas that should have reduced average grades over which its passenger trains ran. Based on this reasoning and information it is assumed that the average speed of passenger trains on the Central Pacific System was 20 miles per hour in 1864–1875, 25 miles per hour in 1876–1885, and 30 miles per hour in 1886–1889.

Information on scheduled time for various stagecoach trips that appear to be some of the fastest indicates average speeds of 7 to 10 miles per hour.[19] Far slower speeds are also reported.[20] Eight miles per hour is assumed to be the average stagecoach speed.

The fastest steamship trip between San Francisco and Sacramento in the early 1860's, is reported as 5 hours, 19 minutes.[21] The usual steamship time is reported as 14 hours for this trip in the early 1850's.[22] The distance between San Francisco and Sacramento by water is given as 125 miles at that time, making the fastest trip 23.58 miles per hour and the usual trip 8.95 miles per hour.[23] Average steamship speed is assumed to be 15 miles per hour. Assuming half the passenger miles by water and half by stagecoach, the average alternative speed is 11.5 miles per hour. This and the average miles per rail passenger produce the annual average hours required for the average rail passenger trip by alternatives. Subtracting the estimated average rail trip time from the average time required by alternatives gives the estimated annual average time saved per Central Pacific System passenger trip shown in Table G-2.

This time saving per passenger is valued on the basis of the average daily wage rate for nonharvest work in the Western Division of the United States reported in Holmes' study.[24] Conversion to an hourly wage is made on the assumption of a 10-hour day. Table G-2 shows the annual estimated value of time saved per Central Pacific System passenger by year. It is assumed that one-fourth of all rail passengers had an opportunity cost of the time saved by rail travel. Table G-2 gives the estimated annual 1869 dollar value of indirect external benefits to Central Pacific System passengers.

---

[19] Oscar D. Winther, "The Express and Stagecoach Business in California, 1848–1860", p. 265; and Oscar D. Winther, *The Transportation Frontier: Trans-Mississippi: West, 1865–1890*, pp. 46 and 66.
[20] Winther, *The Transportation Frontier*, p. 72.
[21] Wilson and Taylor, *Southern Pacific*, p. 193.
[22] Jerry MacMullen, *Paddle-Wheel Days in California*, p. 24.
[23] *Ibid.*, p. 144.
[24] Holmes, *Wages of Farm Labor*, p. 45.

The estimated annual 1869 dollar total value of the external benefits to passengers for the Central Pacific System is shown in the final column of Table G-2. In passing it should be noted that this is about one-half the magnitude if the stagecoach is chosen as the only alternative to the railroad.

Other Systems

Tables G-3 through G-8 present the passenger data and the passenger external benefits estimates for the other six systems. Adjustments and estimates of the basic data are indicated in footnotes to the tables.

TABLE G-3

Passenger External Benefits for the Union Pacific System by Year

Year	Rail rate per mile (current ¢)	Saving per mile (current ¢)	Direct benefits (thousand 1869 $)	Miles per trip	Time saved per trip (hours)	Value of time saved (current $)	Indirect benefits (thousand 1869 $)	Total benefits [a] (thousand 1869 $)
1867	5.1	5.9	395	263	9.71	1.33	8	404
1868	5.1	5.6	896	263	9.71	1.33	32	927
1869	5.1	5.4	2,330	525	19.41	2.83	108	2,437
1870	5.1	4.5	2,008	525	19.41	2.83	110	2,118
1871	4.2	5.1	2,317	567	20.94	3.06	112	2,428
1872	4.2	5.4	2,588	487	17.99	2.63	118	2,706
1873	4.1	5.3	3,050	547	20.21	2.95	143	3,194
1874	3.8	5.3	3,425	557	20.57	2.67	146	3,571
1875	3.3	5.4	4,534	632	23.35	3.04	192	4,726
1876	3.3	4.9	4,212	636	29.87	3.88	251	4,463
1877	3.3	4.6	3,470	581	27.27	2.97	182	3,652
1878	3.3	4.1	2,992	511	24.01	2.62	175	3,167
1879	3.3	4.0	3,015	511	24.01	2.62	181	3,196
1880	3.3	4.4	5,003	190	8.93	1.07	308	5,311
1881	3.3	4.7	4,886	190	8.94	1.06	280	5,166
1882	3.2	5.0	5,230	161	7.54	0.87	274	5,504
1883	3.1	4.9	5,008	126	5.90	0.68	268	5,276
1884	2.9	4.6	4,796	113	5.30	0.62	278	5,074
1885	2.7	4.5	4,927	107	5.01	0.59	286	5,216
1886	2.1	5.0	7,395	114	6.10	0.72	450	7,845
1887	2.3	4.9	7,415	85	4.56	0.53	454	7,869
1888	2.2	5.1	7,795	80	4.27	0.50	464	8,259
1889	2.1	5.1	7,685	87	4.65	0.54	452	8,137

[a] May not equal the sum of direct and indirect benefits because of rounding.

G. Passenger Benefits

TABLE G-4

Passenger External Benefits for the Texas and Pacific System by Year

Year	Rail rate per mile (current ¢)	Saving per mile (current ¢)	Direct benefits (thousand 1869 $)	Miles per trip	Time saved per trip (hours)	Value of time saved (current $)	Indirect benefits (thousand 1869 $)	Total benefits [a] (thousand 1869 $)
1872	6.8	2.8	48	49	1.80	0.18	2	49
1873	6.8	2.6	45	49	1.80	0.18	2	47
1874	6.8	2.2	71	49	1.80	0.17	4	74
1875	6.8	1.8	70	49	1.80	0.17	5	75
1876	3.9	4.3	318	66	3.12	0.29	14	332
1877	3.8	4.1	423	63	2.96	0.26	19	442
1878	4.0	3.4	400	61	2.87	0.25	22	422
1879	3.9	3.3	318	61	2.85	0.25	17	335
1880	4.0	3.7	329	59	2.76	0.25	16	345
1881	3.8	4.2	548	65	3.04	0.28	26	573
1882	3.6	4.6	983	81	3.82	0.33	41	1,024
1883	2.9	5.0	1,823	72	3.39	0.29	72	1,895
1884	2.9	4.6	1,586	71	3.33	0.30	71	1,657
1885	5.8	1.4	284	55	2.59	0.23	39	324
1886	2.6	4.5	1,777	73	3.93	0.35	92	1,869
1887	2.6	4.6	2,012	70	3.76	0.34	102	2,115
1888	2.7	4.7	1,998	61	3.28	0.30	100	2,099
1889	2.7	4.5	2,058	58	3.13	0.29	109	2,168
1890	2.6	4.7	2,495	59	3.14	0.29	127	2,622
1891	2.7	4.6	2,396	57	3.04	0.28	127	2,523
1892	2.6	4.6	2,440	61	3.25	0.30	128	2,568
1893	2.5	4.5	2,439	61	3.28	0.28	120	2,560
1894	2.4	4.3	2,412	65	3.48	0.27	116	2,528
1895	2.5	4.3	2,202	63	3.39	0.25	100	2,302
1896	2.5	4.1	1,996	60	3.53	0.26	102	2,097
1897	2.5	4.3	1,994	58	3.41	0.25	98	2,092
1898	2.4	4.5	2,588	62	3.60	0.30	137	2,725
1899	2.4	4.9	2,824	60	3.53	0.30	139	2,964
1900	2.5	5.0	3,063	57	3.33	0.28	148	3,211

[a] May not equal the sum of direct and indirect benefits because of rounding.

To calculate time saving, the train speed schedule used with the Central Pacific is taken, with the assumed average speed of 30 miles per hour continued for the decade 1885–1895 and average speed for 1896–1900 assumed to be 35 miles per hour. The average speed of alternatives estimated for the Central Pacific is also used for the remaining systems. Data to conduct separate estimates for each individual system are virtually nonexistent.

TABLE G-5

Passenger External Benefits for the Atchison, Topeka and Santa Fe System by Year

Year	Rail rate per mile (current ¢)	Saving per mile (current ¢)	Direct benefits (thousand 1869 $)	Miles per trip	Time saved per trip (hours)	Value of time saved (current $)	Indirect benefits (thousand 1869 $)	Total benefits [a] (thousand 1869 $)
1871	5.1	4.3	166	47	1.75	0.26	5	171
1872	5.1	4.5	234	87	3.21	0.47	9	243
1873	5.1	4.4	249	87	3.21	0.47	10	259
1874	4.5	4.5	291	109	4.03	0.52	11	301
1875	4.7	4.0	254	98	3.63	0.47	10	264
1876	4.2	4.0	522	127	5.98	0.78	33	555
1877	3.4	4.6	766	133	6.25	0.68	37	804
1878	3.1	4.2	1,069	147	6.90	0.75	58	1,128
1879	2.9	4.3	1,554	147	6.92	0.75	85	1,639
1880	2.9	4.8	2,100	160	7.53	0.90	117	2,216
1881	2.9	5.1	3,488	203	9.52	1.13	186	3,673
1882	2.9	5.3	4,331	173	8.11	0.94	218	4,549
1883	2.9	5.0	3,609	134	6.30	0.73	191	3,800
1884	2.6	4.8	4,678	90	4.23	0.50	264	4,941
1885	2.6	4.7	5,152	81	3.81	0.45	300	5,451
1886	2.3	4.9	6,416	99	5.31	0.63	409	6,824
1887	2.4	4.9	7,807	102	5.46	0.64	493	8,300
1888	2.3	5.1	7,008	99	5.31	0.62	426	7,434
1889	2.4	4.8	6,407	91	4.90	0.57	404	6,811
1890	2.2	5.1	10,842	70	3.74	0.43	653	11,495
1891	2.4	4.9	10,970	69	3.69	0.44	701	11,672
1892	2.4	4.8	10,862	66	3.53	0.42	714	11,576
1893	2.3	4.8	13,798	72	3.85	0.41	810	14,608
1894	2.1	4.6	13,502	78	4.17	0.40	743	14,245
1895	2.1	4.6	9,971	66	3.54	0.34	541	10,512
1896	2.2	4.5	9,973	68	3.95	0.38	612	10,586
1897	3.2	3.6	4,936	80	4.70	0.45	374	5,310
1898	3.5	3.4	5,564	84	4.88	0.53	508	6,071
1899	3.4	3.9	6,814	85	4.92	0.57	577	7,391
1900	2.3	5.2	15,152	86	5.01	0.57	965	16,117

[a] May not equal the sum of direct and indirect benefits because of rounding.

The estimated average cost of passenger travel per mile by alternatives used for the Central Pacific System is also used for the remaining six systems. The rate is extrapolated beyond 1889 using the Snyder–Tucker price index with the 1855 = 100. Given the good water transportation alternative in the Central Pacific's most populous area (California), this

G. Passenger Benefits

TABLE G-6

Passenger External Benefits for the Northern Pacific System by Year

Year	Rail rate per mile (current ¢)	Saving per mile (current ¢)	Direct benefits (thousand 1869 $)	Miles per trip	Time saved per trip (hours)	Value of time saved (current $)	Indirect benefits (thousand 1869 $)	Total benefits [a] (thousand 1869 $)
1873	4.7	4.7	110	63	2.32	0.37	3	113
1874	4.5	4.6	110	78	2.90	0.42	3	114
1875	3.9	4.7	137	109	4.05	0.59	4	142
1876	3.8	4.4	141	116	5.43	0.79	6	148
1877	5.0	2.9	118	139	6.51	0.78	8	126
1878	7.7	−0.4	−16	110	5.14	0.62	8	−8
1879	4.0	3.2	189	97	4.57	0.55	12	201
1880	3.9	3.8	414	73	3.43	0.46	29	443
1881	4.2	3.8	455	90	4.23	0.56	33	488
1882	3.3	4.9	1,273	115	5.41	0.74	79	1,352
1883	3.9	4.1	1,513	99	4.64	0.63	115	1,628
1884	3.7	3.8	3,153	162	7.60	1.03	260	3,395
1885	3.6	3.6	2,273	139	6.54	0.89	195	2,468
1886	3.2	4.0	2,674	129	6.92	0.94	241	2,916
1887	2.9	4.3	3,560	114	6.13	0.82	290	3,850
1888	2.9	4.5	5,139	119	6.36	0.85	408	5,547
1889	2.6	4.6	7,568	139	7.47	0.98	567	8,135
1890	2.7	4.7	7,766	104	5.60	0.73	578	8,345
1891	2.7	4.5	8,021	79	4.21	0.57	637	8,659
1892	2.8	4.4	9,006	75	4.00	0.54	735	9,742
1893	2.8	4.3	6,893	80	4.28	0.54	536	7,429
1894	2.5	4.2	5,378	101	5.44	0.62	385	5,763
1895	2.8	4.0	3,673	94	5.04	0.58	277	3,951
1896	2.7	4.0	4,250	95	5.57	0.64	355	4,605
1897	2.9	3.9	3,570	95	5.57	0.64	304	3,874
1898	2.3	4.6	7,331	132	7.73	1.00	600	7,932
1899	2.4	4.9	7,576	111	6.46	0.89	619	8,195
1900	2.4	5.0	9,069	109	6.37	0.88	724	9,792

[a] May not equal the sum of direct and indirect benefits because of rounding.

may understate the cost of alternatives for passengers in general. To the extent this is the case, the social returns streams and social rates of return are biased downward for the other systems. The reason for adopting this technique in place of attempting to estimate an alternative passenger rate for each system is the extreme paucity of data.

For the United States systems the opportunity cost of time saved per hour by rail travel is assumed to be the average wage rate of outdoor labor

TABLE G-7

Passenger External Benefits for the Great Northern System by Year

Year	Rail rate per mile (current ¢)	Saving per mile (current ¢)	Direct benefits (thousand 1869 $)	Miles per trip	Time saved per trip (hours)	Value of time saved (current $)	Indirect benefits (thousand 1869 $)	Total benefits [a] (thousand 1869 $)
1880	3.2	4.5	1,265	47	2.21	0.29	44	1,309
1881	3.2	4.8	1,439	47	2.21	0.29	52	1,490
1882	2.9	5.3	2,527	75	3.53	0.48	111	2,637
1883	3.0	4.9	2,891	61	2.89	0.39	144	3,034
1884	3.1	4.3	2,261	47	2.19	0.30	120	2,381
1885	2.9	4.3	2,121	40	1.87	0.25	109	2,231
1886	2.5	4.6	2,680	32	1.74	0.24	156	2,835
1887	2.2	5.0	3,163	33	1.75	0.24	173	3,336
1888	2.5	4.9	3,281	32	1.74	0.23	189	3,470
1889	2.6	4.7	3,154	33	1.75	0.23	184	3,338
1890	2.4	4.9	3,338	34	1.80	0.24	186	3,524
1891	2.5	4.8	4,075	43	2.30	0.31	254	4,328
1892	2.6	4.5	3,861	51	2.75	0.37	254	4,115
1893	2.7	4.4	3,875	58	3.11	0.39	246	4,120
1894	2.5	4.2	3,512	71	3.80	0.43	206	3,718
1895	2.7	4.1	3,360	65	3.49	0.40	203	3,563
1896	2.7	4.0	3,760	65	3.79	0.44	260	4,021
1897	2.6	4.2	3,822	65	3.80	0.44	252	4,074
1898	2.2	4.6	6,002	87	5.07	0.65	427	6,429
1899	2.2	5.0	6,931	84	4.90	0.68	493	7,424
1900	2.4	5.1	7,695	79	4.60	0.63	554	8,248

[a] May not equal the sum of direct and indirect benefits because of rounding.

of men on farms for day labor other than harvest work (without board) in the regions within which the systems operated.[25] To establish an hourly rate, the average day is assumed to have been 10 hours. The opportunity cost of time savings for the Canadian Pacific is taken to be the median of the high wages without board reported for general laborers.[26] Again, a 10-hour day is assumed.

Given the particular technique utilized, it should be noted that passenger external benefits produced by the investment projects consid-

---
[25] Ibid.
[26] M. C. Urquhart and K. A. H. Buckley, *Historical Statistics of Canada* (Toronto: Macmillan of Canada, 1965), pp. 94–95.

G. Passenger Benefits

TABLE G-8

Passenger External Benefits for the Canadian Pacific System by Year

Year	Rail rate per mile (current ¢)	Saving per mile (current ¢)	Direct benefits (thousand 1900 $)	Miles per trip	Time saved per trip (hours)	Value of time saved (current $)	Indirect benefits (thousand 1900 $)	Total benefits [a] (thousand 1900 $)
1881	2.1	5.9	314	80	3.76	0.51	8	322
1882	2.1	6.1	871	73	3.42	0.46	37	908
1883	2.1	5.8	1,636	73	3.42	0.43	75	1,710
1884	2.1	5.3	2,416	80	3.77	0.47	125	2,541
1885	2.1	5.1	3,610	82	3.84	0.53	216	3,826
1886	2.1	5.0	4,058	79	4.25	0.53	259	4,317
1887	2.0	5.3	4,651	85	4.55	0.64	320	4,971
1888	1.8	5.6	5,745	93	5.00	0.75	404	6,149
1889	1.8	5.5	6,792	96	5.16	0.77	488	7,280
1890	1.7	5.6	7,616	98	5.28	0.79	535	8,150
1891	1.7	5.5	8,657	101	5.43	0.81	616	9,273
1892	1.7	5.5	9,477	101	5.41	0.81	685	10,162
1893	1.7	5.4	9,104	100	5.37	0.80	672	9,775
1894	1.9	4.8	6,992	87	4.65	0.70	570	7,561
1895	1.8	5.0	7,515	87	4.68	0.70	593	8,108
1896	1.8	4.9	7,874	87	5.08	0.76	695	8,568
1897	1.8	5.0	9,385	100	5.84	0.88	813	10,199
1898	1.5	5.4	12,823	117	6.84	1.03	1,035	13,858
1899	1.8	5.5	11,996	104	6.08	0.91	947	12,943
1900	1.9	5.5	11,727	97	5.64	0.85	918	12,645

[a] May not equal the sum of direct and indirect benefits because of rounding.

ered are understated, so that the social returns streams and social rates are also understated. A major reason for this is that no attempt is made to estimate the value of passenger external benefits beyond the terminal year in each case.

Appendix H

Loan Subsidy Cost

Two of the systems studied, the Central Pacific and Union Pacific, include firms that received loans for construction purposes from the United States government. The terms upon which the loans were given to the companies were such that the loans involved a subsidy to the firms and a cost to society that must be considered in estimating the social rate of return for the systems involved.

To estimate the loan subsidy cost, it is assumed that the railroads could have otherwise obtained funds equal in value to those they received from the government construction loans. That is, the railroads could have obtained private loans of the same face value at the same coupon rate (6%) and conditions as the government loans.[1] This undoubtedly understates the loan subsidy cost, and hence unfortunately tends to overstate the

---

[1] When the loans were renewed at later dates the current coupon rate on mortgage bonds is used.

H. Loan Subsidy Cost

social rate of return. For example, the government took only a second mortgage as collateral for its loan, which allowed the railroads to sell a like value of first mortgage bonds. There is no doubt that private lenders would not have provided such lenient terms. The annual interest the railroads would have paid on the construction loan over its life was calculated as follows. First, it was determined when interest began and ended on each group of bonds.[2] Next, the interest for 1 year at 6% was calculated for each group of bonds. The number of days of interest due in the year in which each group of bonds was issued and the year they were payable were determined and converted into percentages of 1 year. The product of these percentages and the annual interest on the group of bonds provided the interest due in the first and last year for each group. The sum of the interest due on all outstanding bonds became the annual interest payable on the construction loan, which is included in the interest payable column of Table H-1 for the Central Pacific System and Table H-2 for the Union Pacific System. From 1895 through 1898 this includes a continuance of the interest due on matured bonds that had not been paid.

Also included in the interest payable column of Table H-1 (starting in 1899) is the interest which it is assumed the railroads of the Central Pacific System would have had to pay if they had received the same new loan from private lenders that the government in effect gave them when it extended the time to pay off the construction loan and accumulated unpaid interest. The railroads paid the government 3% interest semiannually on the declining balance of this new loan. At the same time the Central Pacific issued new 4% mortgage bonds.[3] It is assumed that the railroads would have had to pay 4% to private investors for a loan of the same face value yielding the same funds as the new loan received from the government. During the period of the new loan, interest payments to the government at 3% are included (starting in 1899) in the interest paid column.

Payments on the construction loan and accumulated interest were made into a sinking fund in the United States Treasury between 1865 and 1897. These payments were made under the provisions of the Thurman Act of 1878 and the acts of 1862 and 1864 that required the government to withhold one-half the payment due the railroads for transportation services provided the government, and the railroad to pay a certain percentage of its net earnings.[4] The annual payments (for 1865–1897) shown in Table H-1 were determined by calculating the annual increase in the U.S. Transportation and Sinking Fund Account in the annual balance sheet of

---

[2] U.S. Congress, Senate, *PRC*, p. 2528.
[3] Daggett, *Chapters in the History of the Southern Pacific*, p. 418.
[4] *Ibid.*, pp. 376 and 381.

TABLE H-1

Estimate of Loan Subsidy Cost for the Central Pacific System by Year

Year	Interest Payable (thousand $)	Interest Paid (thousand $)	Loan subsidy cost (thousand current $)	Loan subsidy cost (thousand 1869 $)
1865	86.9	12.0	74.8	65
1866	195.2	13.2	182.0	164
1867	300.0	—	300.0	285
1868	552.3	—	552.3	538
1869	1,421.8	197.8	1,224.0	1,224
1870	1,664.2	317.5	1,346.7	1,465
1871	1,665.3	100.4	1,564.9	1,755
1872	1,665.3	242.2	1,423.2	1,549
1873	1,665.3	244.0	1,421.3	1,578
1874	1,665.3	304.6	1,360.8	1,573
1875	1,665.3	443.5	1,221.9	1,474
1876	1,665.3	358.4	1,307.0	1,668
1877	1,665.3	419.0	1,246.3	1,647
1878	1,665.3	521.8	1,143.5	1,627
1879	1,665.3	1,367.1	298.2	430
1880	1,665.3	958.3	707.0	957
1881	1,665.3	1,246.9	418.4	546
1882	1,665.3	1,169.3	496.1	633
1883	1,665.3	616.5	1,048.8	1,386
1884	1,665.3	333.6	1,331.7	1,748
1885	1,665.3	385.9	1,279.5	1,844
1886	1,665.3	418.3	1,247.1	1,821
1887	1,665.3	371.5	1,293.9	1,865
1888	1,665.3	467.2	1,198.1	1,705
1889	1,665.3	458.2	1,207.1	1,740
1890	1,665.3	524.0	1,141.4	1,624
1891	1,665.3	1,018.6	646.7	932
1892	1,665.3	577.0	1,088.3	1,589
1893	1,665.3	584.8	1,080.6	1,599
1894	1,665.3	599.7	1,065.6	1,666
1895	1,655.3	648.4	1,017.0	1,568
1896	1,665.3	644.6	1,020.8	1,596
1897	1,665.3	715.2	950.1	1,465
1898	1,665.3	—	1,665.3	2,532
1899	1,184.6	705.8	478.8	690
1900	1,883.2	1,411.5	471.6	663
1901	1,882.0	1,411.5	470.5	645
1902	1,705.6	1,279.2	426.4	563
1903	1,470.3	1,102.7	367.6	474
1904	1,235.1	926.3	308.8	399
1905	999.8	749.9	250.0	315
1906	764.6	573.4	191.1	233
1907	529.3	397.0	132.3	158
1908	294.1	220.5	73.5	90
1909	58.8	44.1	14.7	17

H. Loan Subsidy Cost

TABLE H-2

Estimate of Loan Subsidy Cost for the Union Pacific System by Year

Year	Interest Payable (thousand $)	Interest Paid (thousand $)	Loan subsidy cost (thousand current $)	Loan subsidy cost (thousand 1869 $)
1866	118.0	—	118.0	106
1867	366.7	—	366.7	348
1868	838.9	—	838.9	817
1869	1,570.0	—	1,570.0	1,570
1870	1,629.1	1,289.6	339.5	369
1871	1,634.2	450.9	1,183.3	1,327
1872	1,634.2	414.5	1,219.7	1,327
1873	1,634.2	201.4	1,432.7	1,590
1874	1,634.2	433.2	1,201.0	1,389
1875	1,634.2	688.7	945.5	1,141
1876	1,634.2	574.9	1,059.3	1,352
1877	1,634.2	707.3	925.9	1,225
1878	1,634.2	1,065.8	568.4	809
1879	1,634.2	201.6	1,432.6	2,065
1880	2,108.4	1,785.4	322.9	437
1881	2,108.4	1,687.7	420.7	549
1882	2,108.4	2,131.3	−22.9	−29
1883	2,108.4	1,913.1	195.3	258
1884	2,108.4	1,197.3	911.0	1,280
1885	2,108.4	1,241.4	867.0	1,250
1886	2,108.4	827.2	1,281.1	1,871
1887	2,108.4	1,014.7	1,093.7	1,577
1888	2,108.4	1,177.1	931.3	1,325
1889	2,108.4	1,183.4	925.0	1,218
1890	2,108.4	1,263.9	844.6	1,202
1891	2,108.4	1,214.1	894.3	1,289
1892	2,108.4	1,485.3	623.0	910
1893	2,108.4	1,434.3	674.1	998
1894	2,108.4	1,263.0	845.4	1,322
1895	2,108.4	1,151.2	957.2	1,476
1896	2,108.4	1,756.9	351.5	550
1897	2,031.8	1,451.5	580.4	895
1898	1,915.9[a]	0.0	1,915.9	2,913
1899	6,802.4[b]	821.9	5,980.5	8,621

[a] Includes $1,600,000 loan to the Central Branch of the Union Pacific, which was never paid.

[b] Includes $6,588,900 in accrued interest on the Kansas Pacific loan of $6,303,000, which was not paid.

the Central Pacific.[5] For the Union Pacific System the data on payments are taken from *PRC* and *Poor's Manual*.[6]

The difference between the interest-payable column and the interest-paid columns of Tables H-1 and H-2 is the loan subsidy cost. This is shown in both current and 1869 dollars. The Snyder–Tucker general price index is used to convert the current dollars into 1869 dollars.

---

[5] For 1865–1879 from U.S. Congress, Senate, *PRC*, p. 4657, and for 1880–1897 from *Poor's Manual*, appropriate annual volumes.

[6] U.S. Congress, Senate, *PRC*, p. 962 and *Poor's Manual*, appropriate annual volumes. The exception is 1897. No data on payments are available through October 1897. The amount shown is 10/12 of the 1896 total for the Union Pacific and Kansas Pacific companies plus the payment made by the Central Branch of the Union Pacific.

Appendix I

Capital Stocks

Capital stock is estimated for each of the seven systems using the perpetual inventory method. Both end-of-period and midperiod stocks are estimated and used in the estimates of Chapter 6. End-of-period stock is calculated by

$$K_t = (1 - \delta)K_{t-1} + (GI_t)\left(\frac{1 - \delta}{2}\right), \tag{1}$$

where

K_t = capital stock end-of-period t,
GI = gross investment,
δ = double-declining balance depreciation rate,
t = a time subscript.

As can be seen from (1), it is assumed that investment is uniformly distributed over the year. While this does not, of course, correspond with the actual distribution, the divergence of the latter from the assumed distribution is not likely to be great enough to greatly alter the estimate of K. The double-declining balance depreciation rates used in each case are those discussed in Chapter 4. The gross investment series are from Appendix A.

TABLE I-1

End-of-Period and Midperiod Capital Stocks[a] (Thousands of 1869 Dollars)

Year	Central Pacific K	Central Pacific KM	Union Pacific K	Union Pacific KM	Texas and Pacific K	Texas and Pacific KM
1863	680	343	—	—	—	—
1864	1,146	915	152	77	—	—
1865	2,739	1,949	1,510	837	—	—
1866	5,794	4,279	10,039	5,809	—	—
1867	9,034	7,428	19,538	14,737	—	—
1868	22,716	15,931	42,146	30,846	—	—
1869	41,375	32,123	50,552	46,388	—	—
1870	51,832	46,650	52,298	51,438	—	—
1871	51,953	51,899	50,843	51,570	—	—
1872	58,776	55,398	50,453	50,652	1,024	514
1873	58,462	58,624	48,994	49,723	5,699	4,271
1874	61,740	60,121	48,175	48,587	5,770	5,774
1875	61,783	61,769	47,247	47,713	8,610	6,165
1876	80,306	71,126	51,187	49,239	13,086	10,870
1877	82,437	81,389	52,669	51,940	12,828	12,957
1878	83,812	83,139	52,202	52,439	13,163	12,997
1879	87,406	85,634	54,790	53,512	13,158	13,158
1880	90,879	89,166	91,155	73,124	19,889	16,544
1881	90,738	90,818	101,209	96,233	54,661	37,363
1882	94,162	92,404	110,289	105,797	53,584	54,123
1883	97,652	95,932	118,174	114,276	56,103	54,582
1884	96,096	96,879	117,592	117,895	55,344	55,724
1885	94,923	95,516	115,963	116,785	54,254	54,799
1886	99,100	97,039	122,020	119,029	53,184	53,720
1887	99,545	99,336	128,390	125,245	56,728	54,968
1888	98,280	98,919	129,960	129,196	57,100	56,917
1889	98,682	98,493	126,075	128,017	56,327	56,714
1890	—	—	—	—	55,383	55,855
1891	—	—	—	—	54,407	54,837
1892	—	—	—	—	53,870	54,140
1893	—	—	—	—	52,998	53,435
1894	—	—	—	—	52,004	52,476
1895	—	—	—	—	51,458	51,732
1896	—	—	—	—	50,774	50,952
1897	—	—	—	—	50,166	50,274
1898	—	—	—	—	49,422	49,795
1899	—	—	—	—	49,618	49,523
1900	—	—	—	—	49,529	49,576

[a] K is end-of-period stock; KM is midperiod stock.

I. Capital Stocks

(Table I-1 continued)

Santa Fe		Great Northern		Northern Pacific		Canadian Pacific	
K	KM	K	KM	K	KM	K	KM
—	—	—	—	—	—	—	—
—	—	—	—	—	—	—	—
—	—	—	—	—	—	—	—
—	—	—	—	—	—	—	—
—	—	—	—	—	—	—	—
427	214	—	—	—	—	—	—
2,211	1,324	—	—	3,618	1,818	—	—
3,006	2,611	—	—	10,184	6,917	—	—
10,982	7,014	—	—	15,311	12,761	—	—
10,957	10,970	—	—	20,809	18,075	—	—
12,998	11,983	—	—	20,400	20,604	—	—
13,886	13,445	—	—	19,998	20,199	—	—
13,884	13,885	—	—	19,604	19,801	—	—
15,675	14,784	—	—	20,714	20,163	—	—
16,985	16,334	—	—	21,277	20,998	—	—
36,806	26,946	11,883	5,971	22,475	21,880	—	—
58,313	47,615	11,909	11,896	26,600	24,549	—	—
72,374	65,381	16,122	14,026	35,158	30,902	25,620	20,111
79,643	76,030	21,131	18,639	50,288	42,763	46,117	35,921
81,670	80,665	31,990	26,588	81,691	66,070	67,962	57,096
89,192	85,453	38,593	35,310	91,010	86,378	104,555	86,353
93,043	91,131	39,643	39,122	92,466	91,746	128,589	116,637
114,519	103,839	41,032	40,343	97,405	94,952	139,640	134,148
186,173	150,530	64,344	52,748	104,595	101,023	145,346	142,514
203,438	194,858	93,782	79,139	111,068	107,853	150,148	147,766
200,758	202,101	101,237	97,533	123,772	117,457	155,162	152,675
201,928	201,355	100,294	100,768	127,583	125,693	165,564	160,442
199,763	200,850	115,871	108,126	136,879	132,260	168,750	167,218
203,552	201,677	125,057	120,493	141,097	139,005	173,380	171,085
201,802	202,683	153,271	139,240	140,773	136,640	176,319	174,865
199,387	200,598	152,168	152,725	138,000	133,949	175,446	175,889
196,787	198,090	149,946	151,059	135,281	132,116	173,124	174,288
195,842	196,322	147,969	148,960	132,616	131,328	172,018	172,577
221,341	208,665	155,532	147,549	131,608	132,346	175,207	173,629
224,207	222,792	158,235	151,354	131,039	135,171	188,036	181,662
231,476	227,871	147,119	156,898	133,627	140,941	191,967	190,020
237,258	234,393	159,326	158,791	136,686	139,386	199,259	195,640

Midperiod stock is estimated by

$$KM_t = \left(\frac{1-\delta}{2}\right)(K_t - 1) + 0.5(GI_t)\left(\frac{1-\delta}{4}\right), \qquad (2)$$

where KM_t is midperiod stock in period t.

Estimates of end-of-period and midperiod stock for each system are presented in Table I-1.

Index

A

Acre-weight
  defined, 207
Additional subsidy required, 85n
Alternative private rate
  earnings/price ratio, 76
  railroad bond yield, 76
  real rate calculation, 76
Ames, Oakes, 39
Andrews, Frank, 207 and n, 239n
Asa Whitney, 4
Atchison Associates, 47
Atchison, Topeka and Santa Fe, 47
  construction, 47–48
  subsidiary railroads, 48–52
Atchison, Topeka and Santa Fe System
  building ahead of demand, 139
  capacity utilization
    regression, 138
    time series, 134
  capital
    earnings, 185
    long-term elasticities, 131
    stock estimates, 261
  external benefits
    intraregional, 230
    passenger, 250
  included railroads, 167
  investment
    demand function, 127
    time series, 168
  land grant policy
    optimality of aid, 143
    rationality, 145–146
  net land grant revenues, 195, 199
  present value (1869)
    investment in system, 80, 87
    land grant subsidy, 80, 87
  rates of return
    accounting (private) time series, 121
    private
      without subsidy, 86
      with subsidy, 86
    social, 114
  zero rent perimeters, 222–223
    related estimates, 222–223

B

Bean, Louis H.
  hay crop used in cities, 216
  grains
    farm value and gross farm income, 217
  sheep live weight equivalent, 214
  swine average live weight, 215
Beard, Charles A. and Mary R., 9–11
Building ahead of demand
  concept, 19–20, 141
  Fishlow hypothesis, 119–123
  system tests, 138–140, 146–147
Buildings
  farm
    value, 220–221

C

California and Texas Construction Company, 44–45
California Pacific Railroad, 35
  construction cost, 159

263

Canadian Pacific Railway Company
  branch lines, 63, 65–66
  construction, 61–65
  government loans, 63–65
  organization, 61–62
  subsidies, 61–62, 66
Canadian Pacific System
  building ahead of demand, 60, 139
  capacity utilization
    regression, 138
    time series, 134
  capital
    earnings, 188
    long-term elasticities, 131
    stock estimates, 261
  excess subsidy, 93–97
  external benefits
    intraregional, 230–232
    passenger, 253
  government construction, 61–62, 173
  included railroads, 174
  investment
    demand function, 127
    time series, 175
  land grant policy
    optimality of aid, 143
    rationality, 145–146
  net land grant revenues, 204–205
  present value (1881)
    investment in system, 80, 92
    land grant subsidy, 80
    all subsidies, 92
  rates of return
    accounting (private) time series, 121
    private
      without subsidy, 91
      with subsidy, 91
    social, 117
Capacity output
  defined, 123, 133
  estimation, 133
Capacity utilization
  defined, 133
  system estimates, 133–134
Capital earnings
  defined, 178
  by system, 179–188
Capital market imperfections, 24–26

Capital stock
  by system, 260–261
  perpetual inventory method, 72–73, 259
Central Pacific Railroad
  construction, 33–34
  construction cost, 152–156
  land grant, 33
  organization, 33
Central Pacific System
  building ahead of demand, 139
  capacity utilization
    regression, 138
    time series, 134
  capital
    earnings, 178–181
    long-term elasticities, 131
    stock estimates, 260
  external benefits
    interregional, 233–239
    intraregional, 230
    passenger, 240–248
  included railroads, 153
  investment
    demand function, 127–130
    time series, 154
  land grant policy
    optimality of aid, 143
    rationality, 145–146
  loan subsidy
    cost, 256
    1863 present value, 78, 81
  net land grant revenues, 191–194
  present value (1863)
    investment in system, 77, 81
    land grant subsidy, 77
  rates of return
    accounting (private) time series, 121
    private
      without subsidy, 75
      with subsidy, 75
    social, 109
  zero rent perimeters, 208
  related estimates, 208
Colton, David, 36
Contract and Finance Company, 34, 36, 155–156, 158–160
Cooke, Jay and Company, 53
Crédit Mobilier, 5, 39–40
Crocker, Charles, 33, 155

Index

Charles Crocker and Company, 34, 152–155

D

Decker, Leslie E., 8n
Depreciation rates, 73–74, 152n
Dillon, Sidney, 39–40
Durant, Thomas, 38–40

E

Efficiency, 2
Ellis, David Maldwyn, 8n
  land grants
    evaluation for firms, 31
  land grant policy
    danger of generalizations, 15
    recovery of land grants, 5
Engerman, Stanley L.
  decreasing costs, 20n
  railroads as natural monopolies, 22–23n
  railroad land grants
    acceleration of construction, 111n
    best justification, 26
    economic issues, 18n
    efficiency and political feasibility, 27n
External economies
  concept, 19–20, 141
  intraregional benefits, 99–100
    computation, 228–232
  interregional benefits, 100–105
    computation, 233–239
  passenger benefits, 105–107
    computation, 244

F

Fences
  amount and cost, 221
Fishlow, Albert
  building ahead of demand, 119–123, 139, 146–147
  calculation of passenger benefits, 105–106 and n
  understatement of railroad capital estimates, 151n
Fogel, Robert W.
  interregional social savings, 233n
  investment risk, 25n
  rate of return calculation, 69n
  real farm value rise, 227n, 228n
  zero rent perimeter
    estimation technique, 206–207
    estimate, 212
Fremont, John C., 50
Funk, W. C., 215 and n, 216n

G

Gates, Paul Wallace, 9n
George, Peter J.
  Canadian Pacific
    construction cost estimation, 175n
    government construction expenditures, 173
    investment expenditures, 174n, 176n
    required subsidy, 93–97
    rate of return calculation, 69n, 89–90
Goldsmith, Raymond W., 30n
Goodrich, Carter, 19
Gould, Jay, 37, 41
Government intervention, 1–2
Great Northern Railway Company
  branch lines, 59
  land grant, 59–60, 198–201
  organization, 58–59
Great Northern System
  building ahead of demand, 139
  capacity utilization
    regression, 138
    time series, 134–135
  capital
    earnings, 187
    long-term elasticities, 131
    stock estimates, 261
  external benefits
    intraregional, 230
    passenger, 252
  included railroads, 171
  investment
    demand function, 127, 132
    time series, 172
  land grant policy
    optimality of aid, 143
    rationality, 145–146
  net land grant revenues, 198–203
  present value (1879)
    investment in system, 80, 84
    land grant subsidy, 80

rates of return
  accounting (private) time series, 121
  private
    without subsidy, 83
    with subsidy, 83
  social, 116
  zero rent perimeters, 225
  related estimates, 225
Gwin, William M., 26n

H

Henry, Robert S., 6n, 9, 14–15n, 77n
Hill, James J., 57–58, 62
Holliday, Cyrus K., 47
Holmes, George K., 222 and n
Hopkins, Mark, 33, 36, 155
Huntington, C. P., 33, 155
Hypotheses
  ex ante test, 67
  ex post test, 142–146
  of land grant supporters, 5–6, 26–29

I

Illinois Central land grant, 3

J

Judah, Theodore, 33, 34n

L

Land grant policy
  contribution to economic growth, 148–149
  early debate, 3
  economic rationale, 5, 27–29, 141
  evaluation, 15, 147–149
  goals, 1n
  historiography, 8–15
  income distribution effect, 8 and n, 29–31
  political feasibility, 27n, 148
Land improvement costs
  clearing, 221–222
  cost of irrigation, 222–223

M

Macaulay, Frederick R., 76, 223
McClelland, Peter D.
  external benefits
    assumptions, 110n
    consumer surplus measurement, 105n
    partial equilibrium analysis
      legitimacy, 102–103n
Morgan, Charles S., 8n

N

National defense and political unification, 22, 64, 117–118
Natural monopoly, 22–24
Neal, Larry, 73
Net land grant revenue
  definition, 190–191
  by system, 192–204
Northern Pacific Railroad
  branch lines, 54–56
  charter, 52–53
  construction, 53–54
  land grant, 52, 198
Northern Pacific System
  building ahead of demand, 139
  capacity utilization
    regression, 138
    time series, 134
  capital
    earnings, 186
    long-term elasticities, 131
    stock estimates, 261
  external benefits
    intraregional, 230
    passenger, 251
  included railroads, 169
  investment
    demand function, 127–128
    time series, 170
  land grant policy
    optimality of aid, 143
    rationality, 145–146
  net land grant revenues, 198, 200
  present value (1870)
    investment in system, 80, 88
    land grant subsidy, 80, 88
  rates of return
    accounting (private) time series, 121
    private
      without subsidy, 88
      with subsidy, 88
    social, 115
    zero rent perimeters, 224
    related estimates, 224

Index

O

Onderdonk, Andrew, 61
Overbuilding hypothesis, 136–138

P

Pacific Improvement Company, 36–37, 157–159
Pacific railroads debate, 3–4
Pacific Railway Acts, 4, 33, 38
   Government loan, 33, 38
Partial equilibrium analysis
   effect on estimates, 102–103n, 107–108n
Pecuniary external economies, 98
Political unification and rational defense, 14n, 22, 64, 117–118
Potential wagon haul mileage, 207
Primack, Martin L., 221

R

Railroad land grants
   acreage, 6–7
   categories, 6
   distribution of income impact, 29–31
   net proceeds, 29–30
Ransom, Roger L., 208n
Rate of return calculation
   accounting method, 69
   internal rate of return, 69–71
      terminal adjustment, 71–72
Rent theory, 99–100
Riegel, Robert Edgar, 28n, 111n
Riel, Louis, 64

S

St. Paul, Minneapolis and Manitoba Railway
   construction, 58–59
   organization, 57
   predecessor railroads, 56–57
Samuelson, Paul, 103n
Sanford, John Bell, 3n
Saskatchewan (Second Riel) Rebellion, 64, 117–118
Schumpeter, Joseph, 19
Scitovsky, Tibor, 98–99n
Scott, Thomas A., 44–45
Shannon, Fred, 13–14, 77n
Shantz, H. L., 221 and n
Smith, Garrit, 4

Snow, C. N., 74n
Social returns stream, 107
Soltow, Lee, 30
Southern Pacific Company, 37
Southern Pacific Railroad
   construction, 36
   construction cost, 156–157
   land grant, 35
Stanford, Leland, 33, 155
Stephen, George, 62
Strauss, Frederick
   hay crop used in cities, 216
   grains
      farm value and gross farm income, 217
   sheep live weight equivalent, 214
   swine, average live weight, 215
Strong, William B., 51

T

Texas and Pacific Railroad Company, 43
   acquired railroads, 43–44
   construction, 44–46
   land grant, 195
   Texas land grant and bond subsidy, 43–44
Texas and Pacific System
   building ahead of demand, 139
   capacity utilization
      time series, 134–135
      regression, 138
   capital
      earnings, 183
      long-term elasticities, 131
      stock estimates, 260
   external benefits
      intraregional, 230
      passenger, 249
   included railroads, 165
   investment
      demand function, 127, 132
      time series, 166
   land grant policy
      optimality of aid, 143
      rationality, 145–146
   net land grant revenues, 195, 198
   present value (1872)
      investment in system, 80, 85
      land grant subsidy, 80
   rates of return
      accounting (private) time series, 121

private
  without subsidy, 85
  with subsidy, 85
  social, 113
  zero rent perimeters, 220
    related estimates, 220
Tostlebe, Alvin S., 30n

U

Union Pacific Railroad
  branch lines, 40–43
  construction, 39–40
  construction cost, 160–161
  land grant, 33
Union Pacific System
  building ahead of demand, 139
  capacity utilization
    regression, 138
    time series, 134
  capital
    earnings, 182
    long-term elasticities, 131
    stock estimates, 260
  external benefits
    intraregional, 230
    passenger, 248
  included railroads, 162–163
  investment
    demand function, 127
    time series, 164
  land grant policy
    optimality of aid, 143
    rationality, 145–146
  loan subsidy
    cost, 257

1864 present value, 81–82
net land grant revenues, 194, 196–197
present value (1864)
  investment in system, 81–82
  land grant subsidy, 82
rates of return
  accounting (private) time series, 121
  private
    without subsidy, 81
    with subsidy, 81
  social, 112
  zero rent perimeters, 219
    related estimate, 219

V

Van Horne, W. C., 62, 173n
Villard, Henry, 54 and n

W

Western Improvement Company, 36, 155–156
Western Pacific Railroad, 35
  construction cost, 158
  land grant, 191
Williams, J. L., 73
Williamson, Jeffrey C., 107–108n, 128n

Z

Zero rent perimeter
  estimates by system, 218–225
  estimation technique, 206–212
Ziegler, P. Thomas, 215n
Zon, Ralph, 221 and n

www.ingramcontent.com/pod-product-compliance
Lightning Source LLC
Chambersburg PA
CBHW020641230426
43665CB00008B/274